Current and Classic Readings for Microeconomic Literacy

Second Edition

Edited by Ronald M. Harstad and Sharon Ryan

Australia • Brazil • Japan • Korea • Mexico • Singapore • Spain • United Kingdom • United States

**Current and Classic Readings for
Microeconomic Literacy: Second Edition**

Edited by Ronald M. Harstad and Sharon Ryan

Executive Editors:
Maureen Staudt
Michael Stranz

Project Development Manager:
Linda deStefano

Senior Marketing Coordinators:
Sara Mercurio

Senior Production / Manufacturing Manager:
Donna M. Brown

PreMedia Services Supervisor:
Joel Brennecke

Rights & Permissions Specialist:
Kalina Hintz
Todd Osborne

Cover Image:

Getty Images*

* Unless otherwise noted, all cover images used
by Custom Solutions, a part of Cengage
Learning, have been supplied courtesy of Getty
Images with the exception of the Earthview
cover image, which has been supplied by the
National Aeronautics and Space Administration
(NASA).

© 2009, 2007 Cengage Learning

For product information and technology assistance, contact us at
Cengage Learning Customer & Sales Support, 1-800-354-9706

For permission to use material from this text or product,
submit all requests online at **cengage.com/permissions**
Further permissions questions can be emailed to
permissionrequest@cengage.com

Library of Congress Control Number: 2009926394

ISBN-13: 978-1-4240-7008-4

ISBN-10: 1-4240-7008-2

Cengage Learning
5191 Natorp Boulevard
Mason, Ohio 45040
USA

Cengage Learning is a leading provider of customized learning solutions with
office locations around the globe, including Singapore, the United Kingdom,
Australia, Mexico, Brazil, and Japan. Locate your local office at:
international.cengage.com/region

Cengage Learning products are represented in Canada by Nelson Education, Ltd.

For your lifelong learning solutions, visit **custom.cengage.com**

Visit our corporate website at **cengage.com**

Second Edition

Current and Classic Readings for Microeconomic Literacy

Edited by
Ronald M. Harstad and Sharon Ryan

Table of Contents

Topic III: Government Intervention

Topic IV: PPF and Trade

Topic V: Production, Profit and Costs

Topic VI: Profit Maximization

CREDITS

This page constitutes an extension of the copyright page. We have made every effort to trace the ownership of all copyrighted material and to secure permission from copyright holders. In the event of any question arising as to the use of any material, we will be pleased to make the necessary corrections in future printings. Thanks are due to the following authors, publishers, and agents for permission to use the material indicated.

Economic Scene; Observe, theorize, measure, test and don't overlook what goes wrong. Nobel experiments.

By HAL R. VARIAN (NYT) 1078 words
Published: October 24, 2002

YOU can learn a lot when an experiment goes wrong.

Edward Chamberlain, a professor of economics at Harvard in the 1950's, pioneered the concept of "monopolistic competition," a hybrid of the pure monopoly and pure competition models that were then the staple of economics courses.

To demonstrate the problems with those theories, he would run an experiment in his classroom in which students were given hypothetical values of consuming or costs of supplying a good, and they would wander around the room trying to make deals with one another.

Mr. Chamberlain would tally up the results on the blackboard and point out that they were far from the predictions of received theory.

One student, Vernon L. Smith, was much impressed with the experiment. In 1955, while teaching at Purdue, he decided to run a classroom experiment of his own. He couldn't remember exactly how Mr. Chamberlain had set up his experiment, so he used the rules governing trade on the New York Stock Exchange.

In the simplest version of this sort of game, the class is divided into two groups, buyers and sellers. Each buyer is given a "value" for the good being sold, and each seller is given a "cost." Suppose, for example, that there are three buyers with values (1, 2, 3) and three sellers with costs (1, 2, 3).

Theory predicts an equilibrium price of 2, and either one or two units of the good being sold. (At a price of 2, one buyer and one seller are indifferent about transacting, which is why the quantity is indeterminate.)

The actual experiment Mr. Smith ran was similar, but had more buyers and sellers with different prices, so the outcome was not easily predictable.

Much to Mr. Smith's surprise, the classroom experiment quickly converged on the price predicted by simple demand and supply. He thought there must be something wrong, so he tried again. The same thing happened.

Mr. Smith continued to do these in-class experiments for several years and found that he almost always got the price that theory predicted.

His colleagues weren't impressed: games in the classroom? What could the students learn from games? What could economists learn from experimental markets?

But Mr. Smith persisted in his research and published his first paper on experimental economics six years later. Two weeks ago, he was awarded the Nobel in economic science for his pioneering work.

Experimental economics has had a huge impact on economics, in both theory and practice. Researchers have gone on to examine a variety of social institutions using experimental methods, and today it is firmly established as a legitimate subject.

The discipline of economics, like other sciences, rests on observation, theory, measurement and experimentation. Theory is, necessarily, a simplification of reality. But how do you know you've chosen the right simplification? Experimentation is an antidote to misspecification: one often finds that effects that the theory neglects turn out to be important in practice.

The wording of the instructions or minor variations in the rules of interaction can be critical to the outcome. The wise economist will be on the lookout for this sort of anomaly, just as Mr. Smith was back in 1955, for those anomalies are often the source of a deeper understanding.

Daniel Kahneman, who also received a 2002 Nobel in economic science, is a psychologist by training, but much of his research has focused on how people make decisions. Utility maximization, the workhorse of economics, is a particularly simple theory: people make the choices they most prefer.

Most psychologists would argue this is far too simple. If you define "most preferred" too broadly, the theory is virtually tautological. If you define it too narrowly, simple experiments show the theory is literally false.

As with experimental economics, the challenge is to understand the anomalous behavior. Random departures from the theory could just be error, but systematic departures are worth studying.

Mr. Kahneman did much of his work with Amos Tversky, another Israeli psychologist, who died in 1996. Their work has also found belated recognition in the economics profession, under the name "behavioral economics," which uses both theory and experimentation to study decision making as it relates to market phenomena.

Consider the concept of "loss aversion." This refers to the fact that you have to pay people much more to get them to part with something than they would pay to acquire it. Look at some of those losers in your 401(k). Would you rush to buy them at their current price? No? Then cold-blooded economic analysis says you should sell them. But as Mr. Kahneman and Mr. Tversky point out, few people actually do so.

Mr. Kahneman and Mr. Smith are something of an odd couple intellectually. Mr. Smith is, for the most part, a believer in conventional economic analysis. Much of his recent work has been concerned with market design: how should we design electricity markets or markets for airline landing slots to achieve efficient outcomes?

Mr. Kahneman, on the other hand, sees economics as working with models of human behavior that are much too simplistic. He argues that to understand such strange behavior as stock market bubbles, it is necessary to have better models of how people make investment decisions.

Mr. Smith has generated bubbles in economics experiments in the lab and would no doubt agree that better models of behavior would be useful. On the other hand, his inclination would be to tinker with the market design to see if such bubbles could be dampened or even eliminated, rather than to seek a new theory of economic behavior.

But despite their different approaches, both laureates agree on their approach to economic science: observe, theorize, measure and test -- and watch out for experiments that go wrong. They might just lead to a Nobel prize.

Photos: Daniel Kahneman and Vernon L Smith won the Nobel in economics for trying to explain idiosyncrasies in decision making. Their work helped incorporate psychology and experimental testing into economics. (Bloomberg News, left; Associated Press)

What is Experimental Economics?

by Vernon Smith

Experimental economics applies laboratory methods of inquiry to the study of motivated human interactive decision behavior in social contexts governed by explicit or implicit rules. The explicit rules may be defined by experimenter-controlled move sequences and information events in extensive form n (>1)-person games with specified payoff outcomes. Or the rules may be those at an auction or other market institution in which motivated people buy or sell abstract rights (to consume or produce) information and services (e.g. transportation) within some particular technological context. Implicit rules are the norms, traditions and habits that people bring to the laboratory as part of their cultural and biological evolutionary heritage; they are not normally controlled by the experimenter.

Quite generally we can think of experimental **outcomes** (the observed replicable order in final allocations) as the consequence of individual choice **behavior**, driven by the economic **environment** and mediated by the language and rules governing interactions supplied by the **institution**. The economic environment consists of agent preferences, knowledge, skill endowments, and resource constraints. Abstractly, institutions define the mapping from agent choice of **messages** (e.g., bids, asks, acceptances, moves in a game tree, words, actions) into **outcomes**. Under the operation of these rules, or of norms, people choose messages given the economic environment. *A well-established finding in experimental economics is that institutions matter because the rules matter, and the rules matter because incentives matter.* But the incentives to which people respond are sometimes not those one would expect based on the canons of economic/game theory. It turns out that people are often better, and sometimes worse, at achieving gains for themselves and others than is predicted by standard forms of rational analysis. These contradictions provide important clues to the implicit rules that people may follow and can motivate new theoretical hypotheses for examination in the laboratory.

The design of experiments is motivated by two quite distinct concepts of a rational order. Rejecting or denying either of these concepts should not be construed as irrational. Thus, if people in certain contexts choose outcomes yielding the smaller of two rewards, we ask why, rather than conclude that this is irrational.

The first concept of a rational order derives from today's standard social-economic science model (SSSM) going back to the seventeenth century. The SSSM is an example of what Hayek has called, constructivist rationalism, which, in its modern forms and power, stems from Descartes, who believed and argued that all worthwhile social institutions were and should be created by conscious deductive processes of human reason. Truth is derived and derivable from premises that are obvious and unassailable. Thus, in positive economics it has been argued influentially that you judge the validity of a model by its predictions, not by its assumptions--a methodology that provides limited guidance in experimental studies where one can control the economic environment and institutional rules. In economics the SSSM leads to rational predictive models of decision that motivate research hypotheses that experimentalists have been testing in the laboratory since mid twentieth century. The test results are decidedly mixed, and this has motivated constructivist extensions of game theory, most notably based on other-regarding, in addition to own-regarding, preferences, and on 'learning'--the idea that the predictions of the SSSM might be approached over time by trial-and-error adaptation processes.

For tractability, Cartesian rationalism provisionally requires agents to possess complete information - far more than could ever be given to one mind. In economics the resulting analytical exercises, while yielding insightful theorems, are designed to aid and sharpen thinking - if-then parable. Yet, these exercises may not approximate the level of ignorance that has conditioned institutions, as abstract rules independent of particular parameterizations that have survived as part of the world of experience. The temptation, of course, is to ignore this reality, because it is poorly understood, and to proceed in the implicit belief that our parables capture what is most essential in understanding what we observe.

Our theories and thought processes about social systems involve the conscious and deliberate use of reason. Therefore, it is necessary to constantly remind ourselves that human activity is diffused and dominated by unconscious, autonomic, neuropsychological systems that enable people to function effectively *without* always calling upon the brain's scarcest resource: attentional circuitry. This is an important economizing property of how the brain works. If it were otherwise, no one could get through the day under the burden of self-conscious monitoring and planning every trivial action in detail. Also, no one can express in thoughts, let alone words, all that he or she knows, and does not know, but might need to know for some purposive action. For example, imagine the drain on the brain's resources if at the supermarket a shopper were required to explicitly evaluate the utility from every combination of the tens of thousands of grocery items that are feasible for a given budget. Such mental processes are costly and implicitly we must avoid costs that are not worth the benefit. The challenge of any action or problem triggers first a search by the brain to bring to the conscious mind what one knows that is related to the decision context. Context triggers autobiographical experiential memory, which explains why context surfaces as a nontrivial treatment in small group experiments.

We do not recall learning most of our operating knowledge - natural language is the most prominent example, but, of particular relevance for experimental economics, also virtually everything that constitutes our developmental socialization. We learn the rules of a language and of social intercourse without explicit instruction simply by exposure to family and extended family social networks.

These considerations lead to the second concept of a rational order, an undesigned ecological system that emerges out of cultural and biological evolutionary processes: home grown principles of action, norms, traditions, and morality. Thus, "the rules of morality…are not the conclusions of our reason." According to Hume, who was concerned with the limits of reason and the boundedness of human understanding, rationality was a phenomena that reason **discovers** in emergent institutions. Adam Smith expressed the idea of emergent order in both <u>The Wealth of Nations</u> and <u>The Theory of Moral Sentiments</u>. According to this concept of rationality, truth is discovered in the form of the intelligence embodied in rules and traditions that have formed, inscrutably, out of the ancient history of human social interactions. This is the antithesis of the Cartesian and contemporary belief that if an observed social mechanism is functional, somebody in the unrecorded past must have used reason consciously to create it to serve its currently perceived intended purposes. In experimental economics this tradition is represented by the discovery of emergent order in numerous studies of existing market institutions such as the double auction. To paraphrase Adam Smith, people in these experiments are led to promote welfare enhancing social ends that are not part of their conscious intention. This principle is supported by hundreds of experiments whose environments and institutions exceed the capacity of formal game theoretic analysis. But they do not exceed the functional capacity of collectives of incompletely informed human decision makers whose mental algorithms coordinate behavior through the rules of the institution--social algorithms--to generate high levels of measured performance. ***Acknowledging and recognizing the workings of unseen processes are essential to the growth of our understanding of social phenomena, and we must strive not to exclude them from our inquiry, if we have any hope of understanding data inside or outside of the laboratory.*** In this way we at least can attempt to escape the very significant disadvantage of being a human in studying human behavior. Even those who study primates must deal with natural tendencies to anthropomorphize what they observe; so strongly do we identify with our genetic cousins.

Ironically, the greatest success for non-cooperative equilibrium theory, that has emerged from experimental studies beginning over forty years ago, is its power to predict outcomes when people have **incomplete** (private) information on individual payoffs. This "success" has passed with little fanfare because of the standard assumption that decision-makers, like the theorist/experimentalist, must have complete information in order to construct the equilibrium.

How are the two concepts of a rational order related?

Constructivism takes as given the social structures generated by emergent institutions that we observe in the world, and proceeds to model it formally. An example would be the Dutch auction or a sealed bid auction. Constructivists do not ask why or how that institution arose or what were the ecological conditions that created it; or why there are so many distinct auction institutions. In some cases it is the other way around. Thus, revenue equivalence theorems show that the standard auctions generate identical expected outcomes leaving no apparent economic reason for choosing between them. Using game theory to implement constructivist rationality, one represents a socioeconomic situation with an interactive game tree. The ecological concept of rationality asks from whence came the structure captured by the tree? Why this social practice, or game, and not another? Were there others that lacked survival properties and were successfully invaded by what we observe?

The two types of rational order are both expressed in the experimental methodology developed for economic systems design. This branch of experimental economics uses the lab as a test-bed to examine the performance of proposed new institutions, and modifies their rules and implementation features in the light of the test results. The proposed designs are constructivist, although most applications, such as the design of electricity markets or auctions for spectrum licenses, are far too complicated for a complete formal analysis. But when a design is modified in the light of test results, the modifications tested, modified again, retested, and so on, one is using the laboratory to effect an evolutionary adaptation as in the second concept of a rational order. If the final result is implemented in the field, it certainly undergoes further evolutionary change in the light of practice, and of operational forces not tested in the experiments because they are unknown or beyond current laboratory capability.

Finally, understanding decision requires knowledge beyond the traditional bounds of economics, a challenge to which Hume and Smith were not strangers. This is manifest in recent studies of the neural correlates of strategic interaction using fMRI and other brain imaging technologies. This research explores intentions or "mind reading," and other hypotheses about information, choice, and own versus other payoffs in determining behavior.

Economics in the Laboratory

Vernon L. Smith

Vernon L. Smith is Regents' Professor of Economics, and Research Director of the Economic Science Laboratory, University of Arizona, Tucson, Arizona. In 1992, he was named a Distinguished Fellow of the American Economic Association.

Why do economists conduct experiments? To answer that question, it is first necessary briefly to specify the ingredients of an experiment. Every laboratory experiment is defined by an <u>environment</u>, specifying the initial endowments, preferences and costs that motivate exchange. This environment is controlled using monetary rewards to induce the desired specific value/cost configuration (Smith, 1991, 6).[1] An experiment also uses an <u>institution</u> defining the language (messages) of market communication (bids, offers, acceptances), the rules that govern the exchange of information, and the rules under which messages become binding contracts. This institution is defined by the experimental instructions which describe the messages and procedures of the market, which are most often computer controlled. Finally, there is the observed <u>behavior</u> of the participants in the experiments as a function of the environment and institution that constitute the controlled variables.

Using this framework of environment, institution, and behavior, I can think of at least seven prominent reasons in the literature as to why economists conduct experiments. Undoubtedly, there are more (Davis and Holt, 1992, chapter 1 and passim).

<u>1. Test a theory, or discriminate between theories.</u> This motivation comes from the economic and game theory literature. We test a theory by comparing its message or its outcome implications with the experimental observations. The greater the frequency with which the observations hit these "predictions," in the context of a design in which hits are unlikely to occur by chance, the better the theory.[2] Examples can be found in the auction literature (Smith, 1991, 25-29), where risk averse models of bidding in Dutch and first price sealed bid auctions are favored by the data over risk neutral models, while

---

[1] Where appropriate, references to work by me and my coauthors will be to the paper numbers in Smith (1991).

[2] Selten (1989) offers a measure of predictive success. I use the terms "prediction" and "implication" of a theoretical model interchangeably. Consistency with a "prediction" does not require that the theory be done in advance of an observation.

dominate strategy auctions such as the English, whose outcomes are predicted to be independent of risk attitude, perform well in the laboratory. Of course, theories subjected to sufficiently rigorous tests are nearly always found to need improvement; this leads to the second reason for doing experiments.

2. <u>Explore the causes of a theory's failure</u>. When the observations of an experiment fail to conform to the implications of the theory, the first thing to be done is to reexamine the design, and to be sure that the predictive failure is the fault of the theory. Well-articulated theories formally model the environment and the trading rules, and the experimentalist seeks to reproduce these conditions of the theory. In the course of testing when the experimental design continues to seem appropriate and the theory still fails, this tends to encourage an experimental examination designed to discover the cause. Establishing the anatomy of failure is essential to any research program concerned with modifying the theory. Examples are to be found in the bargaining literature (Roth, 1987; Hoffman and Spitzer, 1985; Hoffman, et al, 1992; Bolton, 1991) and in common value auctions (Kagel and Levin, 1986; Cox and Smith, 1992). Often theories that initially perform poorly show improvement if subjects are given more experience (Cox and Smith, 1992), or the payoffs are increased (Smith and Walker, 1993), but sometimes these measures fail to yield results that improve the theory's performance (Smith and Walker, 1993).

3. <u>Establish empirical regularities as a basis for new theory</u>. Well-formulated theories in most sciences tend to be preceded by much observation, which in turn stimulates curiosity as to what accounts for the documented regularities. Microeconomic theory tends to build upon simplifying assumptions, and to eschew attempts to model many of the complex trading and contracting institutions that we observe. But in the laboratory, especially with computerization, institutions with complex trading rules are as easy to study as are simple single unit auctions. This makes it possible to range beyond the confines of current theory to establish empirical regularities which can enable theorists to see in advance what are the difficult problems on which it is worth their while to work. The continuous double auction, used the world over, is a fine example. In this institution buyers announce bid prices, sellers announce offers, or asking prices. Any new bid (offer) must be at a price which is lower (higher) than the standing bid (offer); i.e. the bid-asked spread must narrow. A binding contract occurs when a buyer accepts a seller's ask, or a seller accepts a buyer's bid. Contracts occur in sequence as new bids, asks and acceptances occur. Because of its robust equilibrating properties with small numbers of traders possessing only private information this institution (Smith, 1991, 1, 2, 6) was studied extensively in the laboratory long before the attempts by R. Wilson, D. Friedman and others to model it (see Friedman and Rust, 1992, for references).

4. <u>Compare environments</u>. Comparing environments using the same institution permits an investigation of the robustness of that institution. The objective is to stress the theory with extreme environmental conditions under which an institution's established properties may begin to break down. Thus, in common value auctions (where the item has the same value to all bidders after the auction is completed), the Nash Model

performs better when there are 3-4 bidders than when there are 6-7 bidders (Kagel and Levin, 1986). Similarly, the Nash equilibrium prediction performs fairly well in the Fouraker and Siegel (1963) bargaining environment, but breaks down in the ultimatum game environment (Hoffman et al, 1992), as discussed below.

5. Compare institutions. Using identical environments, but varying the market rules of exchange, has been the means by which the comparative properties of institutions has been established. Examples include the comparison of English, Dutch, first and second price sealed bid auctions, the comparison of uniform and discriminative price multiple unit auctions, and the comparison of posted (retail) pricing with double auction trading (Smith, 1991, 25, 5, 17).

6. Evaluate policy proposals. Friedman's (1960) original proposal that the Treasury auction securities in one-price auctions led to their comparison with the discriminative rules (Smith, 1991, 5). Bids to buy in this auction are arranged from highest to lowest; if the offering was $2 billion worth of bills, this amount of the highest bids are accepted at a price given by the highest rejected bid. In the past decade, private industry and government sponsors have funded studies of the incentives for off-floor trading in continuous double auction markets, alternative institutions for auctioning emissions permits, mechanisms for allocating space shuttle resources, and market mechanisms for the allocation of airport slots (Plott, 1987).

7. The laboratory as a testing ground for institutional design. A growing use of the laboratory is as a testing ground for examining the performance properties of new forms of exchange. The early experiments studying the one-price sealed bid-offer auction for Treasury securities helped Henry Wallich to motivate the Treasury in the early 1970s to offer some long term bond issues using this procedure (Smith, 1991, pp. 511-512). This led eventually to the use of the procedure in auctioning commercial paper and in setting the dividend rate on variable rate preferred corporate securities. In 1992, Treasury resumed its earlier experiments with the one-price auction because of publicized irregularities in dealer bidding.

A second example is the new Arizona Stock Exchange (AZX). In 1988 we started running our first experiments with the uniform price double auction. In this mechanism, buyers submit bids to buy, and sellers submit offers to sell in real time during the specified market "call" period. All bids, offers, and the tentative market clearing uniform price, are displayed as they are entered, so participants can see the existing state of the market, and alter their own bids or offers accordingly. It turns out that this approach has efficiencies comparable to those of continuous double auction, but with no price discrimination. Subsequently we learned that Steven Wunsch independently developed a similar system, and was seeking SEC authority to operate it as a proprietary stock exchange for institutions. Wunsch Auction Systems opened in New York in 1991. About this time officials of the Arizona Corporation Commission, who had heard of our experimental studies of "electronic exchange," approached us with the idea of starting an Arizona Stock Exchange. We demonstrated the uniform price double auction for them, pointed out its properties, and they were eager to get moving. Our first action was to get them together with Wunsch to explore the possibility of moving his exchange to Arizona. Eventually, Wunsch adopted the new name, AZX, and the new exchange has experienced accelerated growth since its move in March 1992. Had it not been for the experiments we would not have come to understand the comparative properties of the uniform price double auction, and been able to recommend it wholeheartedly as a reasonable direction for a new electronic exchange.

What Have Economists Learned from Experiments?

Hoffman's (1991) "Bibliography of Experimental Economics" contains 1500 entries. I can only attempt to report a small selection of some of the findings.

Institutions Matter

Experimentalists have long known that the continuous double auction rules of trade in securities markets constitutes a mechanism remarkably adept at maximizing the gains from exchange at prices tending to converge to competitive equilibria (Smith, 1991, 1). What we have learned since is that this is just one of many illustrations of the principle that institutions matter. This is because the rules determine the information states and individual incentives in the trading game: institutions matter because incentives and information matter. Consequently, posted offer retail pricing converges more slowly and erratically and is less efficient than continuous double auction (Plott and Smith, 1978). Unlike the latter, sellers receive no continuous bid price information from competing buyers. Also, sellers must quote one price per period for all units making price cuts more costly.

Does this mean that posted offers are inferior to continuous double auction? No. The experiments evaluate only the allocative properties of the two mechanisms, and do not address their different transactions cost properties. With continuous double auction, every trade involves decentralized multilateral negotiation, while pricing is centralized in a posted offer system, and clerks need have no bargaining skills. The latter is cost effective for mass retail distribution, the former has been well-suited to the broker-dealer structure of securities markets.

As early as 1965 (Smith, 1991, 4), an extreme environment was used as a stress-test to explore the limits of the ability of the continuous double auction to generate competitive equilibria. This was the 'swastika' environment in which the demand price is constant up to a maximum quantity, and the supply price (below demand price) is also constant up to a maximum quantity greater than the maximum demand quantity. If you draw these demand and supply curves you see what looks like a swastika emblem. Such markets still performed efficiently, but convergence to the competitive equilibrium was slow and erratic when the excess supply was very small. Van Boening and Wilcox

(1992) have recently reported a much more successful stress-test of continuous double auction. They report experiments in which the sellers' only costs are fixed costs that can be avoided by selling zero units, and the demand price is constant up to a fixed capacity. This lumpy environment is structured so that there is no uniform price competitive equilibrium like that to which continuous double auction usually converges; yet efficient allocations exist. The important result is that continuous double auction cannot handle this environment, and research is under way for new or traditional mechanisms that can handle such cases. The issue is of practical importance. airlines, for example, have large flight costs that can only be avoided by not flying.

One of the better-known predictive failures of expected utility theory is the "preference reversal" phenomenon. A subject reports that gamble A is preferred to B, but in responding with her selling price places a higher price on B (say $10) than on A ($7) (Lichtenstein and Slovic, 1971). But Chu and Chu (1990) report that such reversals are much reduced on the second iteration of a process in which the experimenter arbitrages the inconsistency, and the reversals disappear on the third iteration establishing that subjects are not satisfied with their own choices when they experience the implications of those choices. More subtle experiments have been reported by Cox and Grether (1992), in which each subject's selling price is elicited in an English Clock auction which is known to have good demand revelation properties. In this auction a clock is set at a low price; all buyers respond with their demands. The clock then ticks up to successively higher prices, and buyers respond by reducing their demand until there is but one unit demanded. After five repetitions, subjects' selling prices were in general consistent with their choices. Consequently, this provides another example of the tendency for rational behavior to emerge in the context of a repetitive market institution. But in this case, the market corrects the inconsistency of behavior found in choice elicitation experiments.

Unconscious Optimization in Market Interactions

In his early path-breaking critique of the feasibility of rational calculation in human choice, Simon (1955, p. 104) explicitly did not "rule out the possibility that the unconscious is a better decision-maker than the conscious." Unknown to both of us at the time was the fact that the first of hundreds of continuous double auction experiments reported in Smith (1991, 1, Chart 1) would spotlight the crucial importance of not ruling out the rationality of unconscious decision in rule-governed repeat interaction settings. Consider the typical conditions of a continuous double auction experiment. Subjects have private information on their own willingness-to-pay or willingness-to-accept schedules which bound the prices at which each can profitably trade. No subject has information on market supply and demand. After an experiment, upon interrogation they deny that they could have maximized their monetary earnings or that their trading results could be predicted by a theory. Yet despite these conditions, the subjects tend to converge quickly over time to the competitive equilibrium. Thus "the most common responses to the market question were: unorganized. unstable, chaotic, and confused. Students were both surprised and amazed at the conclusion of the experiment when the entrusted student opened a sealed envelope containing the correctly predicted equilibrium price and quantity" (Gillette and DelMas, 1992, p. 5).

That economic agents can achieve efficient outcomes which are not part of their intention was the key principle articulated by Adam Smith, but few outside of the Austrian and Chicago traditions believed it, circa 1956. Certainly I was not primed to believe it, having been raised by a socialist mother, and further handicapped (in this regard) by a Harvard education, but my experimental subjects revealed to me the error in my thinking.

In many experimental markets, poorly informed, error-prone, and uncomprehending human agents interact through the trading rules to produce social algorithms which demonstrably approximate the wealth maximizing outcomes traditionally thought to require complete information and cognitively rational actors.[3]

Information: Less Can Be Better

Providing subjects with complete information, far from improving market competition, tends to make it worse. In 1976, I reported continuous double auction results, using the "swastika" environment described above, comparing the effect of private with complete information (Smith, 1991, 6). Under private information, convergence to the equilibrium outcome (in this case, the Nash-competitive outcome) was much more rapid and dependable then under complete and common information.[4] Similar results had been reported earlier by Fouraker and Siegel (1963) for Bertrand and Cournot oligopoly, and more recently by Noussair and Porter (1992) and Brown-Kruse (1992). When people have complete information they can identify more self-interested outcomes than Nash (and competitive) equilibria, and use punishing strategies in an attempt to achieve them, which delays reaching equilibrium.

Of course, it can be said that all of this simply supports the "folk theorem" that repetition aids cooperation. But the folk theorem operates in situations with small numbers and complete information -- like the fact that a repeated prisoners' dilemma game tends to converge to cooperation. The argument here is much stronger: competitive tendencies prevail under the private information conditions that pervade markets in the economy.

---

[3]That this description applies to markets in the field has been demonstrated by Forsythe et al. (1992), who report the remarkable forecasting accuracy of their presidential stock market, which beats the opinion polls by a wide margin.

[4]Kachelmeier and Shehata (1992) report that these results also hold in cross-cultural comparisons of subjects from China, the United States and Canada.

The principle that private payoff information can yield "better" results has also been established in the Nash bargaining game (Roth, 1987). Nash assumed that the bargainers knew each other's utilities (preferences). Roth and his coworkers implemented this theory with ingenious simplicity: subjects bargained over the division of 100 lottery tickets, each representing a chance to win fixed large or small prizes for each of the two players, with the prizes generally being different for the two players. When the two players know only their own prizes (and each other's percentage of the lottery tickets), the outcome conforms to the Nash bargaining solution. When the bargainers also know each other's prizes the Nash prediction fails; in short, Nash theory is not falsified, it is just not robust with respect to the bargainers knowing both prizes.

The principle that less information can be advantageous also applies under asymmetric payoff information in which Schelling (1957) argued that the less informed bargainer may have an advantage over a completely informed adversary. In fact Siegel and Fouraker (1960) observed this to be the case. The better informed bargainer, knowing that the other player knew only his own payoff, is more forgiving when his opponent makes large demands. This concessionary posture works to the disadvantage of the completely informed player. Camerer, Loewenstein and Weber (1989) call this the "curse of knowledge" and report new evidence in a market setting.

Common Information is Not Sufficient to Yield Common Expectations or "Knowledge"

It has been argued that game theory requires common knowledge.[5] This arbitrarily limits the value of game theory in organizing experimental data, and directs our attention away from the fact that common knowledge is a condition the process of achieving which we must understand if game theory is to make progress in predicting behavior. This is implicitly recognized by the growing current interest among game theorists in concepts of bounded rationality and of learning. Although I believe these are conceptually the right directions to take, if the exercises are guided by introspective model development, uniformed by observations and testing, they are unlikely to achieve their full predictive potential.

---

[5]Aumann (1987, p. 473) has emphasized in unmistakable terms this requirement of game theory: "It is not enough that each player be fully aware of the rules of the game and the utility functions of the players. Each player must also be aware of this fact ... There is evidence that game theorists had been vaguely cognizant of the need for some such requirement ever since the last fifties or early sixties; but the first to give a clear sharp formulation was the philosopher D. K. Lewis (in 1969). Lewis defined an event as common knowledge among a set of agents if all know it, all know that all know it, and so on ad infinitum. The common knowledge assumption underlies all of game theory and much of economic theory. Whatever be the model under discussion, whether complete or incomplete information, consistent or inconsistent, repeated or one-shot, cooperative or noncooperative, the model itself must be assumed common knowledge; otherwise the model is insufficiently specified, and the analysis incoherent."

Experimentalists have attempted to implement the condition of "common knowledge" by publicly announcing instructions, payoffs, and other conditions in an experiment. Some examples of this process would be Roth (1987) in Nash bargaining games, Smith, Suchanek and Williams (Smith, 1991, 19) in finite horizon asset trading experiments, and McCabe (1989) in finite horizon fiat money experiments, but there are many others. However, it should be noted that administering common instructions in public literally achieves common information -- not common knowledge in the sense of expectations. In other words, there is no assurance that a public announcement will yield common expectations among the players, since each person may still be uncertain about how others will use the information.

In laboratory stock markets each player receives an initial endowment in cash and shares of stock. It is public information that the expected dividend in a given time period will be some fixed number for each of the T periods of the game. With zero interest rate the value of a share of stock in the first time period should be T times the expected dividend. In each time period, the rational expectations hypothesis is that share prices will be equal to the remaining dividends to be paid, and will decline by an amount equal to the expected dividend in each time period.

In fact, first time participants in experiments of this sort -- whether they are undergraduates, graduates, business persons, or stock traders -- produce bell-shaped price bubbles starting below fundamental value, rising well above and crashing to near fundamental value in the last few periods. Trading volume is high. When subjects return for a second session, the price bubbles are dampened, and volume is reduced. When they return for a third session, trading tends to follow the decline in fundamental value, with very thin volume. These experiments illustrate that participants come to have common expectations by experience, not by being given common information and then reasoning that others will expect prices to be near fundamental value.[6]

Unless players have common expectations of behavior in later periods, they cannot reason backwards to the present. This problem, for theories based on backward induction rationality, is illustrated by the wage search experiments of Cox and Oaxaca (1989). In their experiments subjects search a distribution of wages, and must decide in each period whether to accept a certain wage offer; if accepted the subject must forego

---

[6]Of relevance here is the "getting to common knowledge" theorem discussed in this journal by Geanakoplos (1992). The theorem is driven by a process in which all agents observe in turn each agent's action. At some finite time, t^*, all agents have common knowledge of what each agent will do in the future. The asset experiments confirm the predictions of the theorem. But this does not imply that the subjects in the experiments go through a reasoning process like that which is used to prove the theorem.. In fact, subjects would have great difficulty articulating the means whereby they reached their unwillingness to trade away from fundamental value.

continued search and the possibility of receiving a better subsequent offer. In this situation, subjects have only to anticipate their own behavior in later periods in order to properly backward induct. Subjects in these experiments behave as if they are solving the backward induction problem properly. Hence, it would appear that when common expectations exist (because the subject "knows" his or her own expectations) then subjects will backward induct. Of course, this does not mean that subjects are conscious of having solved such a problem, and can tell you about it.

In this journal, Brandenberger (1992) has usefully emphasized that the assumption of common knowledge is sometimes unduly strong; examples are given in which if each of two players are rational and they have mutual knowledge (both know it, but not necessarily that both know that both know it), then a Nash equilibrium follows. These distinctions between various degrees of knowledge are certainly helpful, but if game theory is to have predictive value, it is necessary to go further and seek to discover operationally how to achieve the required conditions of knowledge. Theories based upon abstract conditions make no predictions. Subjects obtain knowledge of the strategy choices of others, by experience. This is why I see no way for game theory to advance independently of experimental (or other) observations. We have to understand the processes whereby the required conditions of knowledge are satisfied -- processes like pregame play, repeated play, cheap talk, or the futures market example discussed in a moment -- before the implications of those conditions can become testable hypotheses.

It has been observed that if the failure of rational expectations in finite horizon trading experiments was due to the lack of common expectations about later periods, then introducing futures markets should hasten convergence to rational expectations equilibria by speeding up the process of creating common expectations of later period behavior (Porter and Smith, 1989). Forsythe, Palfrey and Plott (1982) had reported that convergence in two-period horizon experiments was hastened by introducing a futures market on period two. If our interpretation was correct, then a futures market on period 8 in 15-period asset trading experiments would aid in creating common expectation at mid-horizon (subjects already expect trading at fundamental value near the end), and price bubbles should be retarded in the presence of such a futures market. Porter and Smith (1989) report experiments supporting this hypothesis. The learning suggested by these studies is that the important role of futures markets may be to foster common expectations among traders concerning a future event. This permits the backward induction calculus to yield the appropriate rational expectations in the current period.

Dominated Strategies Are for Playing, Not Eliminating

It is commonly argued that dominated strategies should never rationally be played, and thus can be eliminated in game-theoretic analysis. But players in repeated games do sometimes play dominated strategies and there are sound reasons why.

Consider the two person alternating play game tree in Figure 1, which is played repeatedly for a long time with uncertain termination (McCabe, Rassenti and Smith,

1992). If player 1 moves down at x_1 then at x_2 player 2 can signal a desire to achieve the cooperative outcome (50:50) by moving left, or, by moving right, signal a desire to achieve the subgame noncooperative outcome (40:40). But if player 2 chooses left at x_2, player 1 can defect by moving down at x_3, forcing player 2 at node x_5 to choose between (60:30) and the direct punishment outcomes that result at node x_7. Game theory reasons that player 2 should play left at node x_5, accepting player 1's defection, but punish on the next round of repeated play by choosing right at node x_2 (choosing right at x_2 almost without exception ends at the equilibrium (40:40)). Subject player 2's tend not to do this, but instead to play down at x_5, and thereby to punish immediately. The reason is clear, the resulting message is unambiguous, with no possibility that player 1's will misunderstand. The strategy works: even when 12 subjects are randomly repaired after each play, there is a strong tendency toward the cooperative outcome by round 15-20. (If the game is altered by interchanging the (50:50) and (60:30) payoff boxes, thereby removing player 2's ability to punish immediately, then cooperation fails to emerge). This is not the game-theoretic route to repeated-play cooperation because the bargainers are assumed to have common expectations (knowledge). But, as we have seen, common expectations is achieved by a process of play, not by deductive analysis. Part of this process may be to punish in ways that will be clearly understood.

Figure 1
A Two-Person Alternating-Play Game

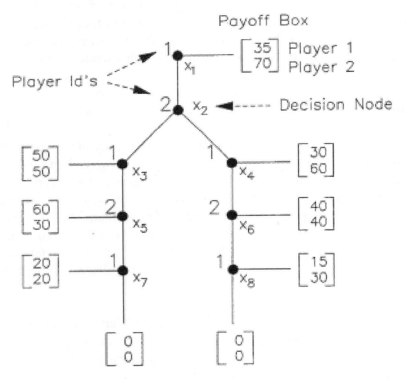

Efficiency and Underrevelation Are Compatible

It is well-known that a market participant, whether a buyer or seller, can sometimes tilt the conditions of the transaction toward personal gain and away from market efficiency, by not revealing true willingness to trade. Consequently, economists often seem to argue as if market efficiency must rely on complete revelation of preferences.

As an empirical counterexample, consider the version of the uniform price double auction mechanism studied in McCabe, Rassenti and Smith (1992). Remember that in this auction format, subjects submit openly displayed bids during a market call period. In this format, subjects greatly underreveal demand and supply, but they adjust their bids and offers so that the market clearing price and quantity approximates a competitive equilibrium. At this equilibrium they produce many bids and offers tied at the same price. This behavior serves to protect each side of the market against manipulation by the other side. That is, if a buyer attempts to lower the market price by bidding lower, that buyer's bid is replaced by another tied bid without moving the price, and similarly if a seller attempts to raise the price.

In short, efficiency only requires enough revelation to allow the marginal units on both sides of the market to trade. This can occur although there is massive under-revelation of the inframarginal units. In uniform price experiments, one frequently observes that subjects capture 100 percent of the surplus while revealing only 10-15 percent of it in their bids.

The Endowment Effect

Thaler (1980) has argued that the observed tendency in survey studies for willingness-to-accept to exceed willingness-to-pay by nontrivial amounts is due to an "endowment" (or ownership) effect which arises because of loss aversion; an example is the man who paid $5 per bottle for a case of wine. A few years later he is offered $100 per bottle, and refuses, although he has never paid more than $35 for a bottle of wine. In this case giving up the wine yields a loss which is more highly weighted than the gain from purchasing an equivalent bottle. The existence of an endowment effect has been suggested by numerous hypothetical survey studies; recently, the experimental focus has been to verify its existence with real goods.

It has been argued by Kahneman, Knetsch and Thaler (1990) that the endowment effect does not apply to goods held for resale; only to goods which are consumed. Similarly, it does not apply to the exchange of rights (or tokens) on which value has been induced by cash payments in experiments. In either case, since what is being acquired is intended from the start to be resold, losses and opportunity costs are transparently equivalent. Kahneman, Knetsch and Thaler (1990) report both choice and exchange experiments confirming the results with tokens, but establishing the willingness-to-accept/willingness-to-pay discrepancy for consumer goods (like emblem mugs, pens, and so on). They also reject empirically the important qualification that the discrepancy is due to income effects (see their experiments 6 and 7). Franciosi, Kujal, Michelitsch and Smith (1993) have reported experiments that narrow the reported willingness-to-accept/willingness-to-pay discrepancy by using a more uniform choice task, and by using the uniform price double auction (with its good revelation properties for marginal units) to establish price. While these results reduce the discrepancy, the endowment effect remains statistically (and economically) significant.

Samuelson and Zeckhauser (1988) suggest that the endowment effect may be a manifestation of a broader "status quo bias;" they provide results showing the existence of such a bias even when the problem is not framed in terms of gains and losses. Models of utility-maximizing when decision costs are taken into account postulate a trade-off between the sum of all the various costs of decision making and the value of the decision outcome (Smith and Walker, 1993). Such models predict a bias in favor of one's current status, since any change is cognitively and information costly.

Fairness: Taste or Expectation?

According to survey studies reported by Kahneman, Knetsch and Thaler (1986), people indicate that it is unfair for firms to raise prices and increase profits in response to certain changes in the environment which are not justified by an increase in costs. Thus, respondents report that it is 'unfair' for firms to raise the price of snow-shovels after a snowstorm, or to raise the price of plywood following a hurricane. In these circumstances, economic theory predicts shortages, an increase in prices toward the new market clearing levels, and, eventually an increase in output. Unfortunately, economic theory does not predict the verbal behavior of agents in this process so that such expressions do not falsify the theory.

Do expressions of unfairness reflect interpersonal utilities that reduce effective demand for the product of offending parties, or do they vent the unpleasant need for expectations to be adjusted? If such results show no more than a lag as aggrieved parties adjust their expectations to the new reality, the standard models will predict the eventual result, as the indignation subsides. But protesting parties may react strategically in their self-interest by withholding demand and punishing price "gougers," or, fearing this, sellers may moderate or forgo their increase in prices. Alternatively, by way of contemporary contract theory, one side or the other may see the reference price and transactions as an implicit contract, not to be lightly tampered with. If an economic agent can extract resources by claiming unfair treatment, then it is consistent with standard theory for the agent to manufacture words to that effect. In such situations, it isn't clear that standard self-interested utility-maximizing models can account fully for the observed market behavior.

Kahneman, Knetsch and Thaler (1986) do not predict the final outcome in these cases; a departure from the reference transaction, initially seen as unfair, may eventually achieve the status of a new reference transaction. This argument is a form of the standard adaptive expectations hypothesis, and has been tested in an experimental market environment (Kachelmeier, et al, 1991; Deng, et al, 1992). In an initial baseline series of trading periods with a 50 percent profits tax on sellers, the after-tax profit of sellers is identical with the consumer's surplus of buyers, and the division of surplus is "fair." Then the reference baseline is altered by substituting a 20 percent sales tax for the 50 percent profit tax on sellers. The effect of the sales tax is to raise the market clearing price, and substantially increase seller after-tax profit relative to buyer profit in comparison with the reference situation. Across experiments, the subjects are divided into three different treatment groups: (1) marginal cost disclosure, in which buyers are informed of the price implications of the sales tax; (2) no disclosure, in which buyers are given no new information; (3) profit disclosure, in which buyers receive a graph showing for each price what the potential split of total surplus is between buyers and sellers.

Deng et al (1992) choose a particular institutional context in which sellers independently post selling prices at the beginning of each period. Buyers, queued at random, choose to make their purchases one at a time. The Kahneman, Knetsch, Thaler argument implies that in the first period, prices will be highest under marginal cost disclosure, where buyers are informed of the price implications of the sales tax, because the disclosure serves to justify price increases and to reduce any resistance to them. Revealing profits, on the other hand, will lead to the lowest prices in the first period, because the change from the reference (baseline) transactions is greatest, and will lead to substantial resistance. The no-information group should, according to the hypothesis, fall between these extremes.

The results strongly and significantly support the Kahneman, Knetsch and Thaler hypothesis. In period one, the price in the marginal cost disclosure group was very near the new competitive equilibrium, with prices much the lowest in the profit disclosure group. But in successive trading periods, the mean prices in the profit disclosure and no disclosure groups increase, and by period 10 none of the three means are statistically different from each other or the competitive price. These results offer strong confirmation of standard theory, as the sellers in the profit disclosure treatment raise prices over time in response to the excess demand. Furthermore, as sellers raise prices they are not deterred by any significant incidence of demand withholding by buyers.

Fairness questions also arise in the ultimatum game where a sum of money, say $10 is to be allocated between two people. Player 1 moves first offering some amount, X, of the $10 to player 2. If player 2 accepts that amount, then player 1 receives the rest; if player 2 rejects that amount, both players receive zero. Game theory predicts that player 1 will offer the smallest possible amount to player 2; player 2 will accept it as better than nothing; and player 1 will take the lion's share. However, in the experimental context when players are anonymously paired, and play only once, the modal offer by player 2 is $5, with a lower median.

These observations have been interpreted as showing that the players have a taste for fairness (see Bolton, 1991, and his references). In particular player 2 is concerned about being treated fairly by player 1, and the latter must take this into account lest her offer be rejected. But this interpretation has been called into question by the results of the "dictator game" in which player 2 <u>must</u> accept the offer of player 1. Forsythe et al (1988) find significantly lower offers in the dictator game than in the ultimatum game. Hoffman et al (1992) corroborate these results and report dramatically lower offers (two-thirds offer zero) when the dictator game is run double blind: the experimenter does not know the decisions or payoffs of any subject. To put it another way, the dictator results are highly sensitive to the degree of anonymity from other persons. This suggests that the ultimatum game results are due primarily to strategic and expectational considerations, and not just to a taste for fair outcomes. The same considerations apply to the above market experiments.

Methodology and Experiment

The fact that the planet Mercury exhibited an orbit that violated Newton's theory did not lead Newtonians to conclude that the theory was falsified; rather, they concluded that there must exist a heretofore unknown planet between the sun and Mercury that perturbed its orbit from the predicted path (they even named it Vulcan, and there was no subsequent shortage of claimed sightings) (Roseveare, 1982). <u>All</u> tests of a theory require various auxiliary hypotheses that are necessary in order to interpret the observations as a test of the theory. These auxiliary hypotheses go under various names: initial conditions, <u>ceteris paribus</u> clauses, background information, and so on. Consequently, all tests of a theory are actually joint tests -- that is, a test of the theory conditional on the auxiliary hypotheses. This leads to the Duhem-Quine theses, according to which one can always rescue a theory from an anomalous observation by <u>ex post hoc</u> recourse to imaginative and persuasive auxiliary hypotheses. Conversely, every observational victory for a theory can be questioned by a suitable revision of the background knowledge in which the theory is embedded. This thesis denies the possibility of direct falsification of any specific testable implication of a theory (and, in its strong form, denies rational rules of selection).

My view is that some philosophers have exaggerated the significance of the Duhem-Quine problem, while experimentalists may be unaware of its power in influencing their day-to-day activities. Experimental economists are intuitively if not formally aware of the problem; this is why they do so many experiments probing the sources of a theory's failure, or success, as in the ultimatum game and other examples discussed above. If you have a confounding problem with auxiliary hypotheses, then you do new experiments to test them. If the auxiliary hypotheses are not testable, this is preeminently your critic's problem.

A recent exchange among experimentalists in the December 1992 <u>American Economic Review</u> is squarely reflective of the Duhem-Quine problem. Harrison (1992) has questioned all falsifying observations in experimental economics as due to a postulated low opportunity cost of deviating from theoretical optimality. This thesis sets the stage for the convenient nihilist belief that all recalcitrant observations must be due to inadequate payoff opportunity cost. (Of course, this argument raises the unanswered question of why there exists validating results with low opportunity cost). But, like most important instances of Duhem-Quine, the proposition can be and has been tested -- in this case many times over the last 30-odd years (Smith and Walker, 1993, offer a review).[7] The results have made it plain that money does matter; that factors besides money also matter; that many anomalies do not disappear by escalating payoffs (and foregone profits); and that inadequate attention has been given to modelling the possible relationship between the performance of a theory and the (monetary and nonmonetary) motivation of decision makers.[8]

But other Duhem-Quine issues regularly arise. Both when the results are favorable and when they are unfavorable to a theory, experimental economists have asked if the observations were affected by increased subject experience. Thus, Alger (1986) reports oligopoly results in which early convergence to Nash behavior does not persist when much longer experiments are run. But Alger (1986) used simulated buyers, and it has been shown that mean prices are uniformly lower in oligopoly competition when real buyers are used (Brown-Kruse, 1991). These and a host of similar Duhem-Quine issues are subject to empirical examination and are part of the day-to-day operating life of experimentalists.

The "replication" problem is also related to Duhem-Quine. It is often claimed that there is inadequate replication in economics. The common complaint is that because

------

[7]At the other pole from Harrison stand some psychologists who downplay the evidence that monetary payoffs can have a significant affect on outcomes. To wit: "We agree with Smith and Walker (1993) that monetary incentives could improve performance under certain conditions by eliminating careless errors" (Tversky and Kahneman, 1992, p. 316). The reader will not find any statement like this in the cited reference to agree with. The "errors" we discuss are not careless; they are deviations from optimality attributed to decision costs. If subjects care less about getting it right when there are zero or low rewards, and decision is costly, this is because it is in their interest to care less. We canvass 31 studies in which increasing rewards relative to baseline either reduces the deviations of the data around the theory's prediction, or moves the ventral tendency of the data closer to this prediction.

[8]Of course, one can always offer the incredible argument that any recalcitrant case would go away if you just made payoff opportunity cost large enough. But this argument simply shows the limitations of a theory that postulates motivated agents, but is devoid of all detail as to that motivation. "Auxiliary" hypotheses in experimental economics that have to do with key issues involving the state of the agent like motivation and experience (learning), must ultimately be incorporated into the theory, not banished to the realm of auxiliary hypotheses for the experimentalists to worry about.

replications are inadequately "original," editors are reluctant to publish them, and researchers are not well-motivated to conduct them. Experimental economists should perform replications, and often do so, as part of the process of reporting new experiments, so that the results can be compared with replications of previous studies. Of course, few such replications are completely pure: seldom does a researcher attempt to replicate exactly all the instructions, procedures, subject type, and other conditions used in a previous study. I would argue that such attempts at pure replication are in order only when the <u>results</u> of a previous study fail to replicate, and it is desirable to investigate why. If I do an experiment similar to yours as a baseline control for comparison with a related experiment I intend to perform, I am testing the robustness of your original results using my instructions, my subjects and a different experimenter. In effect, I am varying some of the more routine auxiliary hypotheses, and asking if the results are nonetheless indistinguishable. As a practical matter they most often are. When they are, then my experiment provides <u>more</u> support for the original theory than if the <u>same</u> (your) experiment was simply repeated. Franklin (1990, p. 107-8) makes this point by noting that if you want to know the correct time, it is more informative to compare your watch with another's than for either of you to look at your own watch twice. Intuitively, experimentalists and editors apply this principle in rejecting routine "pure replication" as not sufficiently original.

Experimentalists and other economists often use the rhetoric of "falsifying" theories, but it is clear from the totality of our professional conduct that falsification is just a means to a different end: the modification of theory in the light of evidence. To pursue this end, we need to know not only the conditions under which extant theory is falsified, but also the conditions under which it is verified. It is naive to suppose that any experiment will deliver the death blow to some theory. Theory always swims in the rough water of anomaly. You don't abandon a theory because of a (or many) falsifying observation(s). When Newton published the <u>Principia</u>, it was well-known that he could not even account for the orbit of the moon. Einstein's famous paper "On the Electrodynamics of Moving Bodies" (<u>Annalen der Physik</u>, 17, 1905) was "refuted" within a year by Kaufman (in the same journal) whose β-ray experiments showed that the deviations from the predictions of the theory were considerably beyond the limits of error that could be attributed to his equipment. Einstein agreed, but rationalized: "Only after a diverse body of observations becomes available will it be possible to decide with confidence whether systematic deviations are due to a <u>not yet recognized</u> source of errors or to the circumstance that the foundations of the theory of relativity do not correspond to the facts" (Einstein, 1907, p. 283, italics are mine). As it turned out, Kaufman's apparatus was later found to be faulty.

If you look at what experimental economists do, not what they say, you get the right picture of science learning. When a theory works well, they push imaginatively to find deliberately destructive experiments that will uncover its edges of validity, setting the stage for better theory and a better understanding of the phenomena. When a theory works poorly, they reexamine instructions for lack of clarity, increase the experience level of subjects, try increased payoffs, and explore sources of "error" in an attempt to find the limits of the falsifying conditions; again, this is for the purpose of better understanding the anatomy of a theory's failure, or the procedures for testing it, and thereby laying the basis for improving the theory. Ultimately, the procedures under which a theory is tested should be part of the theory.[9] But this step requires theorists' models to reflect a close understanding of the circumstances that produced the observations.

* I am indebted to Timothy Taylor, Don McClosky and Alan Kruger for helpful comments and editing of an earlier version.

---

[9]This is recognized by Bicchieri (1988), Brandenberger (1992), Geanokoplos (1992) and others when they model common knowledge as part of the theory of backward induction games. It is common for "background assumption" eventually to be made part of the theory.

References

Alger, Dan, <u>Investigating Oligopolies Within the Laboratory</u>, A Staff Report of the Bureau of Economics of the Federal Trade Commission, January 1986.

Aumann, R. J., "Game Theory," in J. Eatwell, M. Milgate and P. Newman (eds.) <u>The New Palgrave A Dictionary of Economics</u>, vol. 2, Cambridge: The Macmillan Press Limited, 1987, pp. 460-482.

Bicchieri, Cristina, "Backward Induction without Common Knowledge," <u>Philosophy of Science Association</u>, Vol. 2, 1988, 329-343.

Bolton, Gary E., "A Comparative Model of Bargaining: Theory and Evidence," <u>American Economic Review</u>, December 1991, 81, 1096-1136.

Brandenberger, Adam, "Knowledge and Equilibrium in Games," <u>Journal of Economic Perspectives</u>, Fall 1992, 6, 83-101.

Brown-Kruse, Jamie, "Contestability in the Presence of an Alternate Market: An Experimental Examination," <u>Rand Journal of Economics</u>, Spring 1991, 22, 136-147.

_____, "Laboratory Tests of Buyer Rationing Rules in Bertrand-Edgeworth Duopolies," Department of Economics, University of Colorado, 1992.

Camerer, Colin F., George Loewenstein and Martin Weber, "The Curse of Knowledge in Economic Settings: Experimental Analysis," <u>Journal of Political Economy</u>, October 1989, 97, 1232-1254.

Chu, Yun-Peng and Ruey-Ling Chu, "The Subsidence of Preference Reversals in Simplified and Marketlike Experimental Settings: A Note," <u>American Economic Review</u>, September 1990, 80, 902-911.

Cox, James C. and Ronald Oaxaca, "Laboratory Experiments with a Finite Horizon Job Search Model," <u>Journal of Risk and Uncertainty</u>, September 1989, 2, 301-329.

Cox, James C. and David Grether, "The Preference Reversal Phenomenon: Response Mode, Markets and Incentives," Department of Economics, University of Arizona, July 1992.

Cox, James C. and Vernon L. Smith, "Endogenous Entry and Common Value Auctions," Economic Science Laboratory, University of Arizona, July 1992.

Davis, Douglas and Charles A. Holt, <u>Experimental Economics</u>. Princeton: Princeton University Press, 1992.

Deng, Gang, Robert Franciosi, Praveen Kujal, Roland Michelitsch and Vernon Smith, "Fairness: Effect on Temporary and Equilibrium Prices in Posted Offer Markets," Department of Economics, University of Arizona, October 1992.

Einstein, Albert, "On the Relativity Principle and the Conclusions Drawn from it," (1907) in <u>The Collected Papers of Albert Einstein</u> (translated by Anna Beck), volume 2. Princeton: Princeton University Press, 1989.

Forsythe, Robert, Thomas Palfrey and Charles Plott, "Asset Valuation in an Experimental Market," <u>Econometrica</u>, May 1982, 50, 537-567.

Forsythe, R., J. Horowitz, N. Savin and M. Sefton, "Replicability, Fairness and Pay in Experiments with Simple Bargaining Games," University of Iowa Working Paper 88-30, 1988, to appear <u>Games and Economic Behavior</u>.

Forsythe, Robert, Forrest Nelson, George R. Neumann and Jack Wright, "Anatomy of an Experimental Political Stock Market," December 1992, 82, 1142-1161.

Fouraker, Lawrence E. and Sidney Siegel, Bargaining Behavior, New York: McGraw-Hill, 1963.

Franciosi, Robert, Praveen Kujal, Roland Michelitsch and Vernon L. Smith, "Experimental Tests of The Endowment Effect," Economic Science Laboratory, University of Arizona, March 1993.

Franklin, Allan, Experiment, Right or Wrong. Cambridge: Cambridge University Press, 1990.

Friedman, Daniel and John Rust (eds.). The Double Auction Market: Institutions, Theories and Evidence. Reading: Addison Wesley/SFI, 1992.

Friedman, Milton, A Program for Monetary Stability, New York: Fordham University Press, 1960.

Geanakopolos, John, "Common Knowledge," Journal of Economic Perspectives, Fall 1992, 6, 56-82.

Gillette, David and Robert DelMas, "Psycho-Economics: Studies in Decision Making," Classroom Expernomics, Newsletter published by Department of Economics, Management and Accounting, Marietta College, Fall 1992, 1, pp. 1-5.

Harrison, Glenn, "Theory and Misbehavior of First Price Auctions: Reply," American Economic Review, December 1992, 82, pp. 1426-1443.

Hoffman, Elizabeth, "Bibliography of Experimental Economics," Department of Economics, University of Arizona, 1991.

Hoffman, Elizabeth and Matthew Spitzer, "Entitlements, Rights and Fairness: An Experimental Examination of Subjects' Concepts of Distributive Justice," Journal of Legal Studies, June 1985, 14, 259-297.

Hoffman, Elizabeth, Kevin A. McCabe, Keith Shachat and Vernon L. Smith, "Preferences, Property Rights and Anonymity in Bargaining Games," University of Arizona, September 1992, to appear in Games and Economic Behavior.

Kachelmeier, Steven J., Stephen T. Limberg and Michael S. Schadewald, "A Laboratory Market Examination of the Consumer Price Response to Information about Producer's Costs and Profits," The Accounting Review, October 1991, 66, 694-717.

Kachelmeier, Steven J. and Mohamed Shehata, "Culture and Competition," Journal of Economic Behavior and Organization, October 1992, 19, 145-168.

Kagel, John H. and Dan Levin, "The Winner's Curse and Public Information in Common Value Auctions," American Economic Review, December 1986, 76, 894-920.

Kahneman, Daniel, Jack K. Knetsch and Richard Thaler, "Fairness as a Constraint on Profit Seeking: Entitlements in the Market," American Economic Review, December 1986, 76, 447-464.

_____, "Experimental Tests of the Endowment Effect and the Coase Theorem," Journal of Political Economy, December 1990, 98, 1325-1348.

Lichtenstein, Sarah and Paul Slovic, "Reversals of Preference Between Bids and Choices in Gambling Decision," Journal of Experimental Psychology, July 1971, 89, 46-55.

McCabe, Kevin A., "Fiat Money as a Store of Value in an Experimental Market," <u>Journal of Economic Behavior and Organization</u>, October 1989, 12, 215-231.

McCabe, Kevin A., Stephen J. Rassenti and Vernon L. Smith, "Designing a Uniform Price Double Auction," in D. Friedman and J. Rust (eds.) <u>The Double Auction Market: Institutions, Theories and Evidence</u>. Reading: Addison Wesley/SFI, 1992.

Noussair, Charles and David Porter, "Allocating Priority with Auctions," <u>Journal of Economic Behavior and Organization</u>, October 1992, 19, 169-195.

Plott, Charles R. and Vernon L. Smith, "An Experimental Examination of Two Exchange Institutions," <u>Review of Economic Studies</u>, February 1978, 45, 113-153.

Plott, Charles, "Some Policy Applications of Experimental Methods," in A.E. Roth (ed.) <u>Laboratory Experimentation in Economics</u>, Cambridge: Cambridge University Press, 1987, 193-219.

Porter, David and Vernon L. Smith, "Futures Markets, Dividend Certainty and Common Expectations in Asset Markets," Department of Economics, University of Arizona, April 1989 (revised November 1992).

Roseveare, N. T. <u>Mercury's Perihelion from Le Verrier to Einstein</u> Oxford: Clarendon Press, 1982.

Roth, Alvin E., "Bargaining Phenomena and Bargaining Theory," in A. E. Roth (ed.) <u>Laboratory Experimentation in Economics</u>. Cambridge University Press, 1987, 14-41.

Samuelson, William and Richard Zeckhauser, "Status Quo Bias in Decision Making," <u>Journal of Risk and Uncertainty</u>, March 1988, 1, 7-59.

Schelling, T. C., "Bargaining, Communication and Limited War," <u>Journal of Conflict Resolution</u>, 1957, 1, 19-36.

Selten, Reinhard, "Properties of a Measure of Predictive Success," University of Bonn Discussion Paper No. 13-130, October 1989.

Siegel, Sidney and Lawrence E. Fouraker, <u>Bargaining and Group Decision Making: Experiments in Bilateral Monopoly</u>. New York: McGraw-Hill, 1960.

Simon, Herbert A., "A Behavioral Model of Rational Choice," <u>Quarterly Journal of Economics</u>, February 1955, 69, 99-118.

Smith, Vernon L., <u>Papers in Experimental Economics</u>. New York: Cambridge University Press, 1991.

Smith, Vernon L. and James M. Walker, "Monetary Rewards and Decision Cost in Experimental Economics," <u>Economic Inquiry</u>, April 1993, 31, 245-261.

Thaler, Richard, "Toward a Positive Theory of Consumer Choice," <u>Journal of Economic Behavior and Organization</u>, March 1980, 1, 39-60.

Tversky, Amos and Daniel Kahneman, "Advances in Prospect Theory: Cumulative Representation of Uncertainty," <u>Journal of Risk and Uncertainty</u>, 5, October 1992, pp. 297-323.

Van Boening, Mark V. and Nathaniel T. Wilcox, "A Fixed Cost Exception to the Hayek Hypothesis," Economic Science Association Meetings, Tucson, Arizona, October 24, 1992.

New Studies Calculate Cost
Of Doing Household Chores

By JANE SPENCER
Staff Reporter of THE WALL STREET JOURNAL
February 26, 2003

Sarah Kalliney doesn't have time to do her laundry, visit her parents or change the cat's litter box. She eats out six nights a week, uses a personal shopper and gets her groceries delivered to her doorstep.

But the time-starved Manhattan executive, who bills at roughly $200 an hour, recently spent nearly 10 hours battling her cellphone company, Sprint PCS, over $9 in late fees.

Is it possible that was worth her time? It is a question economists are finally beginning to tackle. After decades of using time-value formulas to help companies maximize productivity, researchers and even the U.S. government are looking at how those concepts apply to the home front.

In an economy of convenience, where time can be purchased in everything from bags of prewashed lettuce to dog-walking services, these studies aim to help answer dozens of questions Americans wrestle with daily: Who can afford a babysitter? A lawn service? A personal shopper? "The household is a little firm," says Daniel Hamermesh, an economics professor the University of Texas. "It employs labor, it buys technology, it makes decisions about what services to outsource."

But it is a firm that could use some management consultants. Americans often make drastic miscalculations about the value of their time, taking a do-it-yourself approach to tasks that might be less costly in time and money to hire out. A simple oil change, for example, costs $24.99 at some Jiffy Lube locations. But the supplies to do it yourself can run about $21. Yet about 43 million U.S. residents say they change their own oil.

In the past, economists looked strictly at your income to put a price on your leisure hours. Now, the study of off-the-clock time -- or "household production," as it is formally known -- is getting a fresh look, even beginning to take into account intangible factors such as satisfaction and pleasure. In January, the Bureau of Labor Statistics launched its first study of household time use in an effort to provide reliable data for the emerging field. The monthly survey will ask people to report how much time they spend doing such things as practicing yoga and dropping off their kids.

A flood of academic papers, such as "Taking Household Production Seriously" and "Time Crunch or Yuppie Kvetch?" are also circulating. Other work has looked at the impact of time-saving technology from microwaves to washing machines.

This body of scholarship is gaining new relevance now that pinched budgets are forcing some to work longer hours, putting a higher premium on cost-effective use of free time.

Economists say one of the most common miscalculations is "outsourcing" child-care needs to free both parents to contribute to the household income. While plenty of parents choose to stay in the labor force because they enjoy their jobs, others stay because they think they can't afford not to. Sometimes the math proves otherwise, as Steve and Jan Lira recently discovered. She works three days a week as a tax analyst, bringing their combined income to more than $120,000 a year.

They recently looked at what her job was actually costing them -- from the $18,500 they will spend on daycare to the $14,000 they lose in tax credits. By the time they threw in her work-associated costs (office parking, dry cleaning, the restaurant meals they were consuming because they were both too exhausted to cook), they determined that if she left her job, the couple would lose only a few hundred dollars a month.

But economists recognize that for many families the numbers are just a starting point. You can temper the equations with what economists call "psychic variables." Some divide household activities into two categories: consumption (things you enjoy) and production (anything that feels like work). Love gardening? It is consumption. Hate gardening? That is production -- increasing the argument in favor of hiring someone else to do it.

"It's not just about the money," says Dr. Hamermesh. "I get pleasure from listening to the symphony, other people get pleasure from harassing the airlines."

That is how Sarah Kalliney justifies her epic battle with Sprint: It was worth it for the satisfaction. "These people are jerks, and they're taking money that's not theirs," says Ms. Kalliney. "If they're going to ruin my day, I'm going to ruin theirs." She finally won -- but only after she tracked down the phone number for the president of the company. Sprint PCS says it has since taken steps to improve its customer service.

The traditional approach, which valued a leisure time based on your after-tax hourly wage, was published by Nobel-prize winning economist Gary Becker in 1965. The idea was that any time that went toward leisure could be reinvested in work. But income-based formulas have obvious limitations. For instance, many people on a fixed salary don't have the option of getting extra pay if they work another hour. In addition, some people's work is keeping a house running, which doesn't come with a salary.

Still, in figuring out how to maximize your time, salary is a logical jumping-off point. Economists suggest you begin by calculating what an hour of your time is worth, based on your salary after taxes. Using that figure, you can then compare the cost of doing the job yourself vs. outsourcing it. If you do it yourself, you have to add in the price of any materials; if you hire someone else, of course, you have to factor in the time it takes to hire and manage them.

Then, you are ready to tackle the other half of the calculation, which looks at the nonfinancial costs and benefits. Among the factors to consider: how much you enjoy doing the job yourself, and what you're giving up. All told, these conclusions will steer you in one direction or the other. (See sample worksheet on this page.)

To see how this formula works in the real world, we outsourced tasks from lawnmowing to our tax returns -- and then redid the jobs ourselves to compare. Buying a jar of prechopped garlic, for example, saved us 22 minutes of slicing and dicing. According to the formula, anybody who makes more than $10,000 a year can technically afford it. Emotional downside: fresh garlic tastes better.

Investing in technology -- even a good garlic press -- can change the dynamics of these calculations. That is what we found when we did our taxes. Visiting a walk-in tax preparer was a mere two minutes faster than the software program we used, factoring in our travel time to his office, but he cost $139 more. Under this particular scenario, you would need to make almost $14 million a year to justify hiring someone.

Then there was our messy desk. A $85-an-hour professional organizer whipped half of it into shape. The other half we tackled ourselves. The threshold income for hiring the pro? More than half-a-million dollars -- partly because we had to hang around to help her navigate our piles of papers. But she did throw in a feng shui analysis of our bedroom.

Many hard-core do-it-yourselfers are grappling with these same variables. Mark Berg, a financial planner in Wheaton, Ill., changes his own oil and once rented a 70-pound jackhammer to rip out his concrete basement floor.

But the garage sale he held last summer challenged his view. After hours of planning and a long day in the June sun, he netted a nasty sunburn and a wage of $3.56 an hour -- somewhat short of the $150 an hour he charges at the office.

"We will never do another garage sale," he says.

Write to Jane Spencer at jane.spencer@wsj.com

A market for votes

Nov 2nd 2000
From The Economist print edition

The University of Iowa's electronic futures exchange has already made a name for itself in politics, and could soon do so in financial economics

YOU can buy and sell George W. Bush in a millisecond. Likewise, Al Gore, Hillary Clinton or the entire Congress. On the Iowa Electronic Markets (IEM), investors trade a variety of "futures" whose pay-offs are linked to the outcomes of America's elections next week. These futures are mostly used merely for some light-hearted betting. But speculation plays a crucial role in almost all financial markets, and the Iowa markets provide a useful laboratory for studying how investors behave—and even for exploring the prospects of the growing number of electronic exchanges.

Academics at the University of Iowa set up the IEM in 1988 in order to help teach students about finance. The markets are not for futures in the classical sense—that is, promises to exchange some good or service at a fixed date and price. Rather, they are of the "cash-settled" variety. Consider the IEM's "winner-takes-all" market for the American presidency. Each dollar invested with a central clearing-house, up to $500 per participant, buys a bundle containing one future for every candidate. When a candidate wins, futures linked to him will pay $1 each. As only one candidate can win, each bundle of four Bush/Gore/ Nader/Buchanan futures is sure to be worth $1. Prior to the election, investors can trade individual futures at any price for which they can find a counterparty, presumably reflecting what chance they think a candidate has of winning.

Futures such as these can make investors better off, by allowing them to hedge against unpredictable events. For instance, weather futures, a popular commodity on bigger exchanges, do this: betting on an early frost might reduce the risk faced by a farmer, or by somebody who also sells "real" futures that are linked to farm products. A trader might contract to sell coffee beans at a fixed price after the harvest, only to find that a frost cuts supplies and drives the price up. A bet on frost can then provide insurance against this losing situation.

Weather futures are a convenient method for a hedge that could be done using other securities based on the underlying commodities—eg, options to buy coffee at low prices. Political futures may not have such obvious substitutes. How else could you hedge against the glum feeling that comes from seeing your favourite presidential candidate lose in a landslide?

Do political futures really serve this purpose? After the 1988 election, the Iowa professors looked into whether investors had used the market to hedge their political desires—playing the market with their heads rather than their hearts. If they had been investing solely to make money, supporters of Michael Dukakis and George Bush senior should have been equally likely to place bets on either man. In fact, an investor's partisan loyalty, identified in a questionnaire, tended to make him more likely to invest in his own candidate's futures—increasing the risk of a glum feeling on election night, not hedging it.

Market microcosm

Nevertheless, the final prices in 1988 and at the two presidential elections since have almost perfectly mimicked the vote tallies. Indeed, they proved better predictors than many opinion polls. How so? A small group of investors took advantage of the irrational behaviour of the majority by selling futures of candidates whose prices had been artificially bid up by their supporters. As the majority were passive investors— the electoral equivalent of stockmarket-index investors—the small elite of informed active traders were able to arbitrage away the price impact of blind party loyalty.

Further proof that the market's investors are not fully rational comes from bid prices. Often the sum of such prices for the bundle of futures on all candidates exceeds $1. In this situation, selling one future for all candidates yields a guaranteed profit whatever the result of the election—the seller receives more than $1 for a bundle of futures that will pay out exactly $1.

Besides assessing market rationality, the IEM also provides a test of the efficient-markets hypothesis, a core piece of financial theory which, in its most widely accepted form, states that no information available to the public can be used to predict future prices of securities. Any news, data or expectations about future events should already have been factored into prices. Applied to the IEM, this assumption implies that predictable post-convention "bounces" in the polls should have no effect on futures prices. And indeed, price changes before, during and after this year's conventions were smooth, compared with the volatile opinion polls.

The IEM may have a more useful role besides providing cute tests of economic theory: examining the strengths and weaknesses of different sorts of electronic exchanges. The Iowan professors have allowed students to bet on such prospects as the Federal Reserve's interest-rate policy and Microsoft's share price, to extend the IEM beyond the electoral cycle, and to let them see what happens when they switch between a market that closes once a day and a market that closes continuously. This may show how investors will react when, as seems inevitable, traditional exchanges give way to 24-hours-a-day computer-trading. Another project will examine how much investors rely on information about trading volumes and price histories.

Despite similarities to established commodity markets, the IEM is unregulated. That might change if serious money started to change hands on the exchange. Potential punters should note that this week the IEM was predicting victories for Mr Bush and Mrs Clinton, as well as Republican majorities in the House and Senate. You disagree? Then place your bets.

CHAPTER 18

CURSED WINNERS AND GLUM LOSERS

Why Life Is Full of Disappointments

Economic theory predicts that you are not enjoying this book as much as you thought you would. This is a special case of a more general proposition: *Most* things in life don't turn out as well as you thought they would. While psychologists, poets, and philosophers have often remarked on this phenomenon, few have recognized that it is a necessary consequence of informed, rational decision making.

Choosing a book is a process fraught with risk and uncertainty. Fortunately, your lifetime of experience as a reader is a valuable guide. It enables you to form some expectation of each book's quality. Your expectations are sometimes very wrong, but on average they are far better than random guesses.

Some books are better than you expect them to be and others are worse, but it is unlikely that you err in one direction much more often than the other. If you consistently either overestimated or underestimated quality, you would eventually discover your own bias and correct for it. So it is reasonable to assume that your expectations are too low about as often as they are too high.

This means that if you chose this book randomly off the shelf, it would be as likely to exceed your expectations as to fall short of them. But you didn't choose it randomly off the shelf. Rational consumer that you are, you chose it because it was one of the few available books that you expected to be among the very best. Unfortunately, that makes it one of the few available books whose quality you are most likely to have overestimated. Under the circumstances, to read it is to court disappointment.

The logic of probable disappointment haunts every aspect of life in which we choose among alternatives. Even when your judgments *in general* are free of bias, your judgments about *those activities that you choose to engage in* are usually too optimistic. Your assessments of potential marriage partners might be exactly right on average, but the one who seems the perfect match is the one whose flaws you are most likely to have overlooked.

Things are even worse when you buy a good at auction. When you are the high bidder, you can be certain of one thing: Nobody else in the room thought the item was worth as much as you did. That observation alone implies that you've probably overestimated its true worth. Economists, ever dismal, call this phenomenon the *winner's curse.*

Imagine that you are a knowledgeable real estate developer submitting a sealed bid on a parcel of land. Your expert judgment tells you that if you could acquire this land for $50,000, you would make a handsome profit. You might think that under the circumstances you'd be happy to win that land at auction for $50,000. But if you *do* win the auction at that price, you learn that your competitors' expert judgments led all of them to less optimistic assessments than your own. Unless you are quite sure that your own information is better than anybody else's, you are likely to wonder if $50,000 is such a bargain after all.

When you are deciding how much to bid for a piece of land, the right question is not, "Given what I know now, would I be happy to buy this land for $50,000?" Instead, the right question is, "Given what I know now, and assuming also that no other developer was willing to bid $50,000, would I *still* be happy to buy it for $50,000?" These are very different questions. Those who frequently buy goods at auction must learn to appreciate that difference and to adjust their bids accordingly.

On the other hand, there are circumstances where the winner's curse is not an issue. Some auction goers are quite certain of how much they are willing to pay for an item, without any regard for what others may know or think. If you are bidding on an antique brass candelabrum, and you have examined it closely, and you know exactly how you plan to use it, and you don't care whether it is attractive to others, and you are certain that you will never want to resell it, then buying the candelabrum for $1,000 is an equally good bargain regardless of what the other bidders may think. In such cases there is no winner's curse. There is still the possibility of disappointment—the candelabrum might not look as good on your mantelpiece as you thought it would—but there is not the *probability* of disappointment that constitutes a true winner's curse. After all, it's equally possible that the candelabrum will look *better* than you imagined, and the fact that you have won the auction does nothing to diminish this possibility.

The presence or absence of a winner's curse is of immediate concern to the buyer, who must account for it in his bidding strategy. It is therefore of indirect concern to the seller, who cares very much how buyers behave. But the seller's role is not limited to hoping that buyers will bid high. The seller is also a strategic player in the auction game. He gets only one move, but it is the most important: He sets the rules.

There are many types of auction. The most familiar is the common English auction, where bidders offer successively higher prices and drop out until only one remains. There is the Dutch auction, where an auctioneer calls out a very high price and successively lowers it until he receives an offer to buy. There is the first-price sealed bid auction, where each buyer submits a bid in an envelope, all are opened simultaneously, and the high bidder gets the item for the amount of his bid. There is the second-price sealed bid auction, where the high bidder gets the item but pays only the amount of the *second*-highest bid. There are third-, fourth-, and fifth-price sealed bid auctions. And there are more exotic possibilities. In the Glum Losers auction, the high bidder gets the item for free and everybody else pays the amount of his own bid.

The seller can choose among these or any other rules that he manages to dream up. Ideally, his goal is to maximize the selling price. In practice, he rarely has enough information to achieve that goal. If two bidders are both willing to go very high, an English auction can force them to compete with each other, pushing the price up as high as possible. If only one bidder is willing to go very high, an English auction is disastrous for the seller: Everyone else drops out early and the potential high bidder gets a fabulous bargain.

Is an English auction good for the seller? The answer is yes if there happen to be two high bidders in the audience and no if there happens to be just one. Because bidders are unlikely to reveal their bidding strategies in advance of the auction, the seller can never know for certain on any given night whether an English auction is preferable to, say, a Dutch auction.

Even to decide between a first-price and a second-price sealed bid auction can be difficult for the seller. On the one hand, in a first-price auction he collects the high bid, while in a second-price auction he collects only the amount of the second-highest bid. On the other hand, bidders generally submit higher bids in a second-price auction. They submit even higher bids in a third-price auction. Which is best for the seller? Again the answer depends on who shows up to bid, and what the bidders' strategies are.

Given his limited information, the seller is in no position to choose the rule that will maximize the selling price at any one auction. But he *can* hope to choose the rule that will maximize the *average* selling price over *many* auctions. At some auctions, English rules yield the highest prices, while at others Dutch rules yield the highest prices. Which rules yield the highest prices on average?

At this point, economic theory makes its entrance, to announce an astonishing truth. Under certain reasonable assumptions (about which I will soon say more), and as a matter of mathematical fact, all of the auction rules I've mentioned yield the same revenue to the seller on average over many auctions. If I regularly sell merchandise at English auctions, while you sell at Dutch auctions, your brother sells at first-price sealed bid auctions, your sister sells at second-price sealed bid auctions, and your crazy Uncle Fester sells at Glum Losers auctions, and if we all sell merchandise of comparable quality, then in the long run we must all do equally well.

This result applies as well to a vast number of other auction rules—in fact, to any rule you can imagine that does not involve some entrance fee to the auction hall or its equivalent.

I haven't told you how I know that sellers using vastly different rules all do equally well on average, because the argument is technical and I haven't yet figured out how to translate it into simple English. (Probably this means that I don't yet understand it well enough.) But there is no doubt that the argument is correct.

A result like this is a great joy to a theorist. It is surprising, elegant, and emphatic. There is no need to mince words or to introduce qualifications. We need not make long and ugly catalogues ("The English auction is superior under any of the following seven conditions, while the Dutch auction is superior under any of the following six other conditions . . . "). We can state our conclusion in no more than five words ("All rules are equally good") and we can prove it incontrovertibly to anyone with an undergraduate's knowledge of advanced calculus. The best thing about it is that almost nobody would have guessed it. If theory never did more than confirm what we already know, there would be no need for it.

And yet . . . It remains disturbingly the case that real-world auctioneers show marked preferences for some rules over others. Cattle and slaves have always been sold in English auctions, tulips in Dutch auctions, and oil drilling rights in sealed bid auctions. If all rules are equally good for the seller, why do sellers insist on one rule rather than another?

An economist might feel some temptation to respond that auctioneers are not economists and so are likely to live in ignorance of the latest breakthroughs. Not only do many auctioneers fail to subscribe to the *Journal of Economic Theory,* but all too often their advanced calculus has grown sufficiently rusty that it would be difficult for them to stay abreast of the field even if they made an honest effort. But the economist's temptation is best resisted. It is a fair assumption that people who run auctions for a living know what they are doing, and that if there is some discrepancy between their behavior and the prescriptions of the economic theorist, then it is the theorist who is missing something. Our job as economists is not to tell auctioneers how to run their business. It is to assume that they *know* how to run their business and to figure out why their strategies are the right ones.

On the one hand we have an argument that under certain assumptions, the choice of auction rule is a matter of indifference. On the other hand, we have the behavior of auctioneers, from which we infer that the choice of auction rule is a matter of considerable concern. The inescapable conclusion is that those "certain assumptions" do not always apply. So it is time to be explicit about what they are.

The most important assumption is that there is no winner's curse. More precisely, the argument assumes that a bidder does not change his mind about the item's value when he learns that another bidder disagrees with him. If you are bidding on a van Gogh to hang on your wall, you might be willing to pay $50 million regardless of what anyone else thinks; if you are bidding on the same painting in anticipation of a large profit at resale, you are likely to be chagrined when you learn that none of the other dealers in the room bid more than $10 million. The equivalence of auction rules holds in the first case but not in the second.

In fact, when bidders care about one anothers' opinions, the seller is well advised to choose the English auction. Going into the auction, there may be only one bidder willing to pay above $10 million. When others observe his willingness to go high, they may reason that he knows something and decide to compete with him. A sealed bid auction precludes this outcome. So does a Dutch auction—by the time the high bidder reveals his enthusiasm, the auction is over.

English auctions are by far the most common and appear to be the form most favored by auctioneers. The theory suggests that the only reason why auctioneers would have such a preference is that bidders respond to information about one anothers' assessments. This means in particular that bidders are subject to the winner's curse. So while the curse is initially no more than a theoretical possibility, the prevalence of English auctions suggests that it is a pervasive phenomenon.

Although the argument for the equivalence of auction rules assumes away the winner's curse, this is not the only direction in which it may depart from reality. Another key assumption is that buyers do not have large fractions of their wealth riding on the outcome of the auction. This assumption is important, because in its absence, buyers bid more conservatively, which affects the entire analysis. In that case, the seller should prefer a first-price sealed bid auction to an English auction. Because buyers are loath to risk losing, and because a sealed bid gives them only one chance to win, they tend to shade their bids upward, profiting the seller.

Another questionable assumption in the standard theory is that the population of bidders does not change when the rules change. In reality, a Dutch auction might draw an entirely different class of bidders than an English auction. Some future theorist will earn fame by figuring out how to incorporate this effect into the analysis.

Rather than venture into such uncharted territory, let me take a side path to explore another issue that confronts the seller. Sellers frequently know more about their merchandise than buyers do and can acquire reputations for honesty by always revealing everything they know, good or bad. Does honesty pay?

Honest John holds used-car auctions on a regular basis. He makes it a point always to announce everything that he knows about the cars he sells. If a car burns oil, or if it's been in an accident, Honest John will tell you. People bid lower when John announces that the car on the block is a lemon, but they bid higher at other times because they know that if John were aware of any problems, he would tell them.

John earns less on the lemons than he would if he were secretive, but he earns more on the good cars. These effects can cancel, leaving John no better or worse off than his counterpart, Silent Sam, in the next town, who reveals nothing. So far, we have found no good argument for Honest John's honesty. But John has one additional advantage over Sam: His policy partly alleviates the threat of the winner's curse and so gives buyers an *additional* reason to bid high. In the long run, John is sure to do better than Sam.

To put this another way, the winner's curse is initially the buyer's problem but becomes the seller's problem also because buyers defend against it by shading their bids downward. It is therefore a good idea for the seller to help buyers ward off the curse. A history of honest dealings can be an effective talisman.

The news that honesty is the best policy would not surprise your grandmother, any more than the news that life is full of disappointments. Like auctioneers, grandmothers have a lot of instinctual knowledge that economists work hard to acquire.

The Speculator As Hero
by Victor Niederhoffer, February 1993

I am a speculator. I own seats on the Chicago Board of Trade and Chicago Mercantile Exchange. When my daughters ask me if my job is as important as the butcher's, the doctor's or the scientist's, I answer that the speculator is a hero, and has been throughout history.

Some speculators are discoverers like Christopher Columbus, creators like Henry Ford, or inventors like Thomas Edison. Their job is easy to place on a high plane. My role in the grander order is indirect, relatively invisible and unplanned. The only discoveries I make are the routes that prices will travel. Like hundreds of thousands of other traders, I try to predict the prices of common goods a day or two in the future. If I think the price of an item will go up, I buy today and sell later. If I think that the price is going down, I'll sell at today's higher price. The miracle is that in taking care of ourselves, we speculators somehow ensure that producers all over the world will provide the right quantity and quality of goods at the proper time, without undue waste, and that this meshes with what people want and the money they have available.

Politicians eager to "do something" about high prices often make laws to punish the speculator. A representative incident occurred during the reign of Emperor Diocletian in Rome in A.D. 300. Speculators were withholding scarce provisions from the hoarders, hoping to unload when the demand was even more intense. To remedy this, Diocletian set the highest price for beef, grains, clothing and several hundred other items. Anyone who sold at a higher price would be put to death.

The result? As reported by Lactantius in A.D. 314, "Much blood was shed upon slight and trifling accounts. The people brought no more provisions to the markets, since they could not get a reasonable price for them, and this increased the dearth so much that at last after many had died by it, the law itself was laid aside."

Another representative incident occurred during the siege of Antwerp by the Spanish in 1585. Antwerp was then the leading commercial town of Europe. The Spanish decided to blockade the port to force surrender when supplies gave out. Knowing this, Antwerp farmers and bakers produced large amounts of bread. Privateers ran the blockade at great peril to provide needed supplies. Prices began to rise. Speculators, guessing that bread was going to be scarce, contributed to further price rises through shrewd purchases.

But Antwerp politicians thought it wrong for greedy speculators to profit from war. The politicians fixed a very low maximum price to everything that could be eaten, and prescribed severe penalties for violators. The consequence was inevitable. Privateers stopped running the blockades and the supply of grain dried up. Consumers had no incentive to economize. The citizens ran out of all their provisions after six months of the siege and the Antwerpers starved. They surrendered and were quickly annexed.

Let's consider some of the principles that explain the causes of shortages and surpluses and the role of speculators.

When a harvest is too small to satisfy consumption at its normal rate, speculators come in, hoping to profit from the scarcity by buying. Their purchases raise the price, thereby checking consumption so that the smaller supply will last longer. Producers encouraged by the high price further lessen the scarcity by growing or importing more. On the other side, when the price is higher than the speculators think the facts warrant, they sell. This reduces prices, encouraging consumption and exports and helping to reduce the surplus.

Of course, speculators aren't always correct.

When they am wrong, their actions contribute to scarcities or gluts. Manias such as the Tullipmania, the South Sea Bubble, the Mississippi Bubble, gold panics, stock-market crashes, and violent swings in the value of the dollar are frequently cited as examples of occasions when speculators contributed to instability and imbalance.

But who could do the job better?

Bureaucrats have little incentive to improve, invest or innovate. When speculators are wrong, however, they are punished severely for their mistakes by losses of their own money. If left unchecked, the tendencies of our modern kings to interfere with the natural working of the marketplace would lead to destruction. But speculators, searching for profit, send signals to producers and consumers as to the forces of destruction and good.

Perhaps the most positive impact of our current-day speculators is to check at inception governmental activities that would have an inflationary impact Governments are prone to spend more money on their activities than they take in through taxes. The consequence often has been substantial inflation, followed by war, revolution and destruction of civilization.

Nowadays, however, bond traders are so alert to the long-term consequences of such activities that they immediately send debt yields up significantly at the first sign of inflation. The increased yields have such a negative and immediate impact on government revenue, business activity, and consumer spending that governments have all but given up trying to sneak increased spending past the market. As a result, the rate of inflation slowed markedly throughout the Western world during the 1980s.

Granted, speculators am not angels; many are motivated by gambling and greed, and when given the chance will take advantage of the public as much as the next person. But the efficiency of a competitive marketplace helps to ferret out and reduce unscrupulous conduct.

The intellectual raises his eyebrows at the economic and historical analysis and contemptuously says, "Man cannot live by bread alone." To this I respond that without us, there would be no bread.

I am proud to be a speculator. I am proud that my humble attempts to predict Tuesday's prices on Monday are an indispensable component of our society. By buying low and selling high, I create harmony and freedom.

*Mr. Niederhoffer, a **Freedom Daily** subscriber, is chairman of Niederhoffer Investments, Inc. This is an edited version of a piece which appeared in the February 10, 1989, issue of **The Wall Street Journal.**© Dow Jones and Co., Inc., 1989. Reprinted by permission.*

January 31, 2008

Economists Dissect the 'Yuck' Factor

By PATRICIA COHEN

WASHINGTON — You can kill a horse to make pet food in California, but not to feed a person. You can hoist a woman over your shoulder while running a 253-meter obstacle course in the Wife-Carrying World Championship in Finland, but you can't hold a dwarf-tossing contest in France. You can donate a kidney to prevent a death and be hailed as a hero, but if you take any money for your life-saving offer in the United States, you'll be jailed.

These prohibitions are not imposed because of concerns about health or safety or unfair practices, some economists say, but because people tend to find such activities repugnant. In other words, just hearing about them can cause a queasy sensation in the pit of your stomach.

People don't pay enough attention to how repugnance affects decisions about what can be bought and sold, asserts Alvin Roth, an economist at Harvard University.

Mr. Roth spoke at a recent panel on the economics of repugnance at the American Enterprise Institute, a conservative research organization in Washington. For conservatives the issue can be particularly pointed. Economic conservatives tend to favor eliminating as many hindrances on the market as possible, while social conservatives believe some practices are so "repugnant" — because they violate traditional values or religious and moral prohibitions — that they should be banned from the marketplace altogether.

Of course the dividing line between mercenary, soulless capitalists and defenders of human dignity is not always clear. As Mr. Roth pointed out, ideas about what is repugnant change all the time. Selling oneself into indentured servitude was once thought permissible, while charging interest on loans was not.

In recent years groups have fought over whether it is acceptable to display and sell art that offends religious sensibilities, like a photograph of a crucifix in urine or a sculpture of Jesus on the cross, made out of chocolate. "Bodies ... The Exhibition" and similar shows, which feature the preserved and dissected remains of people, would once have been considered both ghoulish and profane. Although religious leaders, human-rights activists and medical officials have condemned the cadaver exhibitions, the displays have attracted millions of visitors in the United States and around the world.

And last week a woman in Ohio whose ad to sell a horse mistakenly appeared under the heading "Good Things to Eat" in a newspaper's classified section received dozens of calls, some expressing outrage and others from people interested in turning it into dinner.

(In Europe and Japan horse meat on a menu would stir no more comment than macaroni and cheese would in an American diner.)

Arthur C. Brooks, a professor of government and business at Syracuse University who moderated the Washington panel, spoke of how he — like thousands of other Americans — carried $7,000 in hundred dollar bills to ease the adoption of an abandoned baby in China despite a visceral reaction against the idea of buying and selling children.

"It's very hard to predict what's repugnant and what's not," Mr. Roth said. Paul Bloom, a professor of psychology at Yale, agreed. He conducted a two-year study to try to get at why people consider athletes who take steroids to be cheating, but not those who take vitamins or use personal trainers. He and his team offered different possibilities: What if steroids were completely natural? Or were not at all harmful? Or were only effective if the athlete had to work harder than before?

The only change that caused the interviewed subjects to alter their objections to steroids was when they were told that everyone else thought it was all right. "People have moral intuitions," Mr. Bloom said. When it comes to accepting or changing the status quo in these situations, he said, they tended to "defer to experts or the community."

Often introducing money into the exchange — putting it into the marketplace — is what people find repugnant. Mr. Bloom asserted that money is a relatively new invention in human existence and therefore "unnatural."

Economists are asking the wrong question, Mr. Bloom said at the panel. They assume that "everything is subject to market pricing unless proven otherwise."

"The problem is not that economists are unreasonable people, it's that they're evil people," he said. "They work in a different moral universe. The burden of proof is on someone who wants to include" a transaction in the marketplace. (Mr. Roth, who acknowledges that "economists see very few tradeoffs as completely taboo," did not take the criticism personally.)

The theologian Michael Novak, who is also a resident scholar at the American Enterprise Institute, similarly argued that "not all ethical principles fit under economic reasoning," adding, "the resistance to money is very old and very deep."

Money is clearly the issue in situations involving the human body. Paying young women for eggs to be fertilized and men for sperm is now common practice — even though they are still regularly referred to as "donors." Yet the sale of tissue, cells and eggs for stem-cell research or organs for transplant are still the subject of vehement dispute.

Pope John Paul II said that treating human organs as part of any commercial exchange is "morally unacceptable," a view echoed by the Council of Europe's Convention on Human Rights and Biomedicine.

In the United States federal law prohibits the sale or purchase of human organs. The American Kidney Foundation itself opposes payments on the ground that it "devalues life." And the conservative bioethicist Leon Kass, who was chairman of the President's Council on Bioethics from 2002 to 2005, has called the commercialization of body parts "just inherently wrong."

"If we come to think about ourselves like pork bellies, pork bellies we will become," Mr. Kass has written.

Sally Satel, a psychiatrist and resident scholar at the institute who was herself the recipient of a kidney donation in 2006, asserts that the issue does not need to pit human dignity against saving a life. "A salaried fireman who saves a life is not less heroic," she said. "An object or act can have a price and still be invaluable."

She has forcefully argued in The New York Times Magazine and elsewhere that the sale of human organs with proper oversight to prevent exploitation of the poor should be permitted. There are 74,000 people on the waiting list, and in 2006 about 4,400 died before they could get a kidney. The need is too great, she said. The Nobel Prize-winning economist Gary Becker and his colleague Julio Jorge Elias have even calculated how much a kidney should sell for to eliminate the backlog completely.

In recent years Mr. Roth has helped set up "paired kidney donations," in effect, allowing sets of donors and patients to swap kidneys in order to find a compatible one. These kidney exchanges, which started in 2005, have gained growing acceptance nationwide, he said.

To Mr. Novak instinctual human revulsion is an important attribute. Quoting Aristotle, he said "repugnance makes a necessary contribution to the good life, especially when there is not time for intellectual evaluation." A number of psychologists, philosophers and biologists (most recently Stephen Pinker, also in The Times Magazine) have similarly argued that repugnance is morality's early warning system, an alarm bell that warns that a subject deserves moral scrutiny.

Still, such intuitions are "not always the best director," Mr. Novak said. As in the case of kidney transplants, one must choose "between two great moral ends," he said.

That is why, he added, "mere repugnance is not enough."

In flood zone, a new sense of what's valuable

A new bartering economy has emerged among New Orleans survivors.

Monday, September 5, 2005 | 12:00 a.m. CDT
BY ARIANA EUNJUNG CHA, WASHINGTON POST

NEW ORLEANS — The waters raced into Denise Mitchell's home so quickly that she fled with nothing but what she was wearing.

After Mitchell and 10 members of her extended family took refuge in the convention center downtown, she realized they had another problem: Aid workers were giving out water and food, but there wasn't anything for her infant niece. The only thing Mitchell had that she thought might be of value was the silver necklace she was wearing around her neck, so she wandered around the convention center for hours trying to trade it for milk.

There were no takers. The last thing anyone wanted was something whose sole value was that it looked good.

In the most devastated areas in and around New Orleans, the lack of electricity, flooding and shortage of food is shaping an emergency bartering economy that is markedly different from the rest of the country.

Bartering has been most prevalent at places such as the convention center, where food supplies have been limited and where the law-enforcement presence was increased only on Friday, leaving its temporary residents to govern themselves.

For the tens of thousands of people displaced by Hurricane Katrina, the split-second decisions made as they left their homes about what to take and what to leave have gained meaning beyond what they expected. "Green money," as some people in the city and surrounding areas now refer to cash, in some places has become nearly obsolete.

Meanwhile, things people never thought much about had suddenly became fabulously valuable. A clean pillow and blanket, or even a sheet, could buy practically anything, be it diabetes medicine or a piece of meat. Office chairs with wheels, to ferry around the ill and weak, were worth more than DVD players and laptop computers.

Cigarettes and liquor were initially valuable commodities, a comfort in miserable conditions. But after looters flooded the market, there was so much of the stuff that people started giving it away.

In the minutes or seconds that many had to grab their possessions, some were focused squarely on the practical. Butch Upchurch, 38, and his wife, Karen, 41, had about five minutes to leave their home on the western side of New Orleans. They grabbed their bank statements, insurance papers and some water and food and squeezed into their Chrysler 300. There was room for one of their dogs, but pit bull CoCo, the larger one, didn't fit. They kissed her goodbye and prayed she would survive.

The ones in the most difficult situations were people such as Mitchell who had nothing but the shirt on their back.

But Mitchell was resourceful, and it took her only a few hours to figure out the rules of this new economy. After scrounging in some trash bins, she found T-shirts someone had dumped. She went to people who were evacuated in their pajamas or were wearing wet clothes and bartered until she got not only milk but also a bag of Huggies diapers.

Asian demand helps drive up price of dairy

Increased cost also tied to drought, feed.

Published Saturday, August 11, 2007

PARIS (AP) - Got milk? Well, you're going to need more cash these days to get it.

Growing appetites for dairy in Asia and limited worldwide supply are among a number of factors driving prices of milk to record highs.

In China and elsewhere in Asia, chains such as McDonald's and Starbucks are introducing unfamiliar taste buds to cheeseburgers and lattes, increasing the region's demand for dairy.

Rising costs of animal feed, shrinking European production and long-standing drought in Australia and New Zealand, the world's largest milk-exporting region, are also pushing up the price.

Paying more for milk is causing an uproar in Germany, where families consider providing children with an affordable glass of milk a fundamental right. It is also a concern for consumers in the United States and elsewhere in Europe.

Milk prices hit a record last month in the United States, where consumers paid an average $3.80 a gallon, compared to $3.29 in January, according to the U.S. Department of Agriculture. It forecasts prices will remain high throughout the year.

Prices are likely to remain high worldwide until dairy farmers add more cows or shift production to powders, which are more easily traded than the liquid stuff.

International dairy prices increased 46 percent between November and April, with milk powder prices increasing even faster, according to the Food and Agriculture Organization.

Companies such as candy giant Hershey Co. that use dairy for their products are feeling the pinch. But in many parts of the globe, dairy farmers are cheering. "Global demand has been extraordinary for American dairy products, but global supplies of dairy products have been exceptionally tight," said Michael Marsh, head of the Western United Dairymen trade group in California, the top dairy-producing U.S. state. "From the American dairy farmers' perspective, you have almost a perfect storm."

In China, milk consumption has soared along with rising incomes, a massive expansion of the dairy industry and the increasing familiarity with - and taste for - nonnative foods among young urbanites.

Pizza Hut sells its cheese-laden pies even in smaller Chinese cities, and milk, yogurt and individually packaged cheese slices can be found in small local supermarket chains.

Foreign-owned stores such as France's Carrefour, Germany's Metro and America's Wal-Mart cater to slightly more sophisticated tastes, selling crumbly blue cheeses, wheels of gouda and red-waxed balls of Edam.

Products from Chinese dairy giant Mengniu even carry the label of being the official milk of the Chinese space program. Its drinks promise to "fortify the Chinese people," with packaging showing a space-suited boy clutching a glass of creamy goodness.

China's growing love of dairy is a far cry from two decades ago, when the country was just opening up to foreign products and availability was limited to milk, yogurt and, on rare occasions, butter. The Dairy Association of China estimates consumption will rise by 15 percent to 20 percent annually in the coming years.

Premier Wen Jiabao, on a visit to a dairy farm last year, said his "dream" is for each Chinese child to consume a pint per day. He is boosting production to try to keep up with demand, but the world's most-populous nation remains a net importer of dairy products, including milk powders.

The boom in biofuels is also pushing up corn prices and, as a result, making animal feed more expensive. Farmers have responded by raising milk prices.

Corn futures indicate that the price of corn will remain high this year, according to the Washington-based International Dairy Foods Association. Prices have also risen for soybeans, another feed crop, it said.

The impact on the price of a carton of milk differs across the globe because dairy markets significantly vary from region to region, skewed by domestic and trade policies and other factors such as geography.

Governments in the United States, Canada, the European Union and Japan have a range of policies, including tariffs and quotas, that insulate their milk from international prices, according to the Food and Agriculture Organization.

These systems are under strain, as high rewards in the globalized market are inspiring milk producers to challenge the old practices.

In Germany, where milk prices are set annually after negotiations between producers and powerful retailers, retailers have been holding prices down to the tune of almost 15 percent since 2002. Since July, they've been paying producers an extra 5 to 7 cents a quart after the producers threatened to take their milk elsewhere.

Hershey Co.'s chief executive officer, Richard Lenny, said America's largest candy maker might adjust its formula to use less lactose because of rising milk costs. Candy bar prices will also be reviewed, he said.

High gas prices fuel changes in behavior

Published Saturday, September 17, 2005

WASHINGTON (AP) - Diane Utecht of Wisconsin plans to close off most of her house this winter to reduce her heating bill. Elaine Hobbs' husband recently canceled a trip from their home in Rochester, N.Y., to Baltimore to see his daughter on her birthday because gas prices were too high.

With gasoline hovering close to $3 a gallon and the government forecasting big increases in heating fuel costs this fall, these are only a few of the adjustments Americans are making. And they aren't happy about it.

"I have to block off every room except the kitchen, the bathroom and the living room," said Utecht, a retiree from Loconto, Wis.

Seven in 10 people in a recent AP-Ipsos poll said they expect high gas prices to cause financial problems in the coming months - up from half who felt that way in June 2004. Four in 10 of those polled recently - especially women, minorities and older Americans - said gas costs will cause them serious problems.

The cost of gasoline could ease somewhat as domestic oil production returns to August levels in the coming months. Industry officials estimate that natural gas and heating oil prices will rise about 70 percent because already tight supplies were disrupted by Hurricane Katrina.

Those high prices are changing people's behavior, a recent Pew Research Center poll found.

More than two-thirds of people said they're driving less and shop for the best price on gasoline. More than six in 10 said they're adjusting the temperature in their homes to keep a lid on utility bills. Almost that many said they have changed their plans for travel to avoid driving long distances. Almost three in 10 said they've bought a car that gets better gas mileage.

Seven in 10 in the AP-Ipsos poll said they disapprove of how President George W. Bush is handling gasoline prices, and 43 percent of Republicans surveyed said they were unhappy with Bush over fuel costs.

The AP-Ipsos poll of 1,002 adults was conducted Sept. 6-8, and the Pew survey of 1,523 adults was taken Sept. 8 through Sunday. Both have margins of sampling error of plus or minus 3 percentage points.

Poll: People's views on gas depend on where they live

Published Monday, October 17, 2005

WASHINGTON (AP) - Many motorists these days are complaining about the cost of gasoline, but what people consider a fair price varies greatly depending on where they live.

Americans angrily grit their teeth as they pump $3-per-gallon gas. They think $2 is about right. In Britain, $3 sounds fanciful; people there pay about $6.40 a gallon and think $5 would be fair.

AP-Ipsos polling in the United States and eight of its allies turned up wide disparities in people's thoughts on the cost of filling up.

Spaniards would like to see gasoline for just more than $3 a gallon. People in France, Italy, Germany and South Korea put the fair market price at $4 or a little more. Australians and Canadians would like to see it just below $3 a gallon.

The United States has less than 5 percent of the world's population but consumes 20 million barrels of oil a day, about one-fourth of the global total, according to the American Petroleum Institute.

Many Europeans have found alternatives to depending on cars as fuel prices have soared over the past few years. In much of the United States, however, people are addicted to the car and view it as essential to social and economic well-being. When gas prices shoot to record levels, it rattles the U.S. economy and depresses consumer confidence.

"This whole country runs on cheap gas," said Clinton Ahrens, a businessman from Dows, Iowa. Most Americans have come to expect it over the years, he said.

In much of Europe and elsewhere, gas taxes account for two-thirds or more of the price of gasoline. People in those countries look for high-mileage cars. Public transportation is well-developed.

In the United States, taxes vary by state but amount to about 20 percent of gas prices. Fuel is cheaper in this country than in most parts of the world, investment in mass transit is minimal, gas-guzzling SUVs and trucks zoom along highways, and politicians talk about increasing gas taxes - or any taxes - at their own risk.

"We do have a sense of entitlement here in the United States," said Steve Yetiv, a political scientist at Old Dominion University in Virginia who has studied the impact of energy prices.

"This stems partly from the individualism that is part of the American fabric - an individualism that prizes freedom of action and prizes the freedom to buy as big a car as you want to buy," Yetiv said.

Billy Fillers of Sycamore, Ill., drives a Chevy Tahoe on his rounds to do X-ray repairs, and his weekly gasoline bill has gone from $60 to $120. But he likes his SUV. "The bigger your vehicle, the faster your vehicle - it's a status symbol," he said.

People in most of the countries polled agree that the rising price of gasoline is causing financial hardships. From two-thirds to three-fourths of those in Australia, Canada, France, Germany, Italy, Spain, South Korea and the United States said they expect increases in the price of gasoline to cause them hardships. About half in Britain said they worried about financial hardships, and one-third of respondents in Germany felt that way.

Many surveyed said there is little they can do about it. Renato Baldini, dean of a private school in Rome, said: "I have no alternatives. The only thing I can do now is drive slower to try and save gas."

Businesses Feel Price Pinch

By DAVID WALLE
August 18, 2005 | 12:00 a.m. CDT

The cost of gas is taking a toll on local delivery services.

Faced with surging gasoline prices, local businesses are hoping for relief before they must pass costs on to their customers.

Prices in Boone County have increased from $2.18 last month to the current average of $2.40, according to Mike Right of AAA. A year ago the price was $1.79.

Among the hardest hit are local florists, delivery drivers and the city transit system.

Tina Bradley of Allen's Flowers Inc. said the consequence is the trickle-down effect. Farmers who cultivate the flowers must pay more for gasoline to fuel their tractors.

"It cost us more to drive the vans, and the supplier fuel charge is increasing, too," Bradley said.

Because flowers are shipped by plane and semitrailer, suppliers have already raised their prices. For example, the fuel charge from one supplier for a four-hour trip has increased from $7 to $9, Bradley said.

Allen's Flowers is absorbing the extra cost, but that will change if relief at the pumps doesn't come soon.

"If prices stay where they are we'll have to raise it," Bradley said. "We won't have a choice."

Immediate relief doesn't look likely. On Tuesday, the Wall Street Journal reported that national gas prices have surged by almost 70 cents a gallon in the past year. Prices are expected to rise in the next week and may not begin to drop until fall.

"It's had a pretty negative impact on our drivers," said Richard Martin, part-owner of Italian Village in north Columbia.

The tips the drivers receive remain flat as gasoline prices continue to rise.

"Our drivers are paying literally for the cost of increasing gas prices," said Martin, who added that drivers typically spend $8 or more each night on gasoline.

That expense comes out of their wages. When Martin entered the pizza business in 1995, drivers usually made $14-$15 an hour; now they earn $8 to $9 an hour, he said. Long-time employees are beginning to leave their jobs as delivery drivers, he added.

"If prices continue to increase, it will be significantly harder for people to make a decent living in the delivery service," Martin said.

The city has a cushion in its budget to allow for higher gas prices, said Ken Koopmans, Columbia transportation manager. But if the city enters into a budget crunch, residents shouldn't worry about a reduction in services.

"We won't cut services," Koopmans said.

The city worked with its supplier while preparing its budget. Officials anticipated an increase and budgeted for the worst-case scenario.

"In terms of dollars spent and fuel consumed we are 10 percent below budget for the city as a whole," Koopmans said.

Mark Gringstaff, public works supervisor, oversees transit operations in Columbia.

"We are paying more for fuel than we had hoped," he said. "But we have budgeted for a price higher than its current cost."

Customers have not stopped buying new cars but some are choosing smaller vehicles, said Jim Mandle, manager at the Legend Automotive Group.

"People who have large SUVs are downsizing to smaller SUVs," he said. "People with smaller SUVs are downsizing to cars. But there's still a certain type of person who always needs a big vehicle for their job. They don't have the flexibility to change."

Mandle says that last year cars that got more than 30 miles per gallon comprised 20 percent of their sales; that has increased to 40 percent today.

A Marvel of Cooperation:
How Order Emerges without a Conscious Planner

by Russell Roberts<u>*</u>

February 7, 2005

Russell Roberts

One of the great virtues of economics is how it illuminates the unseen and the hidden. Frederic Bastiat, in his classic essay, <u>What Is Seen and What Is Not Seen,</u> analyzed the economic consequences of a simple act of vandalism, the broken window. We see the broken window. We see or can imagine the consequences of the broken window—more money for the glazier. What is harder to see and imagine is what is not seen—the economic activity that will not take place because the window must be fixed.

This simple example is a fundamental reminder of the scarcity that constrains our choices at a point in time. Bastiat used the metaphor of the broken window to critique policy recommendations whose promises of success often ignored the inevitable scarcity that must always apply at a point in time—resources used for one purpose can no longer be used elsewhere.

But Bastiat had another insight about the seen and the unseen that is less appreciated than his classic metaphor of the broken window. In <u>Chapter 18</u> of *Economic Sophisms,* Bastiat asks why is it than no one goes to sleep anxiously in Paris, worried about whether there will be bread and other items available for purchase in the morning:

On coming to Paris for a visit, I said to myself: Here are a million human beings who would all die in a few days if supplies of all sorts did not flow into this great metropolis. It staggers the imagination to try to comprehend the vast multiplicity of objects that must pass through its gates tomorrow, if its inhabitants are to be preserved from the horrors of famine, insurrection, and pillage. And yet all are sleeping peacefully at this moment, without being disturbed for a single instant by the idea of so frightful a prospect... What, then, is the resourceful and secret power that governs the amazing regularity of such complicated movements, a regularity in which everyone has such implicit faith, although his prosperity and his very life depend

> "How is that millions of people every day cooperate with millions of others to get the bagel to your corner coffee shop? There's no office or government agency or central hub where all the commerce originates. The web of connections holding the system together is unseen."

> The full passage from Smith is in <u>Book I, Chapter 1</u> beginning in paragraph 11.

upon it? That power is an absolute principle, the principle of free exchange.

There are really two aspects of the unseen here. The first is to simply marvel that the massive coordination and cooperation problem gets solved every day without anyone being in charge. Does anyone at the bagel shop or newsstand or lunch counter in a major city every stop to savor this extraordinary achievement of civilization? The source for this lack of appreciation is the quality of the coordination. The system works so well, we never even notice that it is functioning at all. We never stop to marvel at it because we so rarely see the system fail. When was the last time you showed at your local coffee shop to find them out scones or croissants or bagels? They are always there, always fresh, and eminently affordable.

The second aspect that is unseen is that if someone does happen to notice that this unmanaged system works beautifully, he or she would struggle to explain how this phenomenon is achieved. How is that millions of people every day cooperate with millions of others to get the bagel to your corner coffee shop? There's no office or government agency or central hub where all the commerce originates. The web of connections holding the system together is unseen.

In this essay, I want to highlight some of the attempts economists have made in the past to illuminate the often unnoticed and uncoordinated order that emerges, creating wealth the daily life we so often take for granted.

Bastiat was not the first to point the marvel of coordination. Ultimately, the cooperation that underlies the process is driven by specialization and the division of labor. So it is not surprising that Adam Smith, who began _The Wealth of Nations_ with a discussion of the division of labor and its wealth-producing properties, asks his readers to marvel at the power of specialization, the division of labor and the unseen cooperation of thousands to produce a simple woolen coat:

Observe the accommodation of the most common artificer or day-labourer in a civilized and thriving country, and you will perceive that the number of people of whose industry a part, though but a small part, has been employed in procuring him this accommodation, exceeds all computation. The woollen coat, for example, which covers the day-labourer, as coarse and rough as it may appear, is the produce of the joint labour of a great multitude of workmen. The shepherd, the sorter of the wool, the wool-comber or carder, the dyer, the scribbler, the spinner, the weaver, the fuller, the dresser, with many others, must all join their different arts in order to complete even this homely production. How many merchants and carriers, besides, must have been employed in transporting the materials from some of those workmen to others who often live in a very distant part of the country!

Henry George, who is known to modern readers—if he is known at all—for his advocacy of taxing land rather than other inputs, was a superb communicator of this concept of unseen cooperation. In *Protection or Free Trade,* he writes of a rural family preparing a meal of bread, fish and tea, all accompanied by a cheery fire:

The settler cut the wood. But it took more than that to *produce* the wood. Had it been merely cut, it would still be lying where it fell. The labor of hauling it was as much a part of its production as the labor of cutting it. So the journey to and from the mill was as necessary to the production of the flour as the planting and reaping of the wheat. To produce the fish the boy had to walk to the lake and trudge back again. And the production of the water in the kettle required not merely the exertion of the girl who brought it from the spring, but also the sinking of the barrel in which it collected, and the making of the bucket in which it was carried. [par. VII.2]

As for the tea, it was grown in China, was carried on a bamboo pole upon the shoulders of a man to some river village, and sold to a Chinese merchant, who shipped it by boat to a treaty port. There, having been packed for ocean transportation, it was sold to the agency of some American house, and sent by steamer to San Francisco. Thence it passed by railroad, with another transfer of ownership, into the hands of a Chicago jobber. The jobber, in turn, in pursuance of another sale, shipped it to the village store-keeper, who held it so that the settler might get it when and in such quantities as he pleased, just as the water from the spring is held in the sunken barrel so that it may be had when needed.

George's point is not so much the marvelousness of all this unseen cooperation but rather the importance of every step along the way that allows us to enjoy the goods we do. We may think of distributors and traders and transporters as less important than say, the baker who bakes the bagel, but the baker could not bake the bagel without the delivery of the flour, the manufacturing of the ovens and so on.

Perhaps the best known example to the modern reader of the marvelousness of unseen cooperation is Leonard Read's wonderful "I, Pencil." Read claims, speaking in first-person, in the voice of the pencil, that no one knows how to make one:

George's elaboration of the complexity underlying even the simplest of products was designed to defend free trade. Making something and swapping it for something from abroad is no different than making it directly. By showing the complexity of modern production, he is trying to counter the charge that such products are full of wasteful or parasitic contributors of transportation and distribution. See Chapter 7.

Does anyone wish to challenge my earlier assertion that no single person on the face of this earth knows how to make me?

Actually, millions of human beings have had a hand in my creation, no one of whom even knows more than a very few of the others. Now, you may say that I go too far in relating the picker of a coffee berry in far off Brazil and food growers elsewhere to my creation; that this is an extreme position. I shall stand by my claim. There isn't a single person in all these millions, including the president of the pencil company, who contributes more than a tiny, infinitesimal bit of know-how. From the standpoint of know-how the only difference between the miner of graphite in Ceylon and the logger in Oregon is in the type of know-how. Neither the miner nor the logger can be dispensed with, any more than can the chemist at the factory or the worker in the oil field—paraffin being a by-product of petroleum.

Read emphasizes the uncoordinated aspect of this incredible coordination:

There is a fact still more astounding: the absence of a master mind, of anyone dictating or forcibly directing these countless actions which bring me into being. No trace of such a person can be found. Instead, we find the Invisible Hand at work.

Yes, it is marvelous that there are bagels waiting for me in the coffeeshop. Yes, it is marvelous that there are pencils at a dozen places where I might stop to shop for something else along the way. There are plenty of woolen coats, plenty of tea, and more impressively, plenty of cars and computers and televisions, products that are infinitely more complex. But what sustains that cooperation that allows those products to be assembled by millions of strangers who toil unknowing that the cooperation is taking place?

One of the deepest attempts to illuminate that process is Hayek's 1945 article in the *American Economic Review,* "The Use of Knowledge in Society." Hayek is not content to simply marvel that there are pencils and bread and coats and televisions. He has something even more marvelous and unseen he wants his readers to see, and that is how the uncoordinated throng of cooperators who work to produce these products respond to a shortage or some other external change.

Hayek wanted to illuminate the incredible coordinating of vastly decentralized knowledge that must happen to cope with any adjustment such as a shortage. Hayek's answer, akin to Bastiat's referring to self-interest and exchange, and Read's invoking of the Invisible Hand, is the price system, which he expounds on in some

Hayek was invoking the marvelousness of uncoordinated knowledge as a counterpoint to the socialists of his day who argued for the superiority of centralized, state-run, top-down coordination. Bastiat, in the same discussion quoted above, contrasts the success of decentralized exchange in providing Paris with all of its citizens needs with how poorly a government bureau would perform the task.

detail.

It is tempting to say that Hayek was referring to what we today call supply and demand. Unfortunately, today's students are too frequently taught that supply and demand requires perfect competition or perfect knowledge. This leads students to view supply and demand as a theoretical construct that is unlikely to apply in the real world other than in the occasional arcane case such as wheat.

But Hayek took a very different view of the process. He viewed it as imperfect but effective:

Of course, these adjustments are probably never "perfect" in the sense in which the economist conceives of them in his equilibrium analysis. But I fear that our theoretical habits of approaching the problem with the assumption of more or less perfect knowledge on the part of almost everyone has made us somewhat blind to the true function of the price mechanism and led us to apply rather misleading standards in judging its efficiency. The marvel is that in a case like that of a scarcity of one raw material, without an order being issued, without more than perhaps a handful of people knowing the cause, tens of thousands of people whose identity could not be ascertained by months of investigation, are made to use the material or its products more sparingly; *i.e.,* they move in the right direction. This is enough of a marvel even if, in a constantly changing world, not all will hit it off so perfectly that their profit rates will always be maintained at the same constant or "normal" level.

I have deliberately used the word "marvel" to shock the reader out of the complacency with which we often take the working of this mechanism for granted. I am convinced that if it were the result of deliberate human design, and if the people guided by the price changes understood that their decisions have significance far beyond their immediate aim, this mechanism would have been acclaimed as one of the greatest triumphs of the human mind. Its misfortune is the double one that it is not the product of human design and that the people guided by it usually do not know why they are made to do what they do.

One of the virtues of Hayek's exposition, though it is stylistically drab in comparison to the other examples I have given here, is its emphasis on how the unseen cooperation solves the central problem of modern economic order. How do you decide how many bagels or pencils or cars a society needs? How do the answers to those questions change as circumstances and knowledge changes? I want to use this as a jumping off point for an example of unseen cooperation that is taking

One of Hayek's favorite quotes was from Adam Ferguson on "the result of human action but not of human design": Mankind, in following the present sense of their minds, in striving to remove inconveniences, or to gain apparent and contiguous advantages, arrive at ends which even their imagination could not anticipate, and pass on, like other animals, in the track of their nature, without perceiving its end...
Every step and every movement of the multitude, even in what are termed enlightened ages, are made with equal blindness to the future; and nations stumble upon establishments, which are

place today.

Over the next five or ten years, hundreds of millions of Chinese are expected to leave the Chinese countryside and move to the city. This extraordinary migration will require millions of adjustments to take place to make sure that our lives here in America are not thrown totally out of whack. All those newly-arrived Chinese city dwellers will use more pencils, drink more coffee, buy more bicycles, buy more cars and so on. Will there be enough to go around for those of us outside of China? Surely this expected migration will cause immense disruption. Should we worry about it? What precautions should we take to make that transition a smooth one?

And yet, like Bastiat's Parisian, we rightly lose little or no sleep worrying about these changes. The transition will be managed not by a Congressional committee or Presidential board charged with averting a crisis. The transition will be handled by the price system and we'll hardly notice it. Past of the reason for my confidence is based on my theoretical understanding of how markets work as Hayek describes them. But much of my confidence comes from the evidence of the past 20 years when a hundred million Chinese made the same trek we're talking about in the future. This is the greatest migration in human history and my guess is that you missed it. Very little changed in the world around us. The Chinese didn't buy up all the bicycles or cedar for the pencils or coffee grounds for more coffee. Somehow, our economic system took care of this transition so effectively, that most of us didn't even know it happened.

Such changes are happening all the time. The price system, along with the profit we allow producers to earn for responding effectively to prices, keeps our economic lives orderly in the face of those changes. Teachers of economics, this one included, should be looking for ways to illuminate the unseen workings of that incredible system. It is a system that is often described as competitive. Yet it is ultimately a system of cooperation. No one designed the system. It works without anyone being in charge. Marvel at it.

indeed the result of human action, but not the execution of any human design.
[From *An Essay on the History of Civil Society* (1767): Part Third. Section II, p. 122 of the Duncan Forbes edition, Edinburgh University Press, 1966. An online edition is at McMaster's.]

For an intellectual history of the idea that order can emerge without a conscious design or plan, see Norman Barry's "The Tradition of Spontaneous Order."

---

* Russell Roberts is professor of economics at George Mason University and the Features Editor at the Library of Economics and Liberty. He is working on a book on how the emergence of order and unplanned cooperation create wealth and our standard of living.

The Economic Organisation of a P.O.W. Camp

By R. A. RADFORD

INTRODUCTION

AFTER allowance has been made for abnormal circumstances, the social institutions, ideas and habits of groups in the outside world are to be found reflected in a Prisoner of War Camp. It is an unusual but a vital society. Camp organisation and politics are matters of real concern to the inmates, as affecting their present and perhaps their future existences. Nor does this indicate any loss of proportion. No one pretends that camp matters are of any but local importance or of more than transient interest, but their importance there is great. They bulk large in a world of narrow horizons and it is suggested that any distortion of values lies rather in the minimisation than in the exaggeration of their importance. Human affairs are essentially practical matters and the measure of immediate effect on the lives of those directly concerned in them is to a large extent the criterion of their importance at that time and place. A prisoner can hold strong views on such subjects as whether or not all tinned meats shall be issued to individuals cold or be centrally cooked, without losing sight of the significance of the Atlantic Charter.

One aspect of social organisation is to be found in economic activity, and this, along with other manifestations of a group existence, is to be found in any P.O.W. camp. True, a prisoner is not dependent on his exertions for the provision of the necessaries, or even the luxuries of life, but through his economic activity, the exchange of goods and services, his standard of material comfort is considerably enhanced. And this is a serious matter to the prisoner : he is not " playing at shops " even though the small scale of the transactions and the simple expression of comfort and wants in terms of cigarettes and jam, razor blades and writing paper, make the urgency of those needs difficult to appreciate, even by an ex-prisoner of some three months' standing.

Nevertheless, it cannot be too strongly emphasised that economic activities do not bulk so large in prison society as they do in the larger world. There can be little production ; as has been said the prisoner is independent of his exertions for the provision of the necessities and luxuries of life ; the emphasis lies in exchange and the media of exchange. A prison camp is not to be compared with the seething crowd of higglers in a street market, any more than it is to be compared with the economic inertia of a family dinner table.

Naturally then, entertainment, academic and literary interests, games and discussions of the " other world " bulk larger in everyday life than they do in the life of more normal societies. But it would be wrong to underestimate the importance of economic activity. Everyone receives a roughly equal share of essentials; it is by trade that individual preferences are given expression and comfort increased. All at some time, and most people regularly, make exchanges of one sort or another.

Although a P.O.W. camp provides a living example of a simple economy which might be used as an alternative to the Robinson Crusoe economy beloved by the text-books, and its simplicity renders the demonstration of certain economic hypotheses both amusing and instructive, it is suggested that the principal significance is sociological. True, there is interest in observing the growth of economic institutions and customs in a brand new society, small and simple enough to prevent detail from obscuring the basic pattern and disequilibrium from obscuring the working of the system. But the essential interest lies in the universality and the spontaneity of this economic life; it came into existence not by conscious imitation but as a response to the immediate needs and circumstances. Any similarity between prison organisation and outside organisation arises from similar stimuli evoking similar responses.

The following is as brief an account of the essential data as may render the narrative intelligible. The camps of which the writer had experience were Oflags and consequently the economy was not complicated by payments for work by the detaining power. They consisted normally of between 1,200 and 2,500 people, housed in a number of separate but intercommunicating bungalows, one company of 200 or so to a building. Each company formed a group within the main organisation and inside the company the room and the messing syndicate, a voluntary and spontaneous group who fed together, formed the constituent units.

Between individuals there was active trading in all consumer goods and in some services. Most trading was for food against cigarettes or other foodstuffs, but cigarettes rose from the status of a normal commodity to that of currency. RMk.s existed but had no circulation save for gambling debts, as few articles could be purchased with them from the canteen.

Our supplies consisted of rations provided by the detaining power and (principally) the contents of Red Cross food parcels—tinned milk, jam, butter, biscuits, bully, chocolate, sugar, etc., and cigarettes. So far the supplies to each person were equal and regular. Private parcels of clothing, toilet requisites and cigarettes were also received, and here equality ceased owing to the different numbers despatched and the vagaries of the post. All these articles were the subject of trade and exchange.

THE DEVELOPMENT AND ORGANISATION OF THE MARKET

Very soon after capture people realised that it was both undesirable and unnecessary, in view of the limited size and the equality of supplies, to give away or to accept gifts of cigarettes or food. " Goodwill " developed into trading as a more equitable means of maximising individual satisfaction.

We reached a transit camp in Italy about a fortnight after capture and received $\frac{1}{4}$ of a Red Cross food parcel each a week later. At once exchanges, already established, multiplied in volume. Starting with simple direct barter, such as a non-smoker giving a smoker friend his cigarette issue in exchange for a chocolate ration, more complex exchanges soon became an accepted custom. Stories circulated of a padre who started off round the camp with a tin of cheese and five cigarettes and returned to his bed with a complete parcel in addition to his original cheese and cigarettes ; the market was not yet perfect. Within a week or two, as the volume of trade grew, rough scales of exchange values came into existence. Sikhs, who had at first exchanged tinned beef for practically any other foodstuff, began to insist on jam and margarine. It was realised that a tin of jam was worth $\frac{1}{2}$ lb. of margarine plus something else ; that a cigarette issue was worth several chocolate issues, and a tin of diced carrots was worth practically nothing.

In this camp we did not visit other bungalows very much and prices varied from place to place ; hence the germ of truth in the story of the itinerant priest. By the end of a month, when we reached our permanent camp, there was a lively trade in all commodities and their relative values were well known, and expressed not in terms of one another—one didn't quote bully in terms of sugar—but in terms of cigarettes. The cigarette became the standard of value. In the permanent camp people started by wandering through the bungalows calling their offers—" cheese for seven " (cigarettes)—and the hours after parcel issue were Bedlam. The inconveniences of this system soon led to its replacement by an Exchange and Mart notice board in every bungalow, where under the headings " name ", " room number ", " wanted " and " offered " sales and wants were advertised. When a deal went through, it was crossed off the board. The public and semi-permanent records of transactions led to cigarette prices being well known and thus tending to equality throughout the camp, although there were always opportunities for an astute trader to make a profit from arbitrage. With this development everyone, including non-smokers, was willing to sell for cigarettes, using them to buy at another time and place. Cigarettes became the normal currency, though, of course, barter was never extinguished.

The unity of the market and the prevalence of a single price varied directly with the general level of organisation and comfort in the camp. A transit camp was always chaotic and uncomfortable : people were overcrowded, no one knew where anyone else was living, and few took the trouble to find out. Organisation was too slender to include an Exchange and Mart board, and private advertisements were the most that appeared. Consequently a transit camp was not one market but many. The price of a tin of salmon is known to have varied by two cigarettes in 20 between one end of a hut and the other. Despite a high level of organisation in Italy, the market was morcellated in this manner at the first transit camp we reached after our removal to Germany in the autumn of 1943. In this camp— Stalag VIIA at Moosburg in Bavaria—there were up to 50,000 prisoners of all nationalities. French, Russians, Italians and Jugo-Slavs were free to move about within the camp : British and Americans were confined to their compounds, although a few cigarettes given to a sentry would always procure permission for one or two men to visit other compounds. The people who first visited the highly organised French trading centre, with its stalls and known prices, found coffee extract—relatively cheap among the tea-drinking English—commanding a fancy price in biscuits or cigarettes, and some enterprising people made small fortunes that way. (Incidentally we found out later that much of the coffee went " over the wire " and sold for phenomenal prices at black market cafés in Munich : some of the French prisoners were said to have made substantial sums in RMk.s. This was one of the few occasions on which our normally closed economy came into contact with other economic worlds.)

Eventually public opinion grew hostile to these monopoly profits— not everyone could make contact with the French—and trading with them was put on a regulated basis. Each group of beds was given a quota of articles to offer and the transaction was carried out by accredited representatives from the British compound, with monopoly rights. The same method was used for trading with sentries elsewhere, as in this trade secrecy and reasonable prices had a peculiar importance, but as is ever the case with regulated companies, the interloper proved too strong.

The permanent camps in Germany saw the highest level of commercial organisation. In addition to the Exchange and Mart notice boards, a shop was organised as a public utility, controlled by representatives of the Senior British Officer, on a no profit basis. People left their surplus clothing, toilet requisites and food there until they were sold at a fixed price in cigarettes. Only sales in cigarettes were accepted—there was no barter— and there was no higgling. For food at least there were standard prices : clothing is less homogeneous and the price was decided around a norm by the seller and the shop manager in agreement ; shirts would average say 80, ranging from 60 to 120 according to quality and age. Of food, the shop carried small stocks for convenience ; the capital was provided by a loan from the bulk store of Red Cross cigarettes and repaid by a small commission taken on the first transactions. Thus the cigarette attained its fullest currency status, and the market was almost completely unified.

It is thus to be seen that a market came into existence without labour or production. The B.R.C.S. may be considered as " Nature " of the text-book, and the articles of trade—food, clothing and cigarettes—as free gifts—land or manna. Despite this, and despite a roughly equal distribution of resources, a market came into spontaneous operation, and prices were fixed by the operation of supply and demand. It is difficult to reconcile this fact with the labour theory of value.

Actually there was an embryo labour market. Even when cigarettes were not scarce, there was usually some unlucky person willing to perform services for them. Laundrymen advertised at two cigarettes a garment. Battle-dress was scrubbed and pressed and a pair of trousers lent for the interim period for twelve. A good pastel portrait cost thirty or a tin of " Kam ". Odd tailoring and other jobs similarly had their prices.

There were also entrepreneurial services. There was a coffee stall owner who sold tea, coffee or cocoa at two cigarettes a cup, buying his raw materials at market prices and hiring labour to gather fuel and to stoke ; he actually enjoyed the services of a chartered accountant at one stage. After a period of great prosperity he overreached himself and failed disastrously for several hundred cigarettes. Such large-scale private enterprise was rare but several middlemen or professional traders existed. The padre in Italy, or the men at Moosburg who opened trading relations with the French, are examples : the more subdivided the market, the less perfect the advertisement of prices, and the less stable the prices, the greater was the scope for these operators. One man capitalised his knowledge of Urdu by buying meat from the Sikhs and selling butter and jam in return : as his operations became better known more and more people entered this trade, prices in the Indian Wing approximated more nearly to those elsewhere, though to the end a " contact " among the Indians was valuable, as linguistic difficulties prevented the trade from being quite free. Some were specialists in the Indian trade, the food, clothing or even the watch trade. Middlemen traded on their own account or on commission. Price rings and agreements were suspected and the traders certainly co-operated. Nor did they welcome newcomers. Unfortunately the writer knows little of the workings of these people : public opinion was hostile and the professionals were usually of a retiring disposition.

One trader in food and cigarettes, operating in a period of dearth, enjoyed a high reputation. His capital, carefully saved, was originally about 50 cigarettes, with which he bought rations on issue days and held them until the price rose just before the next issue. He also picked up a little by arbitrage ; several times a day he visited every Exchange or Mart notice board and took advantage of every discrepancy between prices of goods offered and wanted. His knowledge of prices, markets and names of those who had received cigarette parcels was phenomenal. By these means he kept himself smoking steadily—his profits—while his capital remained intact.

Sugar was issued on Saturday. about Tuesday two of us used to visit Sam and make a deal; as old customers he would advance as much of the price as he could spare then, and entered the transaction in a book. On Saturday morning he left cocoa tins on our beds for the ration, and picked them up on Saturday afternoon. We were hoping for a calendar at Christmas, but Sam failed too. He was left holding a big black treacle issue when the price fell, and in this weakened state was unable to withstand an unexpected arrival of parcels and the consequent price fluctuations. He paid in full, but from his capital. The next Tuesday, when I paid my usual visit he was out of business.

Credit entered into many, perhaps into most, transactions, in one form or another. Sam paid in advance as a rule for his purchases of future deliveries of sugar, but many buyers asked for credit, whether the commodity was sold spot or future. Naturally prices varied according to the terms of sale. A treacle ration might be advertised for four cigarettes now or five next week. And in the future market " bread now " was a vastly different thing from " bread Thursday ". Bread was issued on Thursday and Monday, four and three days' rations respectively, and by Wednesday and Sunday night it had risen at least one cigarette per ration, from seven to eight, by supper time. One man always saved a ration to sell then at the peak price: his offer of " bread now " stood out on the board among a number of " bread Monday's " fetching one or two less, or not selling at all—and he always smoked on Sunday night.

The Cigarette Currency

Although cigarettes as currency exhibited certain peculiarities, they performed all the functions of a metallic currency as a unit of account, as a measure of value and as a store of value, and shared most of its characteristics. They were homogeneous, reasonably durable, and of convenient size for the smallest or, in packets, for the largest transactions. Incidentally, they could be clipped or sweated by rolling them between the fingers so that tobacco fell out.

Cigarettes were also subject to the working of Gresham's Law. Certain brands were more popular than others as smokes, but for currency purposes a cigarette was a cigarette. Consequently buyers used the poorer qualities and the Shop rarely saw the more popular brands: cigarettes such as Churchman's No. 1 were rarely used for trading. At one time cigarettes hand-rolled from pipe tobacco began to circulate. Pipe tobacco was issued in lieu of cigarettes by the Red Cross at a rate of 25 cigarettes to the ounce and this rate was standard in exchanges, but an ounce would produce 30 home-made cigarettes. Naturally, people with machine-made cigarettes broke them down and re-rolled the tobacco, and the real cigarette virtually disappeared from the market. Hand-rolled cigarettes were not homogeneous and prices could no longer be quoted in them with safety: each cigarette was examined before it was accepted and thin ones were rejected, or extra demanded as a make-weight. For a time we suffered all the inconveniences of a debased currency.

Machine-made cigarettes were always universally acceptable, both for what they would buy and for themselves. It was this intrinsic value which gave rise to their principal disadvantage as currency, a disadvantage which exists, but to a far smaller extent, in the case of metallic currency;—that is, a strong demand for non-monetary purposes. Consequently our economy was repeatedly subject to deflation and to periods of monetary stringency. While the Red Cross issue of 50 or 25 cigarettes per man per week came in regularly, and while there were fair stocks held, the cigarette currency suited its purpose admirably. But when the issue was interrupted, stocks soon ran out, prices fell, trading declined in volume and became increasingly a matter of barter. This deflationary tendency was periodically offset by the sudden injection of new currency. Private cigarette parcels arrived in a trickle throughout the year, but the big numbers came in quarterly when the Red Cross received its allocation of transport. Several hundred thousand cigarettes might arrive in the space of a fortnight. Prices soared, and then began to fall, slowly at first but with increasing rapidity as stocks ran out, until the next big delivery. Most of our economic troubles could be attributed to this fundamental instability.

PRICE MOVEMENTS

Many factors affected prices, the strongest and most noticeable being the periodical currency inflation and deflation described in the last paragraphs. The periodicity of this price cycle depended on cigarette and, to a far lesser extent, on food deliveries. At one time in the early days, before any private parcels had arrived and when there were no individual stocks, the weekly issue of cigarettes and food parcels occurred on a Monday. The non-monetary demand for cigarettes was great, and less elastic than the demand for food : consequently prices fluctuated weekly, falling towards Sunday night and rising sharply on Monday morning. Later, when many people held reserves, the weekly issue had no such effect, being too small a proportion of the total available. Credit allowed people with no reserves to meet their non-monetary demand over the week-end.

The general price level was affected by other factors. An influx of new prisoners, proverbially hungry, raised it. Heavy air raids in the vicinity of the camp probably increased the non-monetary demand for cigarettes and accentuated deflation. Good and bad war news certainly had its effect, and the general waves of optimism and pessimism which swept the camp were reflected in prices. Before breakfast one morning in March of this year, a rumour of the arrival of parcels and cigarettes was circulated. Within ten minutes I sold a treacle ration, for four cigarettes (hitherto offered in vain for three), and many similar deals went through. By 10 o'clock the rumour was denied, and treacle that day found no more buyers even at two cigarettes.

More interesting than changes in the general price level were changes in the price structure. Changes in the supply of a commodity, in the German ration scale or in the make-up of Red Cross parcels, would raise the price of one commodity relative to others. Tins of oatmeal, once a rare and much sought after luxury in the parcels, became a commonplace in 1943, and the price fell. In hot weather the demand for cocoa fell, and that for soap rose. A new recipe would be reflected in the price level: the discovery that raisins and sugar could be turned into an alcoholic liquor of remarkable potency reacted permanently on the dried fruit market. The invention of electric immersion heaters run off the power points made tea, a drug on the market in Italy, a certain seller in Germany.

In August, 1944, the supplies of parcels and cigarettes were both halved. Since both sides of the equation were changed in the same degree, changes in prices were not anticipated. But this was not the case: the non-monetary demand for cigarettes was less elastic than the demand for food, and food prices fell a little. More important however were the changes in the price structure. German margarine and jam, hitherto valueless owing to adequate supplies of Canadian butter and marmalade, acquired a new value. Chocolate, popular and a certain seller, and sugar, fell. Bread rose; several standing contracts of bread for cigarettes were broken, especially when the bread ration was reduced a few weeks later.

In February, 1945, the German soldier who drove the ration waggon was found to be willing to exchange loaves of bread at the rate of one loaf for a bar of chocolate. Those in the know began selling bread and buying chocolate, by then almost unsaleable in a period of serious deflation. Bread, at about 40, fell slightly; chocolate rose from 15; the supply of bread was not enough for the two commodities to reach parity, but the tendency was unmistakable.

The substitution of German margarine for Canadian butter when parcels were halved naturally affected their relative values, margarine appreciating at the expense of butter. Similarly, two brands of dried milk, hitherto differing in quality and therefore in price by five cigarettes a tin, came together in price as the wider substitution of the cheaper raised its relative value.

Enough has been cited to show that any change in conditions affected both the general price level and the price structure. It was this latter phenomenon which wrecked our planned economy.

Paper Currency—Bully Marks

Around D-Day, food and cigarettes were plentiful, business was brisk and the camp in an optimistic mood. Consequently the Entertainments Committee felt the moment opportune to launch a restaurant, where food and hot drinks were sold while a band and variety turns performed. Earlier experiments, both public and private, had pointed the way, and the scheme was a great success. Food was bought at market prices to provide the meals and the small profits were devoted to a reserve fund and used to bribe Germans to provide grease-paints and other necessities for the camp theatre. Originally meals were sold for cigarettes but this meant that the whole scheme was vulnerable to the periodic deflationary waves, and furthermore heavy smokers were unlikely to attend much. The whole success of the scheme depended on an adequate amount of food being offered for sale in the normal manner.

To increase and facilitate trade, and to stimulate supplies and customers therefore, and secondarily to avoid the worst effects of deflation when it should come, a paper currency was organised by the Restaurant and the Shop. The Shop bought food on behalf of the Restaurant with paper notes and the paper was accepted equally with the cigarettes in the Restaurant or Shop, and passed back to the Shop to purchase more food. The Shop acted as a bank of issue. The paper money was backed 100 per cent. by food ; hence its name, the Bully Mark. The BMk. was backed 100 per cent. by food : there could be no over-issues, as is permissible with a normal bank of issue, since the eventual dispersal of the camp and consequent redemption of all BMk.s was anticipated in the near future.

Originally one BMk. was worth one cigarette and for a short time both circulated freely inside and outside the Restaurant. Prices were quoted in BMk.s and cigarettes with equal freedom—and for a short time the BMk. showed signs of replacing the cigarette as currency. The BMk. was tied to food, but not to cigarettes : as it was issued against food, say 45 for a tin of milk and so on, any reduction in the BMk. prices of food would have meant that there were un-backed BMk.s in circulation. But the price of both food and BMk.s could and did fluctuate with the supply of cigarettes.

While the Restaurant flourished, the scheme was a success : the Restaurant bought heavily, all foods were saleable and prices were stable.

In August parcels and cigarettes were halved and the Camp was bombed. The Restaurant closed for a short while and sales of food became difficult. Even when the Restaurant reopened, the food and cigarette shortage became increasingly acute and people were unwilling to convert such valuable goods into paper and to hold them for luxuries like snacks and tea. Less of the right kinds of food for the Restaurant were sold, and the Shop became glutted with dried fruit, chocolate, sugar, etc., which the Restaurant could not buy. The price level and the price structure changed. The BMk. fell to four-fifths of a cigarette and eventually farther still, and it became unacceptable save in the Restaurant. There was a flight from the BMk., no longer convertible into cigarettes or popular foods. The cigarette re-established itself.

But the BMk. was sound ! The Restaurant closed in the New Year with a progressive food shortage and the long evenings without lights due to intensified Allied air raids, and BMk.s could only be spent in the Coffee Bar—relict of the Restaurant—or on the few unpopular foods in the Shop, the owners of which were prepared to accept them. In the end all holders of BMk.s were paid in full, in cups of coffee or in prunes. People who had bought BMk.s for cigarettes or valuable jam or biscuits in their heyday were aggrieved that they should have stood the loss involved by their restricted choice, but they suffered no actual loss of market value.

PRICE FIXING

Along with this scheme came a determined attempt at a planned economy, at price fixing. The Medical Officer had long been anxious to control food sales, for fear of some people selling too much, to the detriment of their health. The deflationary waves and their effects on prices were inconvenient to all and would be dangerous to the Restaurant which had to carry stocks. Furthermore, unless the BMk. was convertible into cigarettes at about par it had little chance of gaining confidence and of succeeding as a currency. As has been explained, the BMk. was tied to food but could not be tied to cigarettes, which fluctuated in value. Hence, while BMk. prices of food were fixed for all time, cigarette prices of food and BMk.s varied.

The Shop, backed by the Senior British Officer, was now in a position to enforce price control both inside and outside its walls. Hitherto a standard price had been fixed for food left for sale in the shop, and prices outside were roughly in conformity with this scale, which was recommended as a " guide " to sellers, but fluctuated a good deal around it. Sales in the Shop at recommended prices were apt to be slow though a good price might be obtained : sales outside could be made more quickly at lower prices. (If sales outside were to be at higher prices, goods were withdrawn from the Shop until the recommended price rose : but the recommended price was sluggish and could not follow the market closely by reason of its very purpose, which was stability.) The Exchange and Mart notice boards came under the control of the Shop : advertisements which exceeded a 5 per cent. departure from the recommended scale were liable to be crossed out by authority : unauthorised sales were discouraged by authority and also by public opinion, strongly in favour of a just and stable price. (Recommended prices were fixed partly from market data, partly on the advice of the M.O.)

At first the recommended scale was a success : the Restaurant, a big buyer, kept prices stable around this level : opinion and the 5 per cent. tolerance helped. But when the price level fell with the August cuts and the price structure changed, the recommended scale was too rigid. Unchanged at first, as no deflation was expected, the scale was tardily lowered, but the prices of goods on the new scale remained in the same relation to one another, owing to the BMk., while on the market the price structure had changed. And the modifying influence of the Restaurant had gone. The scale was moved up and down several times, slowly following the inflationary and deflationary waves, but it was rarely adjusted to changes in the price structure. More and more advertisements were crossed off the board, and black market sales at unauthorised prices increased : eventually public opinion turned against the recommended scale and authority gave up the struggle. In the last few weeks, with unparalleled deflation, prices fell with alarming rapidity, no scales existed, and supply and demand, alone and unmellowed, determined prices.

Public Opinion

Public opinion on the subject of trading was vocal if confused and changeable, and generalisations as to its direction are difficult and dangerous. A tiny minority held that all trading was undesirable as it engendered an unsavoury atmosphere ; occasional frauds and sharp practices were cited as proof. Certain forms of trading were more generally condemned ; trade with the Germans was criticised by many. Red Cross toilet articles, which were in short supply and only issued in cases of actual need, were excluded from trade by law and opinion working in unshakable harmony. At one time, when there had been several cases of malnutrition reported among the more devoted smokers, no trade in German rations was permitted, as the victims became an additional burden on the depleted food reserves of the Hospital. But while certain activities were condemned as anti-social, trade itself was practised, and its utility appreciated, by almost everyone in the camp.

More interesting was opinion on middlemen and prices. Taken as a whole, opinion was hostile to the middleman. His function, and his hard work in bringing buyer and seller together, were ignored ; profits were not regarded as a reward for labour, but as the result of sharp practices. Despite the fact that his very existence was proof to the contrary, the middleman was held to be redundant in view of the existence of an official Shop and the Exchange and Mart. Appreciation only came his way when he was willing to advance the price of a sugar ration, or to buy goods spot and carry them against a future sale. In these cases the element of risk was obvious to all, and the convenience of the service was felt to merit some reward. Particularly unpopular was the middleman with an element of monopoly, the man who contacted the ration wagon driver, or the man who utilised his knowledge of Urdu. And middlemen as a group were blamed for reducing prices. Opinion notwithstanding, most people dealt with a middleman, whether consciously or unconsciously, at some time or another.

There was a strong feeling that everything had its " just price " in cigarettes. While the assessment of the just price, which incidentally varied between camps, was impossible of explanation, this price was nevertheless pretty closely known. It can best be defined as the price usually fetched by an article in good times when cigarettes were plentiful. The "just price" changed slowly; it was unaffected by short-term variations in supply, and while opinion might be resigned to departures from the "just price", a strong feeling of resentment persisted. A more satisfactory definition of the "just price" is impossible. Everyone knew what it was, though no one could explain why it should be so.

As soon as prices began to fall with a cigarette shortage, a clamour arose, particularly against those who held reserves and who bought at reduced prices. Sellers at cut prices were criticised and their activities referred to as the black market. In every period of dearth the explosive question of "should non-smokers receive a cigarette ration?" was discussed to profitless length. Unfortunately, it was the non-smoker, or the light smoker with his reserves, along with the hated middleman, who weathered the storm most easily.

The popularity of the price-fixing scheme, and such success as it enjoyed, were undoubtedly the result of this body of opinion. On several occasions the fall of prices was delayed by the general support given to the recommended scale. The onset of deflation was marked by a period of sluggish trade; prices stayed up but no one bought. Then prices fell on the black market, and the volume of trade revived in that quarter. Even when the recommended scale was revised, the volume of trade in the Shop would remain low. Opinion was always overruled by the hard facts of the market.

Curious arguments were advanced to justify price fixing. The recommended prices were in some way related to the calorific values of the foods offered: hence some were overvalued and never sold at these prices. One argument ran as follows:—not everyone has private cigarette parcels: thus, when prices were high and trade good in the summer of 1944, only the lucky rich could buy. This was unfair to the man with few cigarettes. When prices fell in the following winter, prices should be pegged high so that the rich, who had enjoyed life in the summer, should put many cigarettes into circulation. The fact that those who sold to the rich in the summer had also enjoyed life then, and the fact that in the winter there was always someone willing to sell at low prices were ignored. Such arguments were hotly debated each night after the approach of Allied aircraft extinguished all lights at 8 p.m. But prices moved with the supply of cigarettes, and refused to stay fixed in accordance with a theory of ethics.

Conclusion

The economic organisation described was both elaborate and smooth-working in the summer of 1944. Then came the August cuts and deflation. Prices fell, rallied with deliveries of cigarette parcels in September and December, and fell again. In January, 1945, supplies of Red Cross cigarettes ran out: and prices slumped still further: in February the supplies of food parcels were exhausted and the depression became a blizzard. Food, itself scarce, was almost given away in order to meet the non-monetary demand for cigarettes. Laundries ceased to operate, or worked for £s or RMk.s: food and cigarettes sold for fancy prices in £s, hitherto unheard of. The Restaurant was a memory and the BMk. a joke. The Shop was empty and the Exchange and Mart notices were full of unaccepted offers for cigarettes. Barter increased in volume, becoming a larger proportion of a smaller volume of trade. This, the first serious and prolonged food shortage in the writer's experience, caused the price structure to change again, partly because German rations were not easily divisible. A margarine ration gradually sank in value until it exchanged directly for a treacle ration. Sugar slumped sadly. Only bread retained its value. Several thousand cigarettes, the capital of the Shop, were distributed without any noticeable effect. A few fractional parcel and cigarette issues, such as one-sixth of a parcel and twelve cigarettes each, led to momentary price recoveries and feverish trade, especially when they coincided with good news from the Western Front, but the general position remained unaltered.

By April, 1945, chaos had replaced order in the economic sphere: sales were difficult, prices lacked stability. Economics has been defined as the science of distributing limited means among unlimited and competing ends. On 12th April, with the arrival of elements of the 30th U.S. Infantry Division, the ushering in of an age of plenty demonstrated the hypothesis that with infinite means economic organisation and activity would be redundant, as every want could be satisfied without effort.

Last-Minute Bidding and the Rules for Ending Second-Price Auctions: Evidence from eBay and Amazon Auctions on the Internet

By Alvin E. Roth and Axel Ockenfels*

Auctions on the Internet provide a new source of data on how bidding is influenced by the detailed rules of the auction. Here we study the second-price auctions run by eBay and Amazon, in which a bidder submits a reservation price and has this (maximum) price used to bid for him by proxy. That is, a bidder can submit his reservation price (called a proxy bid) early in the auction and have the resulting bid register as the minimum increment above the previous high bid. As subsequent reservation prices are submitted, the bid rises by the minimum increment until the second-highest submitted reservation price is exceeded. Hence, an early bid with a reservation price higher than any other submitted during the auction will win the auction and pay only the minimum increment

above the second-highest submitted reservation price.

eBay and Amazon use different rules for ending an auction. Auctions on eBay have a fixed end time (a "hard close"), while auctions on Amazon, which operate under otherwise similar rules, are automatically extended if necessary past the scheduled end time until ten minutes have passed without a bid. These different rules give bidders more reason to bid late on eBay than on Amazon. We find that this is reflected in the auction data: the fraction of bids submitted in the closing seconds of the auction is substantially larger in eBay than in Amazon, and more experience causes bidders to bid later on eBay, but earlier on Amazon.

Last-minute bidding, a practice called "sniping," arises despite advice from both auctioneers and sellers in eBay that bidders should simply submit their maximum willingness to pay, once, early in the auction. For example, eBay instructs bidders on the simple economics of second-price auctions, using an example of a winning early bid. They discuss last-minute bids on a page explaining that they will not accept complaints about sniping, as follows:[1]

> Bid Sniping (last-minute bidding).
> eBay always recommends bidding the absolute maximum that one is willing to pay for an item early in the auction. eBay uses a proxy bidding system: you may bid as high as you wish, but the current bid that is registered will only be a small increment above the next lowest bid. The remainder of your Maximum Bid is held, by the system, to be used in the event someone bids against you ... Thus, if one is outbid, one should be at worst, ambivalent toward being outbid. After all, someone else was simply willing to pay

* Roth: Harvard University, Department of Economics and Graduate School of Business Administration, Soldiers Field Road, Baker Library 183, Boston, MA 02163 (e-mail: aroth@hbs.edu; URL: ⟨http://www.economics.harvard.edu/~aroth/alroth.html⟩); Ockenfels: Max Planck Institute for Research into Economic Systems, Strategic Interaction Group, Kahlaische Strasse 10, D-07745 Jena, Germany (e-mail: ockenfels@mpiew-jena.mpg.de; URL: ⟨http://www.mpiew-jena.de/esi/ockenfels/index.html⟩). We gratefully acknowledge helpful conversations on this subject with Estelle Cantillon, Scott Cook, Jeff Ely, Ed Glaeser, Seungjin Han, Ehud Kalai, Bertrand Koebel, Eric Maskin, Muriel Niederle, Martin Osborne, Ariel Pakes, Jack Porter, Jean-Francois Richard, Uri Rothblum, Hal Varian, and comments from audiences at the following universities and colleges: Berkeley, Berlin, Bielefeld, Bilbao, Bonn, Columbia, Dortmund, Harvard, Koblenz, London School of Economics, Minnesota, Munich, Northwestern, Stanford, and Wellesley. We also thank two anonymous referees for very helpful comments, the many bidders who allowed us to interview them, and the readers of a *New York Times* column by Hal Varian and a *Wall Street Journal* article by Joel Rosenblatt that mentioned an earlier version of this paper for many stimulating opinions. Most of the work was done while Ockenfels was a postdoctoral research fellow at the Harvard Business School. This project received financial support from the National Science Foundation, the Harvard Business School, and the Deutsche Forschungsgemeinschaft (DFG).

[1] Online: ⟨http://pages.ebay.com/aw/notabase.html⟩ (1999).

more than you wanted to pay for it. If someone does outbid you toward the last minutes of an auction, it may feel unfair, but if you had bid your maximum amount up front and let the proxy bidding system work for you, the outcome would not be based on time.

Sellers, when urging potential buyers to bid early, are concerned that very late bids run the risk of not being successfully transmitted, which causes lower expected revenues. The following paragraph, posted by a seller (Axis Mundi) together with item descriptions, is representative advice:

THE DANGERS OF LAST-MINUTE BIDDING: Almost without fail after an auction has closed we receive e-mails from bidders who claim they were attempting to place a bid and were unable to get into eBay. There is nothing we can do to help bidders who were "locked out" while trying to place a "last minute" bid. All we can do in this regard is to urge you to place your bids early. If you're serious in your intent to become a winning bidder please avoid eBay's high traffic during the close of an auction. It's certainly your choice how you handle your bidding, but we'd rather see you a winner instead of being left out during the last-minute scramble.

Other warnings about late bidding come from auctionwatch.com, a rich source of information for users of Internet auctions ("There are inherent risks in sniping. If you wait too long to bid, the auction could close before your bid is processed")[2] and from esnipe.com, an online agent that places late bids on behalf of its users (" ... network traffic and eBay response time can sometimes prevent a bid from being completed successfully. This is the nature of sniping").[3] Despite all this advice, however, there is an active exchange of tips in eBay's chat rooms about how to snipe effectively, and there is even a market for bidding software that makes sniping easy. The following excerpt from a software ad reflects the inclination to bid late:

... our bidding program BidMaster 2000 provides you complete control. ... Set a bid 7 days ahead, track the item's price during the week, edit your bid time, and amount; when the end of the auction nears WHAM your bid will be placed automatically.

One reason we might see snipers on eBay is that sniping can be a best response to a variety of strategies. For example, inexperienced bidders might make an analogy with first-price "English" auctions, and be prepared to continually raise their bids to maintain their status as high bidder. In an eBay-style auction with a hard close, bidding very late might be a best response to "incremental bidding" of this sort. That is, bidding very near the end of the auction would not give the incremental bidder sufficient time to respond, and so a sniper competing with an incremental bidder might win the auction at the incremental bidder's initial, low bid. In contrast, bidding one's true value early in the auction, when an incremental bidder is present, would win the auction only if one's true value were higher than the incremental bidder's, and in that case would have to pay the incremental bidder's true value. Of course, late bidding may also be a best response to other incremental bidding (or "price war") behaviors, including that of a dishonest seller who attempts to raise the price by using "shill bidders" to bid against a proxy bidder.[4] So, in an eBay auction, even with purely private values, it is not a dominant strategy to bid one's true value early, which might be suggested by false analogy to one-time sealed-bid second-price auctions.[5]

The advantage that sniping confers in an auction with a fixed deadline is eliminated or greatly attenuated in an Amazon-style auction with an automatic extension.[6] In such an auc-

[2] Online: ⟨http://www.auctionwatch.com/awdaily/tipsandtactics/buy-bid2.html⟩ (2000).

[3] Online: ⟨http://www.esnipe.com/faq.asp⟩ (2000).

[4] Dan Ariely et al. (2002) provide lab evidence for incremental-bidding behavior in second-price Internet auctions. See Judith H. Dobrzynski (2000) in the *New York Times* or Glenn R. Simpson (2000) in the *Wall Street Journal* for well-publicized examples of shill bidding.

[5] A related observation, the failure of the dominance criterion in English-auction models, has been made in a theoretical contribution by Ulrich Kamecke (1998).

[6] The relevant Amazon rules are the following: "We know that bidding may get hot and heavy near the end of many auctions. Our Going, Going, Gone feature ensures that you always have an opportunity to challenge last-second bids.

tion, an attentive incremental bidder can be provoked to respond whenever a bid is placed. So there is no advantage in bidding late, and certainly no advantage in delaying one's bid until so late that there is some probability that there will not be time to successfully submit it.

In fact, sniping in an auction with a fixed deadline, in which very late bids have some probability of not being successfully transmitted, need not depend on the presence of irrational bidders. There can be equilibria even in purely private-value auctions in which bidders have an incentive to bid late, even though this risks failing to bid at all. This kind of equilibrium can be interpreted as a kind of implicit collusion against the seller, because it has the effect of probabilistically suppressing some bids, and hence giving higher profits to the successful bidders.[7] But in Amazon-type auctions, in which a successful late bid extends the auction, this kind of equilibrium does not persist (see Ockenfels and Roth [2002] for precise statements and proofs).

Another way to explain late bidding without positing inexperience or irrationality on the part of the bidders is to note that, if an auction is common value rather than private value, bidders can get information from others' bids that causes them to revise their willingness to pay. In general, late bids motivated by information about common values arise either so that bidders can incorporate into their bids the information they have gathered from the earlier bids of others, or so bidders can avoid giving information to others through their own early bids. In an auction with a fixed deadline, a sharp form of this latter cause of late bidding may arise when some bidders are better informed than others. For example, in auctions of antiques, there

may be bidders who are dealers/experts and who are better able to identify high-value antiques. These well-informed bidders (who may be identifiable because of their frequent participation) may wish to bid late because other bidders will recognize that their bid is a signal that the object is unusually valuable. Bidding just before the deadline of an auction with a fixed deadline allows them to profit from their information without allowing other bidders enough time to respond. Again, in an Amazon-type auction with an automatic extension, the ability to bid without providing information to attentive competitors would be eliminated or substantially attenuated.[8]

Thus there are a variety of rational, strategic reasons for sniping (i.e., for bidding very near the scheduled end of an eBay auction), despite the risk that late bids may not be transmitted successfully. It is a best response to naïve incremental-bidding strategies, and can arise even at equilibrium in both private-value and common-value auctions.[9]

Here's how it works: whenever a bid is cast in the last ten minutes of an auction, the auction is automatically extended for an additional ten minutes from the time of the latest bid. This ensures that an auction can't close until ten 'bidless' minutes have passed. The bottom line? If you're attentive at the end of an auction, you'll always have the opportunity to vie with a new bidder" (online: ⟨http://www.amazon.com/exec/varzea/ts/help/going-going-gone/002-3341436-6525260, 1999⟩).

[7] The probability that some late bids will not be successfully transmitted is a risk for each bidder, but a benefit for his opponents, and it is this "public good" aspect of the risk of bidding late that creates the possibility of a profitable collusive late-bidding equilibrium in eBay (but not in Amazon).

[8] This is the intuition reflected in the following bit of advice to bidders: "The greatest advantage of sniping is it affords you anonymity among the other bidders. If you're a long-time bidder, others who bid on the same items as you will recognize your user ID. Some might even 'ride your coattails,' performing site searches on what you're bidding on, then perhaps bidding against you. If you choose to snipe, the other bidders won't know where you'll strike next, and that can mean more wins and frequently better prices for you" (online: ⟨http://www.auctionwatch.com/awdaily/tipsandtactics/buy-bid2.html⟩, 1999; see Ockenfels and Roth [2002] for a more formal treatment that captures this intuition).

[9] Esnipe.com, a site that offers to automatically place a predetermined bid a few seconds before the end of the eBay auction, nicely summarizes some of these reasons but also speaks to the risks involved: "There are many reasons to snipe. A lot of people that bid on an item will actually bid again if they find they have been outbid, which can quickly lead to a bidding war. End result? Someone probably paid more than they had to for that item. By sniping, you can avoid bid wars. That's not all. Experienced collectors often find that other bidders watch to see what the experts are bidding on, and then bid on those items themselves. The expert can snipe to prevent other bidders from cashing in on their expertise.... Will esnipe guarantee that my bids are placed? We certainly wish we could, but there are too many factors beyond our control to guarantee that bids always get placed" (online: ⟨http://www.esnipe.com/faq.asp 2000⟩). In fact, esnipe.com recently started to publish statistics on success rates, time to place bids and hourly trends based on an average of more than 4,200 bids per day (online: ⟨esnipe.com/stats.asp⟩, 2000). While the time it takes to place a bid varies considerably over weekdays and hours, on average 4.5 percent of esnipe's late bids failed to be successfully transmitted in September 2000. (Esnipe was sold

TABLE 1—HYPOTHESES ABOUT THE CAUSES OF LATE BIDDING

Hypotheses	Predicted contribution to late bidding
Strategic hypotheses	
Rational response to naïve English-auction behavior or to shill bidders: bidders bid late to avoid bidding wars with incremental bidders	All three strategic hypotheses suggest more late bidding on eBay than on Amazon, with a bigger effect for more experienced bidders. Also (via the third point), more late bidding in categories in which expertise is important than in categories in which it is not.
Collusive equilibrium: bidders bid late to avoid bidding wars with other like-minded bidders	
Informed bidders protecting their information (e.g., late bidding by experts/dealers)	
Nonstrategic hypotheses	
Procrastination	No difference between eBay and Amazon.
Search engines present soon-to-expire auctions first	
Desire to retain flexibility to bid on other auctions offering the same item	
Bidders remain unaware of the proxy bidding system	
Increase in the willingness to pay over time (e.g., caused by an endowment effect)	
Bidders do not like to leave bids "hanging"	

Of course, there can also be nonstrategic reasons why bidders bid late, some of which are listed in Table 1. These nonstrategic reasons, however, should be relatively unaffected by the difference in rules between eBay and Amazon. (The hypotheses are not mutually exclusive; they could each be contributory causes of late bidding.)

The strategic differences between eBay-style (hard close auctions) and Amazon-style (automatic extension) auctions suggest that the hypotheses about the causes of late bidding can be investigated by examining the timing of bids on eBay and Amazon. So, we compare the timing of bids in eBay and Amazon in the categories Antiques and Computers, which might reasonably be expected to have different scope for expert information. We also survey late bidders on eBay to shed light on the observed behavior.

I. Description of the Data Sample

Amazon and eBay publicly provide data about the bid history and other features of auctions that have been completed within the last four weeks on eBay and eight weeks on Amazon. We downloaded data from both auction

sites in the categories "Computers" and "Antiques." In the category of Computers, retail prices of most items are easily available, because most items are new.[10] Each bidder's willingness to pay, however, remains private information. In the Antiques category, retail prices are usually not available and the value of an item is often ambiguous and sometimes requires an expert to appraise. So the bids of others are likely to convey information about the item's value, allowing the possibility that experts may wish to conceal their information.

Our data set consists of randomly selected auctions completed between October 1999 and January 2000 that met certain selection criteria.[11] For the category Computers we selected computer monitors and laptop auctions. For Antiques, we did not restrict our search to a particular subset of items. This is partly to avoid the danger that the data are dominated by atypical behavioral patterns that might have evolved in thin markets for specific antiques, and partly

on eBay in an auction ending at 18:08:38 PST on 12/1/00, and the winning bid of \$35,877.77 arrived at 18:08:24 PST on 12/1/00 along with three other bids that were submitted in the last minute.)

[10] We did not collect data about retail prices, which would depend on many details of each item offered for sale.

[11] Most importantly, auctions were only included if they attracted at least two bidders, and auctions with a hidden reserve price were only considered if the reserve price was met. In this paper, we focus on our main results; a much more detailed account of the sampling criteria and of the data, including the distributions of number of bidders per auction and feedback numbers across auction houses, can be found in Ockenfels and Roth (2002).

because of a lack of data on Amazon, since relatively few antiques are auctioned there. In total, the data from 480 auctions with 2,279 bidders were included in all analyses of this paper. We have 120 eBay Computers with 740 bidders, 120 Amazon Computers with 595 bidders, 120 eBay Antiques with 604 bidders, and 120 Amazon Antiques with 340 bidders.[12] For each auction, we recorded the number of bids, number of bidders, and whether there was a reserve price. On the bidder level, we recorded the "timing" of the last bid and each bidder's "feedback number." Both variables are described in detail next.

Both auction houses provide information about when each bidder's last bid is submitted.[13] For each bidder we downloaded how many seconds before the deadline the last bid was submitted. (If the bid came in before the last 12 hours of the auction end, we just count this bid as "early"). While this information is readily provided in eBay's bid histories of completed auctions, the end time of an auction in Amazon is endogenously determined since an auction continues past the initially scheduled deadline until ten minutes have passed without a bid. We therefore computed for each last bid in Amazon the number of seconds before a "hypothetical" deadline. This hypothetical deadline is defined as the current actual deadline at the time of bidding under the assumption that the bid in hand and all subsequent bids were not submitted.[14]

On eBay, buyers and sellers can give each other positive feedback $(+ 1)$, neutral feedback (0), or negative feedback $(- 1)$ along with a brief comment. A single person can affect a user's feedback number by only one point (even though giving multiple comments on the same user is possible). The total of positive minus negative feedback is eBay's "feedback number." It is prominently displayed next to the bidder's or seller's eBay username. Amazon provides a related, slightly different reputation mechanism. Buyers and sellers are allowed to post 1–5 star ratings of one another. Both the average number of stars and the cumulative number of ratings are prominently displayed next to the bidder's or seller's Amazon username. We refer to the cumulative number of ratings as the "feedback number" on Amazon. Since in both auction sites the feedback numbers (indirectly) reflect the number of transactions, they might serve as approximations for experience and, more cautiously, as an indicator of expertise.[15]

---

[12] eBay maintains a substantially bigger market than Amazon (see David Lucking-Reiley [2000] for a comprehensive survey of internet auctions, their sizes, revenues, institutions, etc.). For instance, on the supply side, the number of listed items that we found for our Computers category exceeds Amazon's number in the same time span by a factor of about ten. There may be other differences besides volume, since buyers as well as sellers self-select themselves into an auction. Following the data analysis, we will argue that this selection might influence the magnitude of the differences between Computers and Antiques within an auction format, but should not influence the direction of the differences we report.

[13] Since October 2000, eBay's bid history for each auction includes all bids.

[14] Suppose, for example, one bid comes in one minute before the initial closing time and another bidder bids eight minutes later. Then, the auction is extended by 17 minutes. The first bid therefore is submitted 18 minutes and the second bid ten minutes before the actual auction close. The

bids show up in our data, however, as one and two minutes (before the hypothetical deadline), respectively. Since we only observe the timing of last bids, this calculation implicitly assumes that no bidder bids more than once later than ten minutes before the initial deadline. The potential effect of this bias is, however, very small. In total, 28 out of 240 Amazon auctions in our sample were extended. In 26 of these auctions, only one bidder and in the other two auctions two bidders bid within the last ten minutes with respect to the initial deadline. Therefore, we may misrepresent the timing of up to 30 out of 935 Amazon bidders. Note that the possible misrepresentation of timing with respect to the hypothetical instead of the actual closing time leads us, if at all, to *overestimate* the extent to which Amazon bidders bid late. This would only strengthen our comparative results of late bidding in Amazon and eBay.

[15] Note that the feedback number on eBay is the sum of positive and negative feedback. Hence, if positive and negative feedbacks were left with comparable probabilities, the feedback numbers could not be interpreted as experience or expertise. The fact, however, that in our eBay sample *no* bidder (but two sellers) had a negative feedback number while more than 25 percent have zero feedback numbers indicates that negative feedbacks are left very rarely. This suggests that both the feedback numbers in eBay and Amazon are proxies for the number of transactions. Other authors empirically examine the effect of feedbacks in eBay on price (Daniel Houser and John Wooders, 2000; Lucking-Reiley et al., 2000; Mikhail I. Melnik and James Alm, 2001), on the emergence of trust (Paul Resnick and Richard Zeckhauser, 2001; see also Gary Bolton et al. [2002] for a related experimental study), and on multiple bidding (Ockenfels and Roth, 2002).

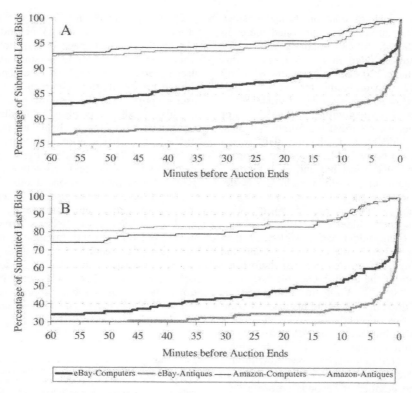

FIGURE 1. CUMULATIVE DISTRIBUTIONS OVER TIME OF (A) BIDDERS' LAST BIDS AND (B) AUCTIONS' LAST BIDS

II. The Timing of Bids

Figure 1 illustrates our central observations regarding the timing of bids. Figure 1A shows the empirical cumulative probability distributions of the timing of last bids for all bidders, and Figure 1B the corresponding graphs for only the last bid in each auction.[16] The graphs show that in both auction houses, a considerable share of last bids is submitted in the very last hour of the auctions. (Recall that the auctions usually run for several days.) However, late bidding is substantially more prevalent on eBay than on Amazon.

Figure 1A reveals that 20 percent of all last bids on eBay compared to 7 percent of all last bids on Amazon were submitted in the last hour. Figure 1B shows that in more than two-thirds of all eBay auctions, at least one bidder is still active in the last hour, while this is only true for about one-quarter of all Amazon auctions. Furthermore, the graphs reveal that, on eBay, a

[16] Recall that the timing of bids in Amazon is defined with respect to a "hypothetical" deadline that differs from the actual closing time if a bid comes in later than ten minutes before the initial end time. Recall also that the last bidder is not necessarily the high bidder since an earlier submitted proxy bid can outbid subsequent incoming bids. Specifically, in eBay 29 (89, 132, 163) *final* bids but only 17 (66, 106, 131) *winning* bids were submitted within the last ten seconds (one minute, ten minutes, one hour). In Amazon the corresponding frequency distributions of final and winning bids are (0, 1, 28, 54) and (0, 0, 20, 43), respectively. We finally note here that it is not too unusual to see the auction price in eBay double in the last 60 seconds, and since it takes some seconds to make a bid, bidders attempt-

ing to submit a bid while the price is rising so rapidly may receive an error message telling them that their bid is under the (current) minimum bid. These eBay bidders, who attempted to bid in the last minute, are not represented in these data, since their last-minute bids did not register as bids in the auction.

considerable share of bidders submit their bid in the last five minutes (9 percent in Computers and 16 percent in Antiques), while only a few bids come in equally late on Amazon (about 1 percent in both Computers and Antiques). The difference is even more striking at the auction level: 40 percent of all eBay Computers auctions and 59 percent of all eBay Antiques auctions as compared to about 3 percent of both Amazon Computers and Amazon Antiques auctions, respectively, have last bids in the last five minutes. The pattern repeats in the last minute and even in the last ten seconds.[17] In the 240 eBay auctions, 89 have bids in the last minute and 29 in the last ten seconds. In Amazon, on the other hand, only one bid arrived in the last minute. The figures also indicate that within eBay, bidders bid later in Antiques than in Computers.[18]

The main differences in the four distributions in each of the two graphs in Figure 1 (more late bidding in eBay than in Amazon in each category, respectively, and more late bidding in eBay Antiques than in eBay Computers) can be statistically supported by various regression analyses on both the bidder and the auction level.[19] Furthermore, the regressions reveal an interesting correlation between bidders' feedback numbers and late bidding. The impact of the feedback number on late bidding is highly significantly positive in eBay and (weakly significantly) negative in Amazon. This suggests that more experienced bidders on eBay go later than less experienced bidders, while experience in Amazon has the opposite effect, as suggested by the strategic hypotheses.[20] It is therefore safe to conclude that last-minute bidding is not simply due to naïve time-dependent bidding. Rather, it responds to the strategic structure of the auction rules in a predictable way. In addition, since significantly more late bidding is found in antiques auctions than in computer auctions on eBay but not on Amazon, behavior responds to the strategic incentives created by the possession of information, in a way that interacts with the rules of the auction.

Because these data do not come from a controlled experiment, self-selection of buyers and sellers into different auctions might affect some of our results. If expert antique buyers prefer to bid on eBay, and if sellers of goods that require expert valuation follow them to eBay, this might increase the size of the difference in late bidding between eBay Antiques and Computers, as compared to Amazon Antiques and Computers. (Of course the difference between late bidding on eBay for computers and for antiques would still support the prediction that there will be more late bidding on items that require expertise to evaluate.) The other personal variable that the theory predicts is important is experience in the sense of learning best responses, as distinct from acquiring expertise related to the items for sale. One might conjecture that the differences in the timing of bids between eBay and Amazon reflect differences

---

[17] In fact, a more detailed theoretical and econometric analysis of the full shape of the distributions in Roth and Ockenfels (2000) reveals that the distributions of the timing of bids in Amazon and eBay are strikingly *self-similar*. That is, it is virtually impossible to say whether a distribution of last bids is drawn from, say, the last hour or from the last 12 hours of the auctions if no information about the time scale is given.

[18] As pointed out by a referee, the timing shown in Figures 1A and 1B cannot be explained by the "naïve" hypothesis that more bidders per auction cause last bids to be later. In fact, Figure 1B shows that last bids in eBay Computers come earlier than last bids in eBay Antiques, while the number of bidders per auction is actually significantly higher in eBay Computers (see Ockenfels and Roth, 2002).

[19] In Roth and Ockenfels (2000), we ran probit, logit, and ordinary least-squares (OLS) regressions using 5-, 10-, and 15-minute thresholds for late bidding, while controlling for the number of bidders per auction and bidders' feedback numbers. All differences in the distributions mentioned above are statistically significant at the 5-percent level (two-sided), while no statistically significant difference between Amazon Antiques and Amazon Computers can be detected, independent of the statistical model or the threshold for late bidding. The results appear to be also robust across different data sets. First, in a pilot study, we downloaded data from eBay and Amazon in 320 auctions of computer monitors and antique books. The data set is less complete since only last bidders and only two feedback categories were considered. To the extent we can compare the data with the data reported in this paper, however, they agree in essentially all qualitative features described here. Second, in an exploratory sample of just over 1,000 eBay auctions with at least one bid in May and June 1999, we found substantial variation in the percentage of last-minute bids, ranging from 56 percent in the category "Antiques: Ancient World" to 0 percent in "Collectibles: Weird Stuff: Totally Bizarre."

[20] Ronald T. Wilcox (2000) examines a sample of eBay auctions and also finds that more experienced bidders bid later.

in the distributions of bidders' experience (as described by Ockenfels and Roth [2002]). A selection bias of this sort cannot explain the fact, however, that the effect of experience on the timing of bids goes in the opposite directions on eBay and Amazon, as suggested by the strategic hypotheses. Furthermore, we think that the fact that all the strategic predictions are that there will be more late bidding on eBay than on Amazon diminishes the likelihood that the positive results for that comparison are primarily due to selection based on buyer and seller characteristics. But there is still room for a controlled experiment in the laboratory, which we will discuss further in the conclusion.[21]

III. Survey

Three hundred and sixty-eight eBay bidders who successfully bid at least once in the last minute of an auction were sent a questionnaire. We included approximately the same number of bidders who bid late in Computers and Antiques. Twenty percent responded to our survey. The survey complements the bid data, by giving bidders' perspectives about what drives late bidding, and by providing information about the (otherwise unobservable) risk that a late bid fails to be transmitted. We very briefly report some patterns in the answers.[22]

A large majority of responders (91 percent) confirm that late bidding is typically part of their early planned bidding strategy. Most of these bidders unambiguously explain that they snipe to avoid a "bidding war" or to keep the price down. In addition, some experienced Antiques bidders (about 10 percent of all responders, mostly with high feedback numbers) explicitly state that late bidding enables them to avoid sharing valuable information with other bidders.[23] At the same time, some bidders say that they are sometimes influenced by the bidding activity of others, although 88 percent of the late bidders in our survey say that they have a clear idea, early in the auction, about what they are willing to pay. But besides this supportive evidence for strategic late bidding, we also find some indications of naïve late bidding. A few bidders (less than 10 percent, mostly with zero feedback number) appear to confuse eBay with an English auction (i.e., they appear to be unaware of eBay's proxy bidding system).[24]

Although more than 90 percent of the responders to our survey never use sniping software, many operate with several open windows and synchronize their computer clock with eBay time in order to improve their late-bidding performance. Nevertheless, when bidding late, 86 percent of all bidders report that it happened

---

[21] Some of our experimenter colleagues have asked at seminars why, if there are unobserved parts of the field data, we did not start from the outset with an experimental investigation. The answer is that field studies and laboratory experiments are complements not substitutes, and as many questions would have been raised about a laboratory study. If late bidding had been observed (only) in the lab, the natural question would be whether it arose because subjects who were already in the lab until the end of the experiment paid no cost to wait and bid at the last minute. Without a field study, it would have been reasonable to conjecture that the same effect would not be observed in the field, in bidding by people who have other things to do than wait for auctions to end.

[22] Not all bidders answered all questions. The percentages we report here refer to the actual number of answers to the corresponding question. See Roth and Ockenfels (2000) for the complete questionnaire and a collection of typical answers to each question. Note also that the fact that late bidders tend to be more experienced is reflected in our survey sample. The average feedback number in our eBay choice data is 29 for all bidders and 64 for all last-minute bidders. The average feedback number in our survey data is 83.

[23] Here are three examples of responses from Antiques bidders: "I know that certain other parties will always chase my bid" (feedback number = 649); "I do so in part because I have found that when I bid early I tend (nearly always) to be outbid, even if I put in a high bid. Maybe this is because I am thought to have special knowledge about what is a good item (e.g., due to my books)" (182); "The most difficult part is ascertaining the genuineness of a particular piece. If it is fake then I lost the game and my knowledge was inadequate. This is where it is important not to bid early on an item. If you are well known as an expert and you bid, then you have authenticated the item for free and invite bidding by others" (47).

[24] One bidder explains his late bidding as follows: "Because I will then know if the price is low enough for the item" (feedback number = 0); another bidder writes: "I would also be sure that other bidders wouldn't outbid me" (0). Interestingly, some more experienced bidders realize that beginners are particularly impatient when bidding: "Many new buyers are particularly aggressive in making sure they are listed as high bidder" (198); "The newbies want only to win and will bid until their money runs out, another reason to wait until the last 30" (43); "If there are first-time bidders (0) then it's best to walk away. They will push the price up just to stay the high bidder" (6).

at least once to them that they started to make a bid, but the auction was closed before the bid was received. But there is another prevalent risk of late bidding: about 90 percent of all bidders say that sometimes, even though they planned to bid late, something came up that prevented them from being available at the end of the auction so that they could not submit a bid as planned. Most bidders gave a quantitative estimation about how often this happened to them. The median response is 10 percent for each kind of risk.

IV. Conclusions

Theoretical considerations suggest that the rule for ending an auction can affect bidding behavior long before the end. The clear difference observed in the amount of late bidding on eBay and Amazon is strong evidence that, as predicted both at equilibrium and when some bidders are unsophisticated, the hard close gives bidders an incentive to bid late, in both private- and common-value auctions. This evidence is strengthened by the observations that (i) the difference is even clearer among more experienced bidders, and (ii) there is more late bidding for eBay Computers than for eBay Antiques, reflecting the additional strategic incentives for late bidding in eBay auctions in which expertise plays a role in appraising values. The substantial amount of late bidding observed on Amazon, (even though substantially less than on eBay) suggests that there are also nonstrategic causes of late bidding, possibly due to naïveté or other nonrational cause, particularly since the evidence suggests that it is reduced with experience.[25]

[25] Of course we do not claim to have exhausted the possible strategic and nonstrategic causes of late bidding in the brief list of hypotheses tested in this study. For example, late bidding in Amazon auctions can arise rationally to the extent that the last ten minutes is a sufficiently short interval so as to present a reduced probability of successful bidding. Preliminary studies (Neeraj Gupta, 2001) suggest that in auctions hosted by Yahoo!, in which the seller may choose either a hard close or an automatic *five*-minute extension, the effect of this choice on late bidding is less clear than the difference between eBay and Amazon auctions. Or perhaps the hard close provides greater entertainment value by concentrating so much of the bidding action at the very end of the auction. Thus, while we find multiple causes, our evi-

The size of the difference between bid distributions on eBay and Amazon suggests that the different rules for ending an auction is an important element of the auction design.[26] On the other hand, the limitations of field data mean that there is room for controlled experiments to help supply a detailed understanding of the difference. Amazon and eBay data reflect not only the behavior of individuals in different auctions, but possibly also the self-selection of individual buyers and sellers with different characteristics into the auctions, and different choices of alternative auctions. We have argued that these uncontrolled differences cannot account for all of the differences we observed, but in the laboratory these differences can be eliminated, and the auction rules compared cleanly. See Ariely et al. (2002) for an experiment that replicates the late-bidding comparisons found in our field data, under controlled conditions in a pure private-value environment. In that experiment, subjects are randomly assigned to different auction conditions, and bid for

dence is not inconsistent with the phenomena discussed by Patrick Bajari and Ali Hortaçsu (2000), Deepak Malhotra and J. Keith Murnighan (2000), and Wilcox (2000). The first two of those papers each looks at an auction of a particular commodity under a fixed set of rules and deduces that the late bidding they observe results from a particular cause (common values, and irrational "competitive arousal," respectively). The third paper looks at auctions of several commodities on eBay, and notes that experienced bidders tend to bid later. But because our empirical design (and our theoretical framework in Ockenfels and Roth [2002]) permits us to compare the auctions of dissimilar commodities using the same auction rules, and similar commodities using different auction rules, the common bidding behavior observed in all three studies can be viewed here in a broader perspective.

[26] The presence of multiple causes for the same phenomena means, however, that it remains difficult to unambiguously assess the effects of the different auction designs. For a fixed set of bidders for a given, private-value object, our findings suggest that a second-price auction with a hard close will raise less revenue than one with an automatic extension, because late bidding causes some bids to be lost. But our theoretical considerations also suggest that bidders with the expertise to identify valuable objects will prefer auctions with a hard close, because in this case late bidding allows the experts to protect their information. So the present evidence does not allow us to suggest which design should be preferred by sellers, although it suggests that the answer may depend on the kind of good being auctioned.

identical, artificial commodities for which they are paid in cash by the experimenter according to values that they know when they bid. As remarked earlier, field studies and laboratory experiments are complements, not substitutes. The present study is a case in which multiple kinds of evidence (theory, transaction data, surveys, anecdotal quotes, experiments) all point in the same direction.

Now that economists are increasingly being called upon to design a variety of markets (see e.g., Roth and Elliott Peranson, 1999; Paul Milgrom, 2001; Roth, 2002; Robert Wilson, 2002), we need to be alert to the fact that small design differences can elicit substantial differences in behavior.[27] In designing new markets, it will be important to consider not only the equilibrium behavior that we might expect experienced and sophisticated players eventually to exhibit, but also how the design will influence the behavior of inexperienced participants, and the interaction between sophisticated and unsophisticated players. The effect of the fixed deadline is no doubt as large as it is because it rewards late bidding both when other bidders are sophisticated and when they are not.

REFERENCES

Ariely, Dan; Ockenfels, Axel and Roth, Alvin E. "An Experimental Analysis of Ending Rules in Internet Auctions." Unpublished manuscript, Harvard University, 2002.

Bajari, Patrick and Hortaçsu, Ali. "Winner's Curse, Reserve Prices and Endogenous Entry: Empirical Insights from eBay Auctions." Working paper, Stanford University, 2000.

Bolton, Gary; Katok, Elena and Ockenfels, Axel. "How Effective Are Online Reputation Mechanisms? An Experimental Investigation." Working paper, Pennsylvania State University, 2002.

[27] In the design of the FCC auctions of radio spectrum, a concern that late bidding would interfere with efficient price discovery led to the inclusion of "activity rules" that prevented bidders from entering the auction only near the end (cf. Milgrom, 2001; Roth, 2002).

Dobrzynski, Judith H. "In Online Auctions, Rings of Bidders." *New York Times,* 2 June 2000, p. 1.

Gupta, Neeraj. "Internet Auctions: A Comparative Study of Seller Options on eBay, Amazon, and Yahoo!" Undergraduate thesis, Harvard College, 2001.

Houser, Daniel and Wooders, John. "Reputation in Auctions: Theory and Evidence from eBay." Working paper, University of Arizona, 2000.

Kamecke, Ulrich. "Dominance or Maximin? How to Solve an English Auction." *International Journal of Game Theory,* October 1998, *27*(3), pp. 407–26.

Lucking-Reiley, David. "Auctions on the Internet: What's Being Auctioned, and How?" *Journal of Industrial Economics,* September 2000, *48*(3), pp. 227–52.

Lucking-Reiley, David; Bryan, Doug; Prasad, Naghi and Reeves, Daniel. "Pennies from eBay: The Determinants of Price in Online Auctions." Working paper, Vanderbilt University, 2000.

Malhotra, Deepak and Murnighan, J. Keith. "Milked for all Their Worth: Competitive Arousal and Escalation in the Chicago Cow Auctions." Working paper, Kellogg School of Management, Northwestern University, 2000.

Melnik, Mikhail I. and Alm, James. "Does a Seller's eCommerce Reputation Matter?" Working paper, Georgia State University, 2001.

Milgrom, Paul. "Auction Theory for Privatization." Unpublished manuscript, Stanford University, 2001.

Ockenfels, Axel and Roth, Alvin E. "Late Bidding in Second Price Internet Auctions: Theory and Evidence Concerning Different Rules for Ending an Auction." Working paper, Harvard University, 2002.

Resnick, Paul and Zeckhauser, Richard. "Trust Among Strangers in Internet Transactions: Empirical Analysis of eBay's Reputation System." Draft prepared for National Bureau of Economic Research workshop, 2001.

Roth, Alvin E. "The Economist as Engineer." *Econometrica,* July 2002, *70*(4), pp. 1341–78.

Roth, Alvin E. and Ockenfels, Axel. "Last Minute Bidding and the Rules for Ending Second-Price Auctions: Theory and Evidence from a Natural Experiment on the Internet." National Bureau of Economic Research (Cambridge, MA) Working Paper No. 7729, 2000.

Roth, Alvin E. and Peranson, Elliott. "The Redesign of the Matching Market for American Physicians: Some Engineering Aspects of Economic Design." *American Economic Review,* September 1999, *89*(4), pp. 748–80.

Simpson, Glenn R. "Ebay Coin Auctions Produce Allegations of 'Shill' Bidding." *Wall Street Journal,* 12 June 2000, pp. A3, A6.

Wilcox, Ronald T. "Experts and Amateurs: The Role of Experience in Internet Auctions." *Marketing Letters,* November 2000, *11*(4), pp. 363–74.

Wilson, Robert. "Architecture of Power Markets." *Econometrica,* July 2002, *70*(4), pp. 1299–1340.

Coke Tests Vending Unit That Can Hike Prices in Hot Weather

By CONSTANCE L. HAYS

[T]aking full advantage of the law of supply and demand, Coca-Cola Co. has quietly begun testing a vending machine that can automatically raise prices for its drinks in hot weather.

"This technology is something the Coca-Cola Co. has been looking at for more than a year," said Rob Baskin, a company spokesman, adding that it had not yet been placed in any consumer market.

The potential was heralded, though, by the company's chairman and chief executive in an interview earlier this month with a Brazilian newsmagazine. Chairman M. Douglas Ivester described how desire for a cold drink can increase during a sports championship final held in the summer heat. "So, it is fair that it should be more expensive," Ivester was quoted as saying in the magazine, Veja. "The machine will simply make this process automatic."

The process appears to be done simply through a temperature sensor and a computer chip, not any breakthrough technology, though Coca-Cola refused to provide any details Wednesday.

While the concept might seem unfair to a thirsty person, it essentially extends to another industry what has become the practice for airlines and other companies that sell products and services to consumers. The falling price of computer chips and the increasing ease of connecting to the Internet has made it practical for companies to pair daily and hourly fluctuations in demand with fluctuations in price -- even if the product is a can of soda that sells for just 75 cents.

The potential for other types of innovations is great. Other modifications under discussion at Coca-Cola, Baskin said, include adjusting prices based on demand at a specific machine. "What could you do to boost sales at off-hours?" he asked. "You might be able to lower the price. It might be discounted at a vending machine in a building during the evening or when there's less traffic."

Vending machines have become an increasingly important source of profits for Coca-Cola and its archrival, Pepsico. Over the last three years, the soft-drink giants have watched their earnings erode as they waged a price war in supermarkets. Vending machines have remained largely untouched by the discounting. Now, Coca-Cola aims to tweak what has been a golden goose to extract even more profits.

"There are a number of initiatives under way in Japan, the United States and in other parts of the world where the technology in vending is rapidly improving, not only from a temperature-scanning capability but also to understand when a machine is out of stock," said Andrew Conway, a beverage analyst for Morgan Stanley. "The increase in the rate of technology breakthrough in vending is pretty dramatic."

Bill Hurley, a spokesman for the National Automatic Merchandising Association in Washington, added: "You are only limited by your creativity, since electronic components are becoming more and more versatile."

Machines are already in place that can accept credit cards and debit cards for payment. In Australia and in North Carolina, Coke bottlers use machines to relay, via wireless signal or telephone, information about which drinks are selling and at what rates in a particular location. The technology is known as intelligent vending, Baskin said, and the information gathered and relayed by Internet helps salespeople to figure out which drinks will sell best in which locations.

"It all feeds into their strategy of micro-marketing and understanding the local consumer," Conway said. "If you can understand brand preferences by geography, that has implications for other places with similar geography."

Coca-Cola and its bottlers have invested heavily in vending machines, refrigerated display cases, coolers and other equipment to sell their drinks cold. Over the last five years, Coca-Cola Enterprises, Coke's biggest bottler, has spent more than $1.8 billion on such equipment. In support, Coca-Cola has spent millions more on employees who monitor and service the equipment. In 1998 alone, it spent $324 million on such support to its biggest bottler.

And last week, Coke's chief marketing officer unveiled the company's plan to pump more sales of its flagship soft drink, Coca-Cola Classic. The program includes a pronounced emphasis on Coke served cold.

Sales of soft drinks from vending machines have risen steadily over the last few years, though most sales still take place in supermarkets. Last year, about 11.9 percent of soft-drink sales worldwide came from vending machines, said John Sicher, the editor of Beverage Digest, an industry newsletter. In the United States, about 1.2 billion cases of soft drinks were sold through vending machines.

In Japan, some vending machines already adjust their prices based on the temperature outside, using wireless modems, said Gad Elmoznino, director of the Trisignal division of Eicon Technology, a Montreal-based modem maker. "They are going to be using more and more communications in these machines to do interactive price setting," he said.

Industry reactions to the heat-sensitive Coke machine ranged from enthusiastic to sanctimonious. "It's another reason to move to Sweden," one beverage industry executive sniffed. "What's next? A machine that X-rays people's pockets to find out how much change they have and raises the price accordingly?"

Bill Pecoriello, a stock analyst with Sanford C. Bernstein, applauded the move to increase profits in the vending-machine business. "This is already the most profitable channel for the beverage companies, so any effort to get higher profits when demand is higher obviously can enhance the profitability of the system further," he said.

He pointed to a possible downside as well. "You don't want to have a price war in this channel, where you have discounting over a holiday weekend, for example," he said. "Once the capability is out there to vary the pricing, you can take the price down."

A Pepsi spokesman said no similar innovation was being tested at the No. 2 soft-drink company. "We believe that machines that raise prices in hot weather exploit consumers who live in warm climates," declared the spokesman, Jeff Brown. "At Pepsi, we are focused on innovations that make it easier for consumers to buy a soft drink, not harder."

Policy Debate: Should there be a market for human organs?

Issues and Background

A new system is needed, one that commercializes organs in a global network. By allowing people to contract for the exchange of organs for monetary consideration, the market opens up financial incentives that increase the available supply of organs.
~David E. Jefferies, "The Body as Commodity: The Use of Markets to Cure the Organ Deficit," International Journal of Global Legal Studies, vol. 5, no. 2

A medically invented, artificial scarcity in human organs for transplantation has generated a kind of panic and a desperate international search them and for new surgical possibilities. Bearing many similarities to the international market in adoption, those looking for transplant organs are so single minded in their quest that they are sometimes willing to put aside questions about how the organ [or 'the baby' in the case of adoption] was obtained. In both instances the language of "gifts" , "donations", " heroic rescues" and "saving lives" masks the extent to which ethically dubious and even illegal practices are used to obtain the desired " scarce" commodity, infant or kidney, for which foreigners (or "better off" nationals) are willing to pay what to ordinary people seems a king's ransom. With desperation built in on both sides of the equation -- deathly ill "buyers" and desperately needy "sellers" -- once seemingly "timeless" religious beliefs in the sanctity of the body and proscriptions against body mutilation have collapsed over night in some parts of the third world under the weight of these new market's demands.
~Nancy Scheper-Hughes

Advances in medical treatments have resulted in a dramatic increase in the number of organ transplants performed each year. A limited supply of organs, however, prevents many individuals from receiving organ replacements that could either save a life or substantially improve the recipient's quality of life.

In the U.S., all states have enacted a variation of the Uniform Anatomical Gift Act of 1968. Under this law, individuals are able to specify that some or all of their body may be donated after their death. The original version of this Act neither allowed, nor prohibited, the sale of human organs. The revised Uniform Anatomical Gift Act of 1987, however, prohibited the sale of human organs.

Restrictions on the sale of human organs in the U.S. came about as a result of markets that appeared in the early 1980s for kidneys that were harvested from living donors in return for a fee. Kidneys were sold primarily by the very poorest members of society. The National Organ Transplant Act of 1984 prohibited payments to those who provided organs for transplantation. While this Act was primarily designed to prevent the sale of organs from living donors, it also prevented the possibility of individuals selling the right to harvest their organs after their death. (The sale of replenishable tissue, such as blood, hair, and sperm, however, is allowed.)

While donors cannot legally be paid for providing organs, there is a very active market for human organs. Organ procurement organizations, operating as local monopolies, collect organs from voluntary donors and then provide them to hospitals that provide transplants. While the National Organ Transplant Act prohibits payments to patients, it allows organ procurement agencies to receive a fee for the removal and transportation of organs.

Opponents of market-based allocation systems argue that individual income and wealth would determine who receives and who supplies organs. They argue that decisions concerning who should receive a transplant should be based upon medical criteria rather than on income and wealth.

Supporters of a market for human organs argue that the chronic shortage of organs for transplant could be reduced or eliminated if donors (or their survivors) were paid for the use of their organs. One popular suggestion is the use of a futures contract in which an individual sells the right to harvest his or her organs if they are suitable for transplant at the time of the individual's death.

One concern that is often raised is the growth of an international black market for organs. Those countries that have a surplus of organs are generally those in which there are the least restrictions on trade in organs. Allegations of human rights violations associated with the acquisition of transplant organs in these countries are not uncommon. Numerous (often well-supported) allegations have been made suggesting that China has executed prisoners to satisfy the demand for organs.

Primary Resources and Data

- *University of Pittsburgh Medical Center, "Organ Transplant System Chronology"*
  http://www.upmc.edu/NewsBureau/tx/chronology.htm
  This site provides a chronology (from 1984 to the present) of the U.S. system for providing organs for transplant.

- *National Organ Transplant Act of 1984*
  http://www.pitt.edu/~htk/documents/1984.act.pdf
  The National Organ Transplant Act of 1984 banned the sale of human organs in the U.S. and

established the current mechanism for distributing donor organs.

- *Uniform Anatomical Gift Act*
  http://www.law.upenn.edu/bll/ulc/fnact99/uaga87.htm
  This document contains the text of the Uniform Anatomical Gift Act (as revised in 1987). This Act establishes the conditions under which individuals can use donor cards to donate organs.

- *National Attorneys' Committee for Transplant Awareness, Inc., "Organ and Tissue Donation and Transplantation: A Legal Perspective""*
  http://www.transweb.org/reference/articles/donation/nacta.html
  This document provides information about the laws governing organ donation.

- *Transweb.org, "Top 10 Myths About Donation & Transplantation"*
  http://www.transweb.org/myths/myths.htm
  This webpage attempts to debunk many of the myths, urban legends, and misconceptions associated with organ transplantation and donation.

- *Michael E. Parmly, "Sale of Human Organs in China"*
  http://www.state.gov/g/drl/hr/rm/index.cfm?docid=3792
  Michael E. Parmly is the Principal Deputy Assistant Secretary of State, Bureau of Democracy, Human Rights, and Labor. In this June 27. 2001 statement, he notes that China harvests the organs of executed prisoners. This has resulted in a growing number of transplant procedures being conducted in China. Parmly raises concerns over the lack of due process and consent in this situation.

- *Dennis Prince, "Organ for Sale--Not Wurlitzer"*
  http://www.vendio.com/awdaily/dailynews/1-090399.html
  In this September 3, 1999 article, Dennis Prince describes the posting of an offer of a kidney for sale on eBay. He notes that the price of this kidney rose from $25,000 to nearly $6 million during the week while this item was listed.

- *OrganSelling.com, "Pennsylvania Reimbursement Plan"*
  http://www.pitt.edu/~htk/pennsylv.htm
  This page contains information about a proposed plan in Pennsylvania to provide up to $300 towards the funeral expenses of organ donors. Links to other resources concerning this plan are also provided.

- *National Center for Policy Analysis, "Pennsylvania to Reward Organ Donors' Families"*
  http://www.ncpa.org/pd/regulat/pd050699c.html
  This May 1999 online news summary article describes a program introduced in Pennsylvania to encourage organ donations. Under this plan, the state pays $300 towards the funeral expenses of

organ donors.

Different Perspectives in the Debate

- *Henry Hansmann, "The Economics and Ethics of Markets for Human Organs"*
  http://www.pitt.edu/~htk/hansmann.htm
  This essay is an excerpt from *Organ Transplantation Policy: Issues and Prospects* (Durham, NC: Duke University Press, 1989), by Henry Hansmann. In this essay, Hansmann argues that a market for human organs would provide incentives that would significantly increase the supply of organs, thereby saving many human lives. He suggests that laws prohibiting sales of human organs were introduced to restrict unethical sales of organs from living donors. Hansmann recommends that a futures market be adopted in which healthy individuals are allowed to sell the right to harvest their organs after their death. He suggests a number of ways in which such a market could be implemented.

- *Donald Boudreaux and A.C. Pritchard, "Organ Donation: Saving Lives through Incentives"*
  http://www.mackinac.org/2482
  In this October 4, 1999 online article, Donald Boudreaux and A.C. Pritchard argue that economic incentives should be used to induce individuals to donate organs. Their suggestion is a relatively modest payment of $10 to $25 to individuals who sign organ donor cards. They suggest that the cost of such a program could be covered by the American Red Cross or a similar organization. Under their plan, charitable organizations that pay individuals to sign the donor card could be compensated by a health insurer whenever an organ is provided by one of these individuals. Boudreaux and Pritchard argue that such a system would provide a Pareto improvement that would benefit potential organ donors, charitable organizations, hospitals, and the recipient of the transplanted organs.

- *Charles T. Carlstrom and Christy D. Rollow, "The Rationing of Transplantable Organs: A Troubled Lineup"*
  http://www.cato.org/pubs/journal/cj17n2-3.html
  Charles T. Carlstrom and Christy D. Rollow discuss the system of rationing transplantable organs in this online article appearing in the *Cato Journal*. They argue that the persistent and growing shortage of organs is the result of the rationing system that is used for allocation purposes. Carlstrom and Rollow suggest that the situation is analogous to the long gas lines that appeared during the price controls on gasoline in the 1970s. The cost of this rationing system, they suggest, is that 10 people awaiting organ transplants die every day. They argue that a market allocation mechanism would save many lives by increasing the supply of organs.

- *Organ Selling Homepage*
  http://www.pitt.edu/~htk/

This website contains an extensive collection of links to resources dealing with the economic and ethical issues associated with the sale of human organs. The sponsors of this website argue that monetary incentives for organ donations will save many lives. Documents on this site include a transcript of the 1983 House of Representatives hearing on the issue of organ selling, including both the pro and con sides of the argument.

- *Libertarian Party, "Online human organ sales: save lives"*
  http://www.bmstahoe.com/Libertarian/onlineorgans.html
  This page contains a statement by the Libertarian Party on its position concerning organ sales. They argue that individuals have the right to dispose of their own bodies. It is also argued that market incentives would eliminate the chronic shortage of organs, thereby saving lives.

- *Ronald Bailey, "The Case for Selling Human Organs"*
  http://www.reason.com/rb/rb041801.html
  In this April 18, 2001 article appearing in *Reason Online*, Ronald Bailey argues that allowing the sale of organs would eliminate the growing shortage of donated organs. He notes that the only person who is not compensated as part of the transplant process is the organ donor.

- *Organ Keeper*
  http://www.organkeeper.com/
  This is the website of an organization that argues that payments to organ donors should be allowed. They note that everyone else involved in the process of providing organs for transplant purposes is compensated except for the actual donor. It is argued that compensation would eliminate the shortage of transplant organs.

- *OrganSales.com*
  http://www.organsales.com/
  This is a website for an organization that tries to locate donor material for patients in need of transplants. The authors of this site are in favor of eliminating the ban on the sale of human organs.

- *Vidya Ram, "International traffic in human organs"*
  http://www.flonnet.com/fl1907/19070730.htm
  Vidya Ram discusses problems associated with organ sales in this March 30-April 12 edition of *Frontline*. He suggests that low-income individuals are often pressured to sell organs, primarily kidneys. Ram argues that organ sellers in low-income countries have often experienced significant health problems after organ removal.

- *Nancy Scheper-Hughes, "The End of the Body: The Global Traffic in Organs"*
  http://sunsite.berkeley.edu/biotech/organswatch/pages/cadraft.html
  In this online May 14, 1998 essay, Nancy Scheper-Hughes raises several concerns about the development of international markets for human organs. She argues that a growing international

black-market harms economically disadvantaged individuals to provide benefits for wealthy individuals. Scheper-Hughes suggests that kidney sales provide funds for low-income households in India and Brazil. She suggests that the "scarcity" of organs is an artificial need that is created by the "human denial and refusal of aging."

- *Payment Subcommittee of the United Network for Organ Sharing Ethics Committee, "Financial Incentives for Organ Donation"*
  http://www.unos.org/resources/bioethics.asp?index=3
  This report provides a nice summary of the arguments for and against the use of financial incentives to encourage organ donations. It is suggested that more study of public opinions and attitudes be done before any such plan is implemented.

- *David J. Rothman, "The International Organ Traffic"*
  http://www.nybooks.com/nyrev/WWWarchdisplay.cgi?19980326014F
  In this March 16, 1998 article, David J. Rothman discusses international trade in human organs. He notes that there have been human rights abuses associated with the provision of organs in several countries, most notably China. Rothman suggests that international medical associations should do more to prevent these abuses from occurring.

- *David G. Young, "An e-Transplant Prophecy"*
  http://www.mitec.net/~jryoung/dgyoung/organs.html
  In this December 7, 1999 online article, David G. Young discusses the controversy stirred up by the attempted sale of a human organ on EBay. He predicts that the growing shortage of organs will result in a change in the law that will allow payments to organ donors.

- *Th. Gutmann and W. Land, "Ethics in living donor organ transplantation"*
  http://www.med.uni-muenchen.de/trans/ethics.htm
  Th. Gutmann and W. Land discuss the ethics of living organ donations in this online essay. They argue that living donor organ transplantation involves complex ethical issues that go beyond the simple Hippocratic Oath. It is suggested that decisions in such cases must weigh the principle of doing no harm to the donor against the overall benefit provided by the transplantation.

- *World Medical Association, "Declaration on Human Organ & Tissue Donation and Transplantation"*
  http://www.wma.net/e/policy/17-180_e.html
  This page contains the text of the World Medical Association's October 2000 declaration on human organ transplantation. This document contains a set of ethical principles concerning organ transplantation. In particular, they state that: "Payment for organs and tissues for donation and transplantation should be prohibited."

- *Claude Earl Fox, "House Testimony: National Organ Transplantation Policy"* http://newsroom.hrsa.gov/speeches/foxOPTN.htm

In this April 8, 1998 testimony, Claude Earl Fox, the Acting Administrator of the Health Resources and Services Administration, discusses shortcomings of the Organ Procurement Network. He argues that the National Organ Transplant Act resulted in improved fairness in organ allocations. Fox argues that a market-based system allocates organs based upon the recipient's wealth rather than medical need. He suggests that the system should be modified to provide equity across geographical regions.

Groups start petition to hike tobacco taxes

Money would go toward prevention, health care, advocates say.

Published Saturday, September 17, 2005

ST. LOUIS (AP) - A coalition of health groups is spearheading a citizen initiative to raise the state's cigarette tax by 80 cents a pack to pay for prevention and cessation programs and health care for those harmed by tobacco.

The Committee for a Healthy Future wants to place the tax increase on the November 2006 election ballot. If approved by voters, the increased tax would raise an estimated $351 million in the first year, said Lori Pickens, senior executive of American Lung Association of Missouri and committee spokeswoman.

The group's petition for a proposed constitutional amendment was filed late yesterday with the secretary of state's office.

Missouri's current cigarette tax rate of 17 cents a pack is second-lowest in the nation, after South Carolina, which is 7 cents a pack. Missouri has one of the highest smoking rates in the country and is the least funded for smoking prevention, Pickens said.

Every day, she said, 28 Missourians die from smoking-related diseases. Nearly 90 percent of the people who smoke begin their habit as teenagers.

Missouri's share of settlement money from a 1998 agreement between tobacco manufacturers and 46 states was aimed at addressing tobacco prevention.

But the money was "squandered, in our opinion," Pickens said, to plug budget gaps under the administrations of Govs. Bob Holden and Matt Blunt.

Janet Wilson, chief of the state's health promotion unit, said the state has relied exclusively on federal grants for tobacco prevention, which this year was reduced 6 percent to $900,000.

"There's solid evidence that prevention strategies are effective, including increasing the price of tobacco products," Wilson said.

Blunt's spokesman, Spence Jackson, said yesterday if the proposal garners the required number of signatures, it would go before the people as a ballot initiative.

However, Blunt doesn't support it in principal and "opposes any effort to increase the tax burden on Missourians," Jackson said.

Besides the American Lung Association, the coalition also includes representatives from the American Cancer Society, American Heart Association and other health groups in the state.

The proposal, which needs nearly 150,000 signatures to get on the ballot, would impose a tax of 4 cents per cigarette - or 80 cents a pack - as well as a 20 percent tax on noncigarette tobacco products.

It would create a "Healthy Future Trust Fund" provision in the Missouri Constitution that requires the tax revenue to be spent on smoking prevention and cessation and disease management for uninsured Missourians who suffer from chronic, smoking-related illnesses such as lung cancer, heart disease and emphysema.

Persons with an annual household income of less than 200 percent of the federal poverty level would be given "health access cards" for outpatient visits, pharmacy and other services to avoid debilitating illness that could force them onto Medicaid. Amounts would vary.

Pickens said 54 percent of the trust fund would beef up Medicaid reimbursement rates to attract doctors and providers who won't accept the current Medicaid reimbursement rate. The higher reimbursement rate could be especially critical for rural Missourians who now have little or no access to care, she said.

The proposal also calls for strict controls on use of the trust fund. Annual audits would ensure no fund money would be diverted to other uses and that no current health-care funding gets replaced by the new cigarette tax revenues.

MORE PROFIT WITH
LESS CARBON

BY AMORY B. LOVINS

Focusing on energy efficiency will do more than protect Earth's climate—it will make businesses and consumers richer

A basic misunderstanding skews the entire climate debate. Experts on both sides claim that protecting Earth's climate will force a trade-off between the environment and the economy. According to these experts, burning less fossil fuel to slow or prevent global warming will increase the cost of meeting society's needs for energy services, which include everything from speedy transportation to hot showers. Environmentalists say the cost would be modestly higher but worth it; skeptics, including top U.S. government officials, warn that the extra expense would be prohibitive. Yet both sides are wrong. If properly done, climate protection would actually *reduce* costs, not raise them. Using energy more efficiently offers an economic bonanza—not because of the benefits of stopping global warming but because saving fossil fuel is a lot cheaper than buying it.

The world abounds with proven ways to use energy more productively, and smart businesses are leaping to exploit them. Over the past decade, chemical manufacturer DuPont has boosted production nearly 30 percent but cut energy use 7 percent and greenhouse gas emissions 72 percent (measured in terms of their carbon dioxide equivalent), saving more than $2 billion so far. Five other major firms—IBM, British Telecom, Alcan, NorskeCanada and Bayer—have collectively saved at least another $2 billion since the early 1990s by reducing their carbon emissions more than 60 percent. In 2001 oil giant BP met its 2010 goal of reducing carbon dioxide emissions 10 percent below the company's 1990 level, thereby cutting its energy bills $650 million over 10 years. And just this past May, General Electric vowed to raise its energy efficiency 30 percent by 2012 to enhance the company's shareholder value. These sharp-penciled firms, and dozens like them, know that energy efficiency improves the bottom line and yields even more valuable side benefits: higher quality and reliability in energy-efficient factories, 6 to 16 percent higher labor productivity in efficient offices, and 40 percent higher sales in stores skillfully designed to be illuminated primarily by daylight.

The U.S. now uses 47 percent less energy per dollar of economic output than it did 30 years ago, lowering costs

BURNING FOSSIL FUELS not only contributes to global warming—it wastes money. Improving the energy efficiency of factories, buildings, vehicles and consumer products would swiftly reduce the consumption of coal and oil, curbing the damage to Earth's climate while saving immense amounts of money for businesses and households.

CARY WOLINSKY (*photography*); JEN CHRISTIANSEN (*photoillustration*)

by $1 billion a day. These savings act like a huge universal tax cut that also reduces the federal deficit. Far from dampening global development, lower energy bills accelerate it. And there is plenty more value to capture at every stage of energy production, distribution and consumption. Converting coal at the power plant into incandescent light in your house is only 3 percent efficient. Most of the waste heat discarded at U.S. power stations—which amounts to 20 percent more energy than Japan uses for everything—could be lucratively recycled. About 5 percent of household electricity in the U.S. is lost to energizing computers, televisions and other appliances that are turned off. (The electricity wasted by poorly designed standby circuitry is equivalent to the output of more than a dozen 1,000-megawatt power stations running full-tilt.) In all, preventable energy waste costs Americans hundreds of billions of dollars and the global economy more than $1 trillion a year, destabilizing the climate while producing no value.

CROSSROADS FOR
ENERGY

THE PROBLEM

- The energy sector of the global economy is woefully inefficient. Power plants and buildings waste huge amounts of heat, cars and trucks dissipate most of their fuel energy, and consumer appliances waste much of their power (and often siphon electricity even when they are turned off).

- If nothing is done, the use of oil and coal will continue to climb, draining hundreds of billions of dollars a year from the economy as well as worsening the climate, pollution and oil-security problems.

THE PLAN

- Improving end-use efficiency is the fastest and most lucrative way to save energy. Many energy-efficient products cost no more than inefficient ones. Homes and factories that use less power can be cheaper to build than conventional structures. Reducing the weight of vehicles can double their fuel economy without compromising safety or raising sticker prices.

- With the help of efficiency improvements and competitive renewable energy sources, the U.S. can phase out oil use by 2050. Profit-seeking businesses can lead the way.

Rooftop solar array

If energy efficiency has so much potential, why isn't everyone pursuing it? One obstacle is that many people have confused efficiency (doing more with less) with curtailment, discomfort or privation (doing less, worse or without). Another obstacle is that energy users do not recognize how much they can benefit from improving efficiency, because saved energy comes in millions of invisibly small pieces, not in obvious big chunks. Most people lack the time and attention to learn about modern efficiency techniques, which evolve so quickly that even experts cannot keep up. Moreover, taxpayer-funded subsidies have made energy seem cheap. Although the U.S. government has declared that bolstering efficiency is a priority, this commitment is mostly rhetorical. And scores of ingrained rules and habits block efficiency efforts or actually reward waste. Yet relatively simple changes can turn all these obstacles into business opportunities.

Enhancing efficiency is the most vital step toward creating a climate-safe energy system, but switching to fuels that emit less carbon will also play an important role. The world economy is already decarbonizing: over the past two centuries, carbon-rich fuels such as coal have given way to fuels with less carbon (oil and natural gas) or with none (renewable sources such as solar and wind power). Today less than one third of the fossil-fuel atoms burned are carbon; the rest are climate-safe hydrogen. This decarbonization trend is reinforced by greater efficiencies in converting, distributing and using energy; for example, combining the production of heat and electricity can extract twice as much useful work from each ton of carbon emitted into the atmosphere. Together these advances could dramatically reduce total carbon emissions by 2050 even as the global economy expands. This article focuses on the biggest prize: wringing more work from each unit of energy delivered to businesses and consumers. Increasing end-use efficiency can yield huge savings in fuel, pollution and capital costs because large amounts of energy are lost at every stage of the journey from production sites to delivered services [*see box on opposite page*]. So even small reductions in the power used at the downstream end of the chain can enormously lower the required input at the upstream end.

The Efficiency Revolution

MANY ENERGY-EFFICIENT PRODUCTS, once costly and exotic, are now inexpensive and commonplace. Electronic speed controls, for example, are mass-produced so cheaply that some suppliers give them away as a free bonus with each motor. Compact fluorescent lamps cost more than $20 two decades ago but only $2 to $5 today; they use 75 to 80 percent less electricity than incandescent bulbs and last 10 to 13 times longer. Window coatings that transmit light but reflect heat cost one fourth of what they did five years ago. Indeed, for many kinds of equipment in competitive markets—motors, industrial pumps, televisions, refrigerators—some highly energy-efficient models cost no more than inefficient ones. Yet far more important than all these better and cheaper technologies is a hidden revolution in the design that combines and applies them.

S. STRONG Solar Design Associates, Inc.

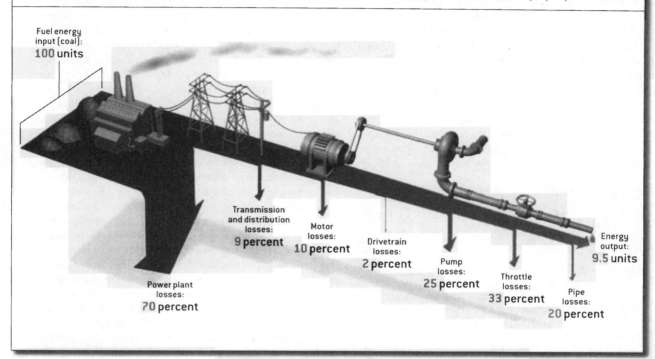

COMPOUNDING LOSSES

From the power plant to an industrial pipe, inefficiencies along the way whittle the energy input of the fuel—set at 100 arbitrary units in this example—by more than 90 percent, leaving only 9.5 units of energy delivered as fluid flow through the pipe. But small increases in end-use efficiency can reverse these compounding losses. For instance, saving one unit of output energy by reducing friction inside the pipe will cut the needed fuel input by 10 units, slashing cost and pollution at the power plant while allowing the use of smaller, cheaper pumps and motors.

Fuel energy input (coal): **100 units**

Transmission and distribution losses: **9 percent**

Motor losses: **10 percent**

Drivetrain losses: **2 percent**

Pump losses: **25 percent**

Throttle losses: **33 percent**

Pipe losses: **20 percent**

Energy output: **9.5 units**

Power plant losses: **70 percent**

For instance, how much thermal insulation is appropriate for a house in a cold climate? Most engineers would stop adding insulation when the expense of putting in more material rises above the savings over time from lower heating bills. But this comparison omits the capital cost of the heating system—the furnace, pipes, pumps, fans and so on—which may not be necessary at all if the insulation is good enough. Consider my own house, built in 1984 in Snowmass, Colo., where winter temperatures can dip to −44 degrees Celsius and frost can occur any day of the year. The house has no conventional heating system; instead its roof is insulated with 20 to 30 centimeters of polyurethane foam, and its 40-centimeter-thick masonry walls sandwich another 10 centimeters of the material. The double-pane windows combine two or three transparent heat-reflecting films with insulating krypton gas, so that they block heat as well as eight to 14 panes of glass. These features, along with heat recovery from the ventilated air, cut the house's heat losses to only about 1 percent more than the heat gained from sunlight, appliances and people inside the structure. I can offset this tiny loss by playing with my dog (who generates about 50 watts of heat, adjustable to 100 watts if you throw a ball to her) or by burning obsolete energy studies in a small woodstove on the coldest nights.

Eliminating the need for a heating system reduced construction costs by $1,100 (in 1983 dollars). I then reinvested this money, plus another $4,800, into equipment that saved half the water, 99 percent of the water-heating energy and 90 percent of the household electricity. The 4,000-square-foot structure—which also houses the original headquarters of Rocky Mountain Institute (RMI), the nonprofit group I cofounded in 1982—consumes barely more electricity than a single 100-watt lightbulb. (This amount excludes the power used by the institute's office equipment.) Solar cells generate five to six times that much electricity, which I sell back to the utility. Together all the efficiency investments repaid their cost in 10 months with 1983 technologies; today's are better and cheaper.

In the 1990s Pacific Gas & Electric undertook an experiment called ACT[2] that applied smart design in seven new and old buildings to demonstrate that large efficiency improvements can be cheaper than small ones. For example, the company built a new suburban tract house in Davis, Calif., that could stay cool in the summer without air-conditioning. PG&E estimated that such a design, if widely adopted, would cost about $1,800 less to build and $1,600 less to maintain over its lifetime than a conventional home of the same size. Similarly, in 1996 Thai architect Soontorn Boonyatikarn built a house near steamy Bangkok that required only one-seventh the air-conditioning capacity usually installed in a structure of that size; the savings in equipment costs paid for the insulating roof, walls and windows that keep the house cool [*see box on opposite page*]. In all these cases, the design approach was the same: optimize the whole building for multiple benefits rather than use isolated components for single benefits.

Such whole-system engineering can also be applied to office buildings and factories. The designers of a carpet factory built in Shanghai in 1997 cut the pumping power required for a heat-circulating loop by 92 percent through two simple changes. The first change was to install fat pipes rather than thin ones, which greatly reduced friction and hence allowed the system to use smaller pumps and motors. The second innovation was to lay out the pipes before positioning the equipment they connect. As a result, the fluid moved through short, straight pipes instead of tracing circuitous paths, further reducing friction and capital costs.

This isn't rocket science; it's just good Victorian engineering rediscovered. And it is widely applicable. A practice team at RMI has recently developed new-construction designs offering energy savings of 89 percent for a data center, about 75 percent for a chemical plant, 70 to 90 percent for a supermarket and about 50 percent for a luxury yacht, all with capital costs lower than those of conventional designs. The team has also proposed retrofits for existing oil refineries, mines and microchip factories that would reduce energy use by 40 to 60 percent, repaying their cost in just a few years.

> Using energy more efficiently offers an economic bonanza—not because of the benefits of stopping global warming but because saving fossil fuel is a lot cheaper than buying it.

Vehicles of Opportunity

TRANSPORTATION CONSUMES 70 percent of U.S. oil and generates a third of the nation's carbon emissions. It is widely considered the most intractable part of the climate problem, especially as hundreds of millions of people in China and India buy automobiles. Yet transportation offers enormous efficiency opportunities. *Winning the Oil Endgame,* a 2004 analysis written by my team at RMI and co-sponsored by the Pentagon, found that artfully combining lightweight materials with innovations in propulsion and aerodynamics could cut oil use by cars, trucks and planes by two thirds without compromising comfort, safety, performance or affordability.

Despite 119 years of refinement, the modern car remains astonishingly inefficient. Only 13 percent of its fuel energy even reaches the wheels—the other 87 percent is either dissipated as heat and noise in the engine and drivetrain or lost to idling and accessories such as air conditioners. Of the energy delivered to the wheels, more than half heats the tires, road and air. Just 6 percent of the fuel energy actually accelerates the car (and all this energy converts to brake heating when you stop). And, because 95 percent of the accelerated mass is the car itself, less than 1 percent of the fuel ends up moving the driver.

Yet the solution is obvious from the physics: greatly reduce the car's weight, which causes three fourths of the energy losses at the wheels. And every unit of energy saved at the wheels by lowering weight (or cutting drag) will save an additional seven units of energy now lost en route to the wheels. Concerns about cost and safety have long discouraged attempts to make lighter cars, but modern light-but-strong materials—new metal alloys and advanced polymer composites—can slash a car's mass without sacrificing crashworthiness. For example, carbon-fiber composites can absorb six to 12 times as much crash energy per kilogram as steel does, more than offsetting the composite car's weight disadvantage if it hits a steel vehicle that is twice as heavy. With such novel materials, cars can be big, comfortable and protective without being heavy, inefficient and hostile, saving both oil *and* lives. As Henry Ford said, you don't need weight for strength; if you did, your bicycle helmet would be made of steel, not carbon fiber.

Advanced manufacturing techniques developed in the past two years could make carbon-composite car bodies competitive with steel ones. A lighter body would allow automakers to use smaller (and less expensive) engines. And because the assembly of carbon-composite cars does not require body or paint shops, the factories would be smaller and cost 40 percent less to build than conventional auto plants. These savings would offset the higher cost of the carbon-composite materials. In all, the introduction of ultralight bodies could nearly double the fuel efficiency of today's hybrid-electric vehicles—which are already twice as efficient as conventional cars—without raising their sticker prices. If composites prove unready, new ultralight steels offer a reliable backstop. The competitive marketplace will sort out the winning materials, but, either way, superefficient ultralight vehicles will start pulling

THE AUTHOR

AMORY B. LOVINS

LOVINS is co-founder and chief executive of Rocky Mountain Institute, an entrepreneurial nonprofit organization based in Snowmass, Colo., and chairman of Fiberforge, an engineering firm in Glenwood Springs, Colo. A physicist, Lovins has consulted for industry and governments worldwide for more than 30 years, chiefly on energy and its links with the environment, development and security. He has published 29 books and hundreds of papers on these subjects and has received a MacArthur Fellowship and many other awards for his work.

How can you keep cool in tropical Thailand while minimizing power usage? Architect Soontorn Boonyatikarn of Chulalongkorn University used overhangs and balconies to shade his 350-square-meter home in Pathumthani, near Bangkok. Insulation, an airtight shell and infrared-reflecting windows keep heat out of the house while letting in plenty of daylight. An open floor plan and central stairwell promote ventilation, and indoor air is cooled as it flows through an underground tube. As a result, the house needs just one seventh of the typical air-conditioning capacity for a structure of its size. To further reduce energy bills, the air-conditioning system's condensers heat the house's water.

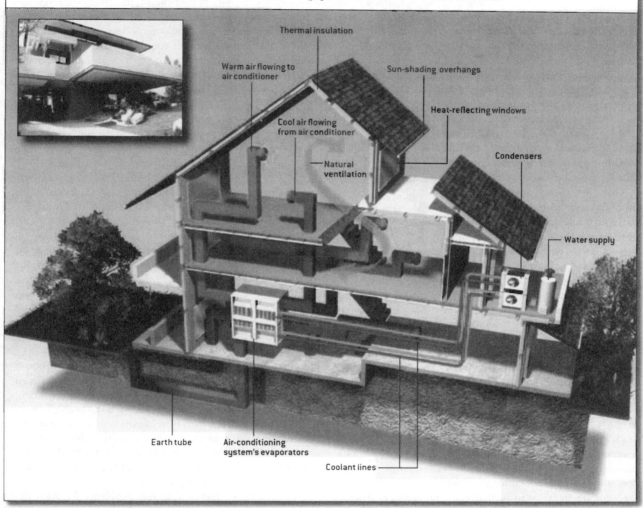

Thermal insulation

Warm air flowing to air conditioner

Sun-shading overhangs

Heat-reflecting windows

Cool air flowing from air conditioner

Condensers

Natural ventilation

Water supply

Earth tube

Air-conditioning system's evaporators

Coolant lines

away from the automotive pack within the next decade.

What is more, ultralight cars could greatly accelerate the transition to hydrogen fuel-cell cars that use no oil at all [see "On the Road to Fuel-Cell Cars," by Steven Ashley; SCIENTIFIC AMERICAN, March]. A midsize SUV whose halved weight and drag cut its needed power to the wheels by two thirds would have a fuel economy equivalent to 114 miles per gallon and thus require only a 35-kilowatt fuel cell—one third the usual size and hence much easier to manufacture affordably [see box on page 81]. And because the vehicle would need to carry only one third as much hydrogen, it would not require any new storage technologies; compact, safe, off-the-shelf carbon-fiber tanks could hold enough hydrogen to propel the

SUV for 530 kilometers. Thus, the first automaker to go ultralight will win the race to fuel cells, giving the whole industry a strong incentive to become as boldly innovative in materials and manufacturing as a few companies now are in propulsion.

RMI's analysis shows that full adoption of efficient vehicles, buildings and industries could shrink projected U.S. oil use in 2025—28 million barrels a day—by more than half, lowering consumption to pre-1970 levels. In a realistic scenario, only about half of these savings could actually be captured by 2025 because many older, less efficient cars and trucks would remain on the road (vehicle stocks turn over slowly). Before 2050, though, U.S. oil consumption could be phased out altogether by doubling the efficiency of oil use and substituting alternative fuel supplies [*see illustration on page 83*]. Businesses can profit greatly by making the transition, because saving each barrel of oil through efficiency improvements costs only $12, less than one fifth of what petroleum sells for today. And two kinds of alternative fuel supplies could compete robustly with oil even if it sold for less than half the current price. The first is ethanol made from woody, weedy plants such as switchgrass and poplar. Corn is currently the main U.S. source of ethanol, which is blended with gasoline, but the woody plants yield twice as much ethanol per ton as corn does and with lower capital investment and far less energy input.

The second alternative is replacing oil with lower-carbon natural gas, which would become cheaper and more abundant as efficiency gains reduce the demand for electricity at peak periods. At those times, gas-fired turbines generate power so wastefully that saving 1 percent of electricity would cut U.S. natural gas consumption by 2 percent and its price by 3 or 4 percent. Gas saved in this way and in other uses could then replace oil either directly or, even more profitably and efficiently, by converting it to hydrogen.

The benefits of phasing out oil would go far beyond the estimated $70 billion saved every year. The transition would lower U.S. carbon emissions by 26 percent and eliminate all the social and political costs of getting and burning petroleum—military conflict, price volatility, fiscal and diplomatic distortions, pollution and so on. If the country becomes oil-free, then petroleum will no longer be worth fighting over. The Pentagon would also reap immediate rewards from raising energy efficiency because it badly needs to reduce the costs and risks of supplying fuel to its troops. Just as the U.S. Department of Defense's research efforts transformed civilian industry by creating the Internet and the Global Positioning System, it should now spearhead the development of advanced ultralight materials.

The switch to an oil-free economy would happen even faster than RMI projected if policymakers stopped encouraging the perverse development patterns that make people drive so much. If federal, state and local governments did not mandate and subsidize suburban sprawl, more of us could live in neighborhoods where almost everything we want is within a five-minute walk. Besides saving fuel, this New Urbanist design builds stronger communities, earns more money for developers and is much

less disruptive than other methods of limiting vehicle traffic (such as the draconian fuel and car taxes that Singapore uses to avoid Bangkok-like traffic jams).

Renewable Energy

EFFICIENCY IMPROVEMENTS that can save most of our electricity also cost less than what the utilities now pay for coal, which generates half of U.S. power and 38 percent of its fossil-fuel carbon emissions. Furthermore, in recent years alternatives to coal-fired power plants—including renewable sources such as wind and solar power, as well as decentralized cogeneration plants that produce electricity and heat together in buildings and factories—have begun to hit their stride. Worldwide the collective generating capacity of these sources is already greater than that of nuclear power and growing six times as fast [*see illustration on page 82*]. This trend is all the more impressive because decentralized generators face many obstacles to fair competition and usually get much lower subsidies than centralized coal-fired or nuclear plants.

Wind power is perhaps the greatest success story. Mass production and improved engineering have made modern wind turbines big (generating two to five megawatts each), extremely reliable and environmentally quite benign. Denmark already gets a fifth of its electricity from wind, Germany a tenth. Germany and Spain are each adding more than 2,000 megawatts of wind power each year, and Europe aims to get 22 percent of its electricity and 12 percent of its total energy from renewables by 2010. In contrast, global nuclear generating capacity is expected to remain flat, then decline.

The most common criticism of wind power—that it produces electricity too intermittently—has not turned out to be a serious drawback. In parts of Europe that get all their power from wind on some days, utilities have overcome the problem by diversifying the locations of their wind turbines, incorporating wind forecasts into their generating plans and integrating wind power with hydroelectricity and other energy sources. Wind and solar power work particularly well together, partly because the conditions that are bad for wind (calm, sunny weather) are good for solar, and vice versa. In fact, when properly combined, wind and solar facilities are more reliable than conventional power stations—they come in smaller modules (wind turbines, solar cells) that are less likely to fail all at once, their costs do not swing wildly with the prices of fossil fuels, and terrorists are much more likely to attack a nuclear

ADDICTED TO OIL

28 million
Barrels of oil that will be consumed each day in the U.S. by 2025 if current trends continue

13 percent
The proportion of a car's fuel energy that reaches its wheels

$70 billion
Annual savings (by 2025) from improving the efficiency of oil use and finding substitutes for oil

Ultralight cars can be fast, roomy, safe and efficient. A concept five-seat midsize SUV called the Revolution, designed in 2000, weighs only 857 kilograms—less than half the weight of a comparable conventional car—yet its carbon-fiber safety cell would protect passengers from high-speed collisions with much heavier vehicles. A 35-kilowatt fuel cell could propel the car for 530 kilometers on 3.4 kilograms of hydrogen stored in its tanks. And the Revolution could accelerate to 100 kilometers per hour in 8.3 seconds.

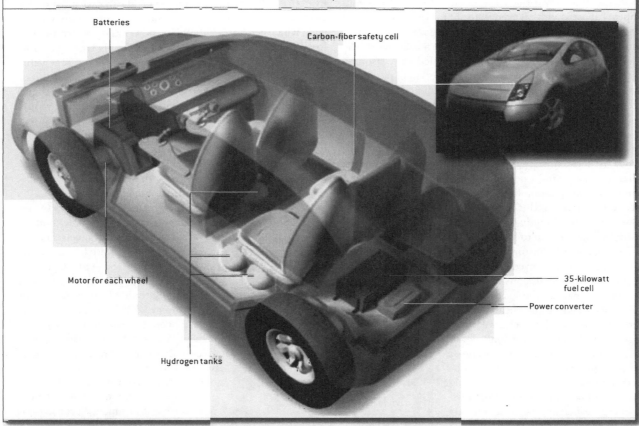

Batteries

Carbon-fiber safety cell

Motor for each wheel

35-kilowatt fuel cell

Power converter

Hydrogen tanks

reactor or an oil terminal than a wind farm or a solar array.

Most important, renewable power now has advantageous economics. In 2003 U.S. wind energy sold for as little as 2.9 cents a kilowatt-hour. The federal government subsidizes wind power with a production tax credit, but even without that subsidy, the price—about 4.6 cents per kilowatt-hour—is still cheaper than subsidized power from new coal or nuclear plants. (Wind power's subsidy is a temporary one that Congress has repeatedly allowed to expire; in contrast, the subsidies for the fossil-fuel and nuclear industries are larger and permanent.) Wind power is also abundant: wind farms occupying just a few percent of the available land in the Dakotas could cost-effectively meet all of America's electricity needs. Although solar cells currently cost more per kilowatt-hour than wind turbines do, they can still be profitable if integrated into buildings, saving the cost of roofing materials. Atop big, flat-roofed commercial buildings, solar cells can compete without subsidies if combined with efficient use that allows the building's owner to resell the surplus power when it is most plentiful and valuable—on sunny afternoons. Solar is also usually the cheapest way to get

electricity to the two billion people, mostly in the developing world, who have no access to power lines. But even in rich countries, a house as efficient as mine can get all its electricity from just a few square meters of solar cells, and installing the array costs less than connecting to nearby utility lines.

Cheaper to Fix

INEXPENSIVE EFFICIENCY improvements and competitive renewable sources can reverse the terrible arithmetic of climate change, which accelerates exponentially as we burn fossil fuels ever faster. Efficiency can outpace economic growth if we pay attention: between 1977 and 1985, for example, U.S. gross domestic product (GDP) grew 27 percent, whereas oil use fell 17 percent. (Over the same period, oil imports dropped 50 percent, and Persian Gulf imports plummeted 87 percent.) The growth of renewables has routinely outpaced GDP; worldwide, solar and wind power are doubling every two and three years, respectively. If both efficiency and renewables grow faster than the economy, then carbon emissions will fall and global warming will slow—buying more time to develop even

ELECTRICITY ALTERNATIVES

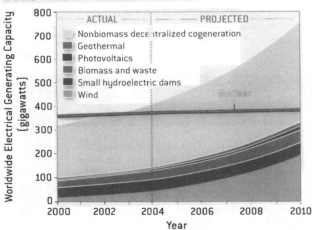

ACTUAL — PROJECTED

- Nonbiomass decentralized cogeneration
- Geothermal
- Photovoltaics
- Biomass and waste
- Small hydroelectric dams
- Wind

Worldwide Electrical Generating Capacity (gigawatts)

800
700
600
500
400
300
200
100
0

2000 2002 2004 2006 2008 2010

Year

DECENTRALIZED SOURCES of electricity—cogeneration (the combined production of electricity and heat, typically from natural gas) and renewables (such as solar and wind power)—surpassed nuclear power in global generating capacity in 2002. The annual output of these low- and no-carbon sources will exceed that of nuclear power this year.

better technologies for displacing the remaining fossil-fuel use, or to master and deploy ways to capture combustion carbon before it enters the air [see "Can We Bury Global Warming?" by Robert H. Socolow; SCIENTIFIC AMERICAN, July].

In contrast, nuclear power is a slower and much more expensive solution. Delivering a kilowatt-hour from a new nuclear plant costs at least three times as much as saving one through efficiency measures. Thus, every dollar spent on efficiency would displace at least three times as much coal as spending on nuclear power, and the efficiency improvements could go into effect much more quickly because it takes so long to build reactors. Diverting public and private investment from market winners to losers does not just distort markets and misallocate financial capital—it worsens the climate problem by buying a less effective solution.

The good news about global warming is that it is cheaper to fix than to ignore. Because saving energy is profitable, efficient use is gaining traction in the marketplace. U.S. Environmental Protection Agency economist Skip Laitner calculates that from 1996 to mid-2005 prudent choices by businesses and consumers, combined with the shift to a more information- and service-based economy, cut average U.S. energy use per dollar of GDP by 2.1 percent a year—nearly three times as fast as the rate for the preceding 10 years. This change met 78 percent of the rise in demand for energy services over the past decade (the remainder was met by increasing energy supply), and the U.S. achieved this progress without the help of any technological breakthroughs or new national policies. The climate problem was created by millions of bad decisions over decades, but climate stability can be restored by millions of sensible choices—buying a more efficient lamp or car, adding insulation or caulk to your home, repealing subsidies for waste and rewarding desired outcomes (for example, by paying architects and engineers for savings, not expenditures).

The proper role of government is to steer, not row, but for years officials have been steering our energy ship in the wrong direction. The current U.S. energy policy harms the economy and the climate by rejecting free-market principles and playing favorites with technologies. The best course is to allow every method of producing or saving energy to compete fairly, at honest prices, regardless of which kind of investment it is, what technology it uses, how big it is or who owns it. For example, few jurisdictions currently let decentralized power sources such as rooftop solar arrays "plug and play" on the electric grid, as modern technical standards safely permit. Although 31 U.S. states allow net metering—the utility buys your power at the same price it charges you—most artificially restrict or distort this competition. But the biggest single obstacle to electric and gas efficiency is that most countries, and all U.S. states except California and Oregon, reward distribution utilities for selling more energy and penalize them for cutting their customers' bills. Luckily, this problem is easy to fix: state regulators should align incentives by decoupling profits from energy sales, then letting utilities keep some of the savings from trimming energy bills.

JEN CHRISTIANSEN; SOURCE: RMI (graph); PROJECTIONS TO 2025 FROM U.S. ENERGY INFORMATION ADMINISTRATION; ESTIMATES AFTER 2025 FROM RMI

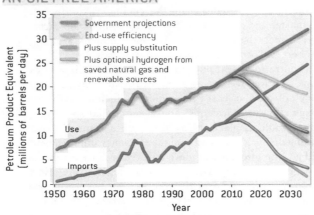

U.S. OIL CONSUMPTION AND IMPORTS can be profitably slashed by doubling the efficiency of vehicles, buildings and industries (*yellow lines in graph*). The U.S. can achieve further reductions by replacing oil with competitive substitutes such as advanced biofuels and saved natural gas (*green lines*) and with hydrogen fuel (*gray lines*).

Superefficient vehicles have been slow to emerge from Detroit, where neither balance sheets nor leadership has supported visionary innovation. Also, the U.S. lightly taxes gasoline but heavily subsidizes its production, making it cheaper than bottled water. Increasing fuel taxes may not be the best solution, though; in Europe, stiff taxes—which raise many countries' gasoline prices to $4 or $5 a gallon—cut driving more than they make new cars efficient, because fuel costs are diluted by car owners' other expenses and are then steeply discounted (most car buyers count only the first few years' worth of fuel savings). Federal standards adopted in the 1970s helped to lift the fuel economy of new cars and light trucks from 16 miles per gallon in 1978 to 22 miles per gallon in 1987, but the average has slipped to 21 mpg since then. The government projects that the auto industry will spend the next 20 years getting its vehicles to be just 0.5 mile per gallon more efficient than they were in 1987. Furthermore, automakers loathe the standards as restrictions on choice and have become adept at gaming the system by selling more vehicles classified as light trucks, which are allowed to have lower fuel economy than cars. (The least efficient light trucks even get special subsidies.)

The most powerful policy response is "feebates"—charging fees on inefficient new cars and returning that revenue as rebates to buyers of efficient models. If done separately for each size class of vehicle, so there is no bias against bigger models, feebates would expand customer choice instead of restricting it. Feebates would also encourage innovation, save customers money and boost automakers' profits. Such policies, which can be implemented at the state level, could speed the adoption of advanced-technology cars, trucks and planes without mandates, taxes, subsidies or new national laws.

In Europe and Japan, the main obstacle to saving energy is the mistaken belief that their economies are already as efficient as they can get. These countries are up to twice as efficient as the U.S., but they still have a long way to go. The greatest op-portunities, though, are in developing countries, which are on average three times less efficient than the U.S. Dreadfully wasteful motors, lighting ballasts and other devices are freely traded and widely bought in these nations. Their power sector currently devours one quarter of their development funds, diverting money from other vital projects. Industrial countries are partly responsible for this situation because many have exported inefficient vehicles and equipment to the developing world. Exporting inefficiency is both immoral and uneconomic; instead the richer nations should help developing countries build an energy-efficient infrastructure that would free up capital to address their other pressing needs. For example, manufacturing efficient lamps and windows takes 1,000 times less capital than building power plants and grids to do the same tasks, and the investment is recovered 10 times faster.

China and India have already discovered that their burgeoning economies cannot long compete if energy waste continues to squander their money, talent and public health. China is setting ambitious but achievable goals for shifting from coal-fired power to decentralized renewable energy and natural gas. (The Chinese have large supplies of gas and are expected to tap vast reserves in eastern Siberia.) Moreover, in 2004 China announced an energy strategy built around "leapfrog technologies" and rapid improvements in the efficiency of new buildings, factories and consumer products. China is also taking steps to control the explosive growth of its oil use; by 2008 it will be illegal to sell many inefficient U.S. cars there. If American automakers do not innovate quickly enough, in another decade you may well be driving a superefficient Chinese-made car. A million U.S. jobs hang in the balance.

Today's increasingly competitive global economy is stimulating an exciting new pattern of energy investment. If governments can remove institutional barriers and harness the dynamism of free enterprise, the markets will naturally favor choices that generate wealth, protect the climate and build real security by replacing fossil fuels with cheaper alternatives. This technology-driven convergence of business, environmental and security interests—creating abundance by design—holds out the promise of a fairer, richer and safer world. **SA**

MORE TO EXPLORE

Hypercars, Hydrogen and the Automotive Transition. A. B. Lovins and D. R. Cramer in *International Journal of Vehicle Design*, Vol. 35, Nos. 1–2, pages 50–85; 2004. Available at www.rmi.org/images/other/Trans/T04-01_HypercarH2AutoTrans.pdf

Winning the Oil Endgame. A. B. Lovins, E. K. Datta, O.-E. Bustnes, J. G. Koomey and N. J. Glasgow. Rocky Mountain Institute, 2004. Available at **www.oilendgame.com**

A complete list of references can be found online at **www.rmi.org/sitepages/pid173.php#C05-05**

Clearing the Haze?

New Evidence on the Economic Impact of Smoking Bans

By Michael R. Pakko

When making decisions about adopting smoke-free laws, advocates often give policymakers a Pollyannaish outlook in which communities can achieve public health benefits with no economic consequences. In particular, the lack of statistically significant economic effects is interpreted as indicating an absence of economic costs. Recent economic research indicates that this is a far too simplistic view of the issue.

A previous article in *The Regional Economist* ("Peering Through the Haze," July 2005) described some early evidence on the economic impact of smoke-free laws and suggested that the findings were far from conclusive.[1]

As more communities have adopted smoke-free laws and more data have been gathered, economists have discovered new, significant findings. As an earlier article suggested, economic costs often focus on specific business categories—those that smokers tend to frequent.

Gambling and Smoking

Several papers have examined the cost of smoke-free laws on the gambling business, using data from slot machine revenue at Delaware racetracks ("racinos").[2] Recent economic research finds conclusive evidence of revenue declines at the racinos after the Delaware Clean Indoor Air Law took effect in December 2002.

In my recent research on the topic, I find statistically significant losses at all three Delaware racinos—ranging from 8.9 percent to 17.8 percent.[3] Overall, the statewide revenue

decline was 14.9 percent. Using slightly different methods that estimate demand for casino gambling, economists Richard Thalheimer and Mukhtar Ali estimate the total revenue loss at 15.9 percent.

These revenue estimates may significantly understate profit losses. For example, the racino that suffered the smallest loss in revenues—Dover Downs—also was the only one with a luxury hotel on site. Dover Downs management responded to initial revenue losses by offering more discounts on hotel rooms.[4] Efforts to prop up revenue may have been partly successful, but at a cost to the bottom line.

Evidence on the effect of smoking bans on gaming revenue shows that when analysis can be narrowly focused on data from specific businesses, statistically significant findings emerge. Another approach is to use very large data sets. As smoking bans have spread across the country, the variety and timing of adopting smoke-free laws have generated data that can help identify effects.

Bar and Restaurant Employment

Two papers, one by Ryan Phelps and the other by Scott Adams and Chad Cotti, have used data available from the Bureau of Labor Statistics to examine the employment effects of smoking bans. Using nationwide county-level data, these two studies examine the changes in employment at bars and restaurants after communities adopt smoking bans. Neither study finds significant employment changes at restaurants, on average, but both find statistically significant employment declines at bars, with loss estimates ranging from 4 percent to 16 percent.

Adams and Cotti also examine some additional factors. For communities in states with

a higher ratio of smokers to nonsmokers than the national average, employment losses at bars were significantly larger, and the employment changes at restaurants went from a small positive effect to a small negative effect (in neither case, statistically significant). Climate also affected restaurant employment.[5] Restaurants in warm climates fared better than those in cooler climates. The authors suggest that the reason for this might be that restaurants in warmer climates can more easily provide outdoor seating where smoking is not prohibited. (See also the sidebar on Columbia, Mo.) Restaurants that suffered the dual curse of being in regions with colder climates *and* a high prevalence of smokers suffered statistically significant employment losses, on average.

California Dreamin'

Another recent economic study examines taxable sales receipts of bars and restaurants in California, the home of the smoke-free movement. Because California communities passed some of the nation's first smoke-free laws, much of the early evidence on the subject was based on these data on California taxable sales receipts; as time has passed, those data have accumulated. The experience of California also provides a case in which a statewide smoking ban was superimposed on a patchwork of local smoke-free laws, providing useful variation in the coverage and jurisdiction of smoking bans that can be exploited in empirical analysis.

This article is based on a presentation at the Sixth Annual ERIE Conference on Local Government and Economics, Erie Pa., Aug.14, 2007.

District Focus: Smoking Ban Singes Columbia, Mo.

Since January 2007, all bars and restaurants in Columbia, Mo., have been required to be smoke-free. Only some sections of outdoor patios are exempt from the requirement.

Some local businesses have continued to oppose the Columbia Clean Air Ordinance, circulating petitions to repeal the law by ballot initiative. According to local press reports, owners of at least four establishments have cited the smoking ban as a factor in their decision to close their doors in 2007.

Recent data from the city of Columbia show a distinct decline in sales tax receipts at bars and restaurants. After rising at an average rate of 6.8 percent from 2002 through 2006, tax revenue declined at an annual rate of 1.3 percent over the first seven months of 2007. (See graph.) Although the data are still preliminary, initial analysis suggests a 5 percent decline in overall sales revenue at Columbia dining establishments since the implementation of the smoking ban. This estimate takes into account past trends, seasonal fluctuations in the data and an overall slowdown in sales tax revenue in Columbia.[6]

One interesting feature of the Columbia story is the response of restaurant owners to the patio exemption. According to an article in the *Columbia Missourian*, owners of at least two bars are building or planning outdoor patio expansions. One owner was quoted as saying, "You have to have a patio to survive."[7] The expenses associated with these renovations may help buffer the sales revenue of these establishments, but they also represent profit losses that are above and beyond the measured sales declines.

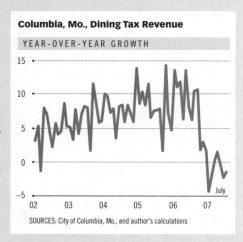

Columbia, Mo., Dining Tax Revenue

YEAR-OVER-YEAR GROWTH

SOURCES: City of Columbia, Mo., and author's calculations

Economists Robert Fleck and Andrew Hanssen analyzed quarterly restaurant sales data for 267 California cities over 25 years. They find that the measured impact of smoking bans differs between local bans and the statewide ban. In what the authors call their "naïve" specification that treats all smoke-free laws the same, they find a statistically significant 4 percent decline in revenues associated with smoking bans.

When they estimate the effects of the statewide ban and local bans independently, they find that the measured decline in restaurant sales is attributable to the statewide ban on cities without local bans. The measured effect of the statewide ban is nearly 4 percent, and it is statistically significant. The independent effect of local smoking ordinances is estimated to be very small and is not significant. These findings are consistent with the interpretation that locally originated smoking bans have little effect, but smoking bans that are imposed on a community by a higher jurisdiction can have a detrimental economic impact.

Fleck and Hanssen go on to uncover an important specification problem: They find that cities that adopted smoke-free laws were systematically different from those that did not. The authors find that sales growth tends to be a predictor of smoking bans, rather than the other way around. This "reverse causality" calls into question many earlier findings, and it poses problems for using data from California in drawing inferences about the economic impact of smoking bans elsewhere.

The Role of Economic Research

Economic effects of smoke-free laws may be difficult to identify and interpret, but analysis suggests that at least some businesses do suffer costs. When they consider passing smoking bans, policymakers should study evidence both from public health professionals and from economists. Ω

Michael R. Pakko is an economist at the Federal Reserve Bank of St. Louis. To see more of Pakko's work, go to http://research.stlouisfed. org/econ/pakko/index.html.

ENDNOTES

[1] Scollo et al. (2003) provide a review of previous literature, much of which has been published in medical and public health journals.
[2] Previous studies of the Delaware racino case study have been published—and disputed—in the public health journal *Tobacco Control*.
[3] See Pakko (forthcoming).
[4] See Dover Downs (2004).
[5] Bar employment was not significantly affected by climate differences.
[6] See Pakko (2007).
[7] See Solberg (2007).

REFERENCES

Adams, Scott; and Cotti, Chad D. "The Effect of Smoking Bans on Bars and Restaurants: An Analysis of Changes in Employment." *The B.E. Journal of Economic Analysis & Policy:* Vol. 7, Issue 1, Contributions, Article 12. See www.bepress.com/bejeap/vol7/iss1/art12.

See Dover Downs Gaming and Entertainment Inc. *Annual Report for the Fiscal Year ended Dec. 31, 2003* (2004).

Fleck, Robert K.; and Hanssen, F. Andrew. "Why Understanding Smoking Bans is Important for Estimating Their Effects: California's Restaurant Smoking Bans and Restaurant Sales." *Economic Inquiry* (forthcoming).

Pakko, Michael R. "The Economics of Smoking Bans: Peering Through The Haze." *The Regional Economist,* Federal Reserve Bank of St. Louis, July 2005, pp. 12-13.

Pakko, Michael. R. "No Smoking at the Slot Machines: The Effect of Smoke-Free Laws on Gaming Revenues." *Applied Economics* (forthcoming).

Pakko, Michael R. "The Economic Impact of a Smoking Ban in Columbia, Missouri: A Preliminary Analysis of Sales Tax Data." *CRE8* Occasional Report, Dec. 11, 2007. See http:// research.stlouisfed.org.regecon/op/CRE8OP-2007-002.pdf.

Phelps, Ryan. "The Economic Impact of 100% Smoking Bans." *Kentucky Annual Economic Report 2006*, Center for Business and Economic Research, Gatton College of Business and Economics, University of Kentucky, 2006, pp. 31-34.

Thalheimer, Richard; and Ali, Mukhtar M. "The Demand for Casino Gaming with Special Reference to a Smoking Ban." *Economic Inquiry* (forthcoming).

Scollo, M.; Lal, A.; Hyland, A.; and Glantz, S. "Review of the Quality of Studies on the Economic Effects of Smoke-free Policies on the Hospitality Industry." *Tobacco Control*, 2003, Vol. 12, pp. 13-20.

Solberg, Christy. "Effects of Smoking Ban Still Debated." *Columbia Missourian*, Sept. 27, 2007. See www.columbiamissourian.com/ stories/2007/09/27/effects-smoking-ban-still-debated/.

July 25, 2005
To Reduce the Cost of Teenage Temptation, Why Not Just Raise the Price of Sin?
By DAVID LEONHARDT

WHEN you look back on all the attempts to curb teenage drinking, smoking and drug use over the last couple of decades, you start to ask yourself a question that countless parents have asked: Does anybody really know how to change a teenager's behavior?

Sometimes the government and advocacy groups have used straight talk, like Nancy Reagan's "Just Say No" campaign. Other times they have tried to play it cool. They drop an egg into a sizzling frying pan and announce, "This is your brain on drugs," or they print mock advertisements that pretend to market cancer. It all feels like a delicate exercise in adolescent psychology.

Much of this back and forth is unnecessary. There is in fact a surefire way to get teenagers to consume less beer, tobacco and drugs, according to one study after another: raise the cost, in terms of either dollars or potential punishment.

In just about every state that increased beer taxes in recent years, teenage drinking soon dropped. The same happened in the early 1990's when Arizona, Maryland, New Jersey and a handful of other states passed zero-tolerance laws, which suspend the licenses of under-21 drivers who have any trace of alcohol in their blood. In states that waited until the late 90's to adopt zero tolerance, like Colorado, Indiana and South Carolina, the decline generally did not happen until after the law was in place.

Teenagers, it turns out, are highly rational creatures in some ways. Budweisers and Marlboros are discretionary items, and their customers treat them as such. Gasoline consumption, by contrast, changes only marginally when the price of a gallon does.

"When people think about drugs, alcohol, even cigarettes, they think about addiction and this strong desire to consume them. They don't think price has an effect," said Sara Markowitz, an economist at Rutgers University in Newark, who studies public health. "That's just wrong. And it holds among kids even more so than among adults."

Not only that, but unprotected sex tended to become less common after the changes in the law, according to studies. Gonorrhea and H.I.V. rates dropped. So did drunken-driving deaths and, for boys, suicides. Whatever the policies' downsides - and they are not insignificant - they have some of the clearest benefits of any government action.

They are also a useful reminder of how often the power of incentives is underestimated. Taste, style, trendiness and advertising all do affect human behavior. A study in the Archives of Pediatric and Adolescent Medicine this month, for example, found that antitobacco television ads do seem to reduce smoking. But nothing has quite the sway that an economic carrot or stick does.

When a big superstore moves into town, many shoppers who claim to prefer the coziness of mom-and-pop stores trek out to the megamall for the lower prices. (You know who you are.) When the government cut welfare payments in the 1990's, many people who had been receiving them went back to work.

Even when inscrutable teenagers and addictive substances are involved, the basic dynamic does not change.

Tax increases on alcohol and tobacco have been fairly common in recent years, allowing researchers to look for the crucial before-and-after effect that helps separate correlation from causation. Alaska, Nebraska, Nevada, Tennessee and Utah have all increased alcohol taxes since 2002. Georgia, Kentucky, Tennessee and Virginia - tobacco-growing states all - are among those that have raised cigarette taxes.

Just because states with higher taxes have lower teenage drinking and smoking rates does not mean that one caused the other. An outside force - like a highly educated population, which might tend to eschew beer and cigarettes but vote for higher taxes - could instead be the underlying cause.

But if drinking or smoking always seems to fall after a tax increase, then the case becomes far stronger. Looking across the states and taking into account all the other factors that can be measured, researchers have found that a 1 percent increase in the price of beer leads to a drop in teenage consumption of between 1 and 4 percent, Dr. Markowitz said. For cigarettes, a 1 percent price increase causes roughly a 1 percent decline in smoking.

Using the same method, researchers can also answer a question that has long occupied public health specialists. It is generally accepted that youngsters who drink, smoke and use drugs are also more likely to take dangerous risks, like having unprotected sex. But does one lead to the other? Or as Christopher Carpenter, an economist at the University of California, Irvine, puts it, are there simply "bad kids" given to misbehaving in all sorts of ways?

Depending on your definition of misbehavior, the answer is both. When alcohol taxes rose, the number of teenagers who reported having had sex in recent months did not change, according to a study by Michael Grossman of the City University of New York and Dr. Markowitz. Nor did the number of partners they had.

But fewer teenagers had unprotected sex. The number of new gonorrhea cases and - though the evidence on this was weaker - new H.I.V. cases also dropped. Since teenagers get these diseases at far higher rates than the rest of the population, any decline can be a big deal.

The enactment of zero-tolerance driving laws also appeared to lead to a fall in sexually transmitted diseases. For boys between the ages of 15 and 20, suicide rates fell 7 percent to 10 percent after a law was put in place, Dr. Carpenter found. (The fact that the effects seem to be concentrated among boys and whites is a mystery that awaits future research.)

"When zero-tolerance laws were being debated, it wasn't like, 'Let's reduce drunk-driving deaths - and gonorrhea and suicide,' " he said. "This is an unintended, surprising consequence."

Zero-tolerance laws also have the advantage of being aimed specifically at teenagers. New alcohol taxes, on the other hand, take money from millions of people who do not spread venereal diseases or drive drunk.

But zero tolerance is now the law of the land in all 50 states, Dr. Carpenter said. There is no more public health uptick to get from it. So until somebody comes up with a smart new incentive, another "Don't Drink and Drive" campaign might be the best tool out there.

Democracy at a price

Sep 18th 1997
From The Economist print edition

Big government, big bill

WHEN it comes to providing social goods—better education, say, or better health as measured by greater life expectancy and lower infant mortality—heavy-spending governments seem to be doing little if any better than governments that spend much less. This only deepens the mystery of the ever-expanding state.

To be fair, up until the 1950s increases in public spending did seem to produce worthwhile improvements in health and education. Certainly up until the 1930s, the larger part of expanding government expenditure was taken up by investment in infrastructure, the supply of essential public services, and the creation of a low-level safety net to guard against poverty. In all these respects, it could be argued, the state was attending to things that the market, left to its own devices, would neglect. In those days, a much larger share of public spending was devoted to dealing with genuine "market failures", as they would now be called.

Later, and especially after 1960, priorities shifted. By now, far fewer gaps in the market remained. Increasingly, the state expanded its role by seizing, and monopolising, activities hitherto left to the market; and by transferring resources in ever more complicated ways from one part of the economy to another, to serve an ever more ambitious (and opaque) range of goals. As a result, in recent decades the connection between increased public spending and improved social outcomes has become much weaker, and in some cases has broken down altogether.

A quick way to demonstrate this is to divide the advanced economies listed earlier into three groups: "big government" countries, where public spending in 1990 was more than 50% of output; "small government" ones, where public spending in 1990 was less than 35% of output; and the rest, which can be disregarded for this purpose. The big-government group takes in Belgium, Italy, the Netherlands, Norway and Sweden; the small-government group Australia, Japan, Switzerland and the United States. For good measure, add to the small-government group two recent arrivals to the ranks of the rich industrial economies: Singapore and Hong Kong, both of whose governments spend less than 35% of GDP. How do these groups compare on broad measures of welfare?

The best single such measure is output per head, adjusted for international differences in purchasing power. By this test, and on the basis of our small, unscientific sample, the small-government countries are just in front. Their adjusted output per head in 1995 was $23,300; the corresponding figure for the big-government countries was $20,400. The small-government economies' growth rates were higher, too: an average rise of nearly 4% a year in income per head between 1960 and 1995, compared with 2.5% for the others (though note that growth in the small-government group comes down to the same lower figure, 2.5%, if Singapore and Hong Kong are left out).

What about health? Spending varies a lot, but outcomes much less. Average life expectancy in big-government and small government countries is very similar, at 78.0 years and 77.8 years respectively. Rates of infant mortality are also much the same in the two groups: 6.0 per 1,000 births in the big-government economies and 5.5 per 1,000 in the small-government ones.

As with health, spending on education varies a good deal; again, however, the results are much closer. The United Nations Development Programme calculates a composite school-enrolment ratio, weighting together the proportion of children attending school at different ages. The higher the ratio, the better a country is doing. In the big-government countries the index is 85%; in the small-government countries it is 78% (or 82% if you exclude Singapore and Hong Kong). The estimated level of adult illiteracy is very low in all the countries in both groups. In a recent international survey of children's skills in mathematics and science, the small-government countries on average did markedly better, particularly in maths, than the big-government countries.

On one social indicator, however, the two groups diverge much more obviously: inequality of incomes. In the big-government countries, the poorest 20% of the population receive 7.4% of the national income, whereas in the small-government economies they get only 5.6%. Even allowing for the fact that incomes overall are higher in the small-government group, in 1995 the poorest 20% there were worse off in absolute terms than their big-government counterparts (see <u>chart</u> 4). Conversely, the richest 20% were much better off in the small-government countries than in the big-government ones, both in absolute terms and relative to the less prosperous in their own economies.

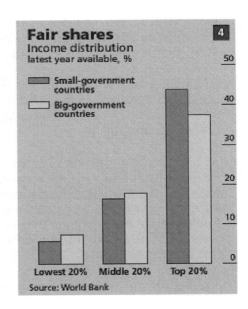

Fair shares
Income distribution
latest year available, %

■ Small-government countries
□ Big-government countries

Lowest 20%   Middle 20%   Top 20%

Source: World Bank

Other things equal

It is possible to argue that the more equal income distribution achieved by transfers in the big-government group is preferable to the greater disparity in the small-government group, even if the relatively small gains at the bottom come at the expense of much larger losses at the top. The question is whether this apparently modest increase in equality justifies surrendering an extra 15-20% of the economy to public control.

The fact that Singapore and Hong Kong qualify for inclusion in the small-government group of advanced economies—they are already richer than Japan and Germany, and still growing fast—suggests a further point. Today's fastest-growing "emerging-market economies", as they are still called, have much smaller governments than most of their western counterparts did at comparable stages of their development. Even in 1960, before their transfer states began to expand in earnest, the big-government countries of the West (and the middle-sized-government countries, too, for that matter) had dedicated 30% of their economies to public spending. Two of the Asian tiger economies have already far surpassed the incomes the West had achieved by 1960. Others are getting there fast, with governments smaller than America's was 40 years ago.

When western analysts reflect on the role of government in East Asia, they concentrate on trade and industrial policies. How much of the rapid growth in East Asia, they ask, is due to clever industrial intervention, and how much to letting markets have their say? This debate seems to have blinded people to an equally important fact: in the world's fastest-growing economies, government, measured by the extent of its spending in the economy, has stayed small. In years to come, will the Asian tigers build transfer states of their own—and if so, will they be able to maintain their faster rates of growth?

In the meantime, a puzzle presents itself. Government in the West has grown to a point where liberty (at least as liberals understand that term) is being seriously infringed. Yet this enormous expansion of the state appears to have yielded little in return. Something seems to have gone wrong. Who, or what, is to blame?

One simple piece of theory sheds a useful light on the question. It shows how taxes, even if they pay for worthwhile things, impose an inescapable economic burden, called a deadweight cost. It also shows that this cost rises more than proportionately as taxes go up (see article).

This analysis, simple as it is, suggests one way in which big government imposes a cost on an economy: every tax-and-transfer destroys some social welfare. No less important, it shows that big government is likely to produce severely diminishing returns. At low levels of government activity, the deadweight cost of taxes may well be outweighed by the gains that flow from essential public goods. But as the scale of government grows, this trade-off seems likely to move in the wrong direction—and at an accelerating pace.

On the spending side of the government's activities, further inefficiencies of various kinds arise, often because the government is usually a monopoly provider of the services it supplies. This is either because it forbids competition, or (as in private health and education) because its service is "free" to users, whereas the private alternatives involve large additional expense. To a much greater extent than a private monopolist, a public monopolist is free from pressures to innovate or become more efficient. Moreover, lack of competition suppresses information that the market would otherwise reveal about the cost of supplying different goods and services and about the value that consumers put on them.

The extreme case of this inefficiency in the allocation of resources was communist central planning. Even those economists who had long doubted the Soviet Union's economic statistics were surprised when the full extent of that failure was laid bare. All across the Soviet empire were enterprises that for decades had been engaged, not in adding value to raw materials but in literally subtracting it: the value of the finished products, measured by the unforced willingness of buyers to pay for them, was less than the value of steel, plastic, glass and other raw materials that went into them. It is well to remember just how badly bureaucrats can fail if allowed to operate as monopolists over a sufficiently wide range of operations.

But memories are short. Those who favour more government intervention in the economy simply point to some market failure, and rest their case. What they are saying, in effect, is that the superiority of markets in allocating resources is strictly theoretical. The textbooks say that given a great many buyers and suppliers, perfect information, homogeneous goods and a complete set of futures markets, perfect competition is bound to follow, bringing "efficiency" in its wake. But if any of these conditions is missing, the whole apparatus will collapse. There will be market failure, and the desired results will not materialise. This is all you need to say to justify government intervention.

This argument, repeated with endless variations, is specious every time. The case for the superiority of markets over planners is empirical, not deductive. Market failure in the sense just defined is not merely common but universal: the textbook conditions are never fully satisfied. But that is not a helpful fact. What matters is to know whether, in practice, imperfect markets work better than imperfect governments. In practice, do competition, incentives to effort and innovation, and survival of the fittest in the marketplace—however flawed that market may be—work better than bureaucrats supposedly pursuing the public interest?

The lessons of history—in the Soviet empire, in China, in Africa and Latin America, in Europe and the United States—suggest that when it is possible to leave the allocation of resources to the market, the results are nearly always better. People who still doubt this are surely no longer entitled to argue that any sign of market failure is sufficient justification for yet another enlargement of government. The deadweight cost of taxes, together with the inefficiencies caused by lack of competition and proper incentives within the public sector, helps to explain why government begins to fail as it grows. But it cannot explain why voters in democracies keep asking for more. Likewise, analysing the components of public spending takes you only so far towards an answer. Government borrowing allows countries to spend beyond their means, or beyond their people's willingness to pay taxes, at least for a while. The fact that transfers have grown so much more quickly than public investment and consumption may also reveal something about the demands that the modern state is expected to satisfy.

But the puzzle remains. Given the evident drawbacks of big government, and given that nobody likes paying higher taxes, why is it that public spending and taxes have both risen so dramatically over the past 50 years?

A brief history of tax

Jan 27th 2000
From The Economist print edition

"NO TAXATION without representation." The slogan of the American revolution has long been a rallying cry for taxpayers and tax evaders alike—though not always with such dramatic consequences. Arguably, the struggle to tax people in ways they find acceptable has been the main force shaping the modern nation-state. But are tax policies designed when the nation-state was all-powerful still appropriate now that globalisation, spurred on by the Internet, is rapidly eroding national borders?

Prostitution may be the oldest profession, but tax collection was surely not far behind. The Bible records that Jesus offered his views on a tax matter, and converted a prominent taxman. In its early days taxation did not always involve handing over money. The ancient Chinese paid with pressed tea, and Jivaro tribesmen in the Amazon region stumped up shrunken heads. As the price of their citizenship, ancient Greeks and Romans could be called on to serve as soldiers, and had to supply their own weapons—a practice that was still going strong in feudal Europe. As Ferdinand Grapperhaus recounts in "Tax Tales" (International Bureau of Fiscal Documentation, Amsterdam, 1998), the origins of modern taxation can be traced to wealthy subjects paying money to their king in lieu of military service.

The other early source of tax revenue was trade, with tolls and customs duties being collected from travelling merchants. The big advantage of these taxes was that they fell mostly on visitors rather than residents. One of the earliest taxes imposed by England's Parliament, in the 13th century, was "tonnage and poundage" on wine, wool and leather, targeted at Italian merchants. Sometimes rulers went a little over the top. Excessive taxation was one reason why King Charles I of England lost his head. Many of those guillotined during the French Revolution of 1789 were much-resented private tax collectors. And the Boston Tea Party was a protest by American patriots against the tea tax imposed by their British rulers.

Income tax, the biggest source of government funds today, is a relatively recent invention, probably because the notion of annual income is itself a modern concept. Governments preferred to tax things that were easy to measure and therefore to calculate liability on. That is why early taxes concentrated on tangible items such as land and property, physical goods, commodities and ships, or the number of windows or fireplaces in a building. The first income tax was levied in 1797 by the Dutch Batavian Republic. Britain followed suit in 1799, and Prussia in 1808. Like most new taxes, these imposts were first introduced as temporary measures to finance war efforts. After the European powers had made peace in Vienna in 1815, Henry Addington, the British prime minister of the day, swore that an income tax would never be imposed again. But in 1842 the British government revived the tax.

What stands out about the 20th century—and particularly its second half—is that governments around the world have been taking a growing share of their countries' national income in tax, mainly to pay for ever more expensive defence efforts and for a modern welfare state. Taxes on consumption, such as the sales tax that is a big source of revenue for America's state and local governments, and the value-added tax on goods and services in Europe, have become increasingly important.

Big differences between countries remain in the overall level of tax. America's tax revenues amount to around one-third of its GDP, whereas Sweden's are closer to half. There are also big differences in the preferred methods of collecting it, the rates at which it is levied and the definition of the "tax base" to which those rates are applied, as well as the division of responsibility for taxation between levels of government.

Global economy, national taxes

The increasing globalisation of economies in the 20th century was accompanied by a rare outbreak of internationalism by the tax authorities. Many countries chose to tax their citizens—individual or corporate—on their global income, whether or not they had already paid their due on some of it abroad.

The League of Nations, the forerunner to the United Nations, in 1921 commissioned a report by financial experts who concluded that this practice of "double taxation" interfered with "economic intercourse and...the free flow of capital". It suggested rules for determining when tax should be paid to the country in which the income is generated, and when to the taxpayer's country of residence. It drafted a model treaty (now updated by the OECD) that spawned many bilateral agreements. Initially intended to stop income being taxed twice, these bilateral treaties opened the way for multinational companies to avoid tax on their profits altogether by setting up in business where taxes were lowest. Combined with greater mobility of capital, this new flexibility encouraged tax competition between countries.

The Big City; Scalping Law Trims Wallets Of Knick Fans

By JOHN TIERNEY (NYT) 803 words
Published: June 3, 1999

IF you wanted to see the Knicks play the Pacers in Indianapolis Tuesday night, you could have bought a seat for $65 from a ticket broker. But if you'd like to see them play this weekend in Madison Square Garden, expect to pay at least $250.

One possible explanation for this price difference is that New York is a much bigger city with more affluent fans competing for seats. But you find a similar gap even when you compare New York with Los Angeles, another metropolis with lots of wealthy fans.

During the first two rounds of the basketball playoffs, when the Lakers were still in contention, brokers were selling tickets to games in Los Angeles for $50. The cheapest seats available in New York during those earlier rounds cost three to four times as much.

Why so much more? Perhaps the main reason is that so many politicians are determined to protect us. Unlike California and Indiana and most other states, New York outlaws ticket scalping, and Attorney General Eliot L. Spitzer has just issued an inch-thick report demanding even stiffer penalties for scalpers.

New York's law, which was renewed this week by the Legislature, makes it illegal to resell a ticket for more than 10 percent above the face value. Ticket brokers have evaded the law by operating in New Jersey and Connecticut, but they still run the risk of prosecution if they make a deal with anyone in New York. These restrictions on the legal flow of tickets have fostered black market practices and prices.

By contrast, people in Los Angeles and Indianapolis can resell tickets for whatever they want, so the holders of season tickets to Laker and Pacer games can readily profit by selling their playoff seats to brokers. And although the brokers are legally free to charge astronomical prices, there are so many tickets on the open market that they cost less than in New York.

"The more you allow tickets to be openly traded, the more you'll see prices come down," said Stephen Happel, a professor of economics at Arizona State University at Tempe. He has seen this process firsthand in Phoenix, where he helped persuade the authorities to establish areas outside sports arenas at which licensed brokers, street scalpers and fans can sell tickets on game day at any price they want.

"New York is such an anomaly," Dr. Happel said. "Right there under the shadow of Wall Street, you're trying to turn people into criminals for buying and selling pieces of paper that are essentially no different from call options. But you can't defeat the laws of demand and supply. The more restrictions you put on selling tickets, the more you'll drive up prices, and the more you'll encourage hard-core criminals to get in the business."

The criminal results of the current law are amply documented in the report issued last week by the Attorney General. His investigators took more than four years studying brokers and box office employees to discover what was already known by economists and citizens of the old Soviet Union: when you fix the price for something below its market value, people will pay bribes to get their hands on it.

THE report says the widespread corruption should be combated by classifying box office bribery and ticket scalping as felonies. (They are now misdemeanors.) But why not eliminate the crime wave by eliminating the crime? In an interview, the Attorney General was asked why a ticket broker shouldn't be as free to set prices as, say, a real estate developer like Mr. Spitzer's father.

"You could make a theoretically powerful argument in favor of lifting price controls on tickets," Mr. Spitzer said. "But a legislative decision was made to impose the controls, and that has created an attendant problem of commercial bribery. All we're trying to do is eliminate the bribery that has become endemic in the ticket industry."

Mr. Spitzer did have some words of encouragement for New Yorkers who would like the same freedom to buy tickets as people in other states. He suggested that box offices at arenas and Broadway theaters could start selling market-priced tickets on the Internet.

"Perhaps they could eliminate the middleman," Mr. Spitzer said, "and auction off tickets on Ebay directly to consumers."

The idea is intriguing, but it's hard to imagine the local box offices doing anything so creative very soon. For now, the cheapest way to see the playoffs is to drive to Indianapolis.

POLICY
BRIEFING

NUMBER 1   MARCH 8, 2006

HOW AN EARNINGS TAX HARMS CITIES LIKE ST. LOUIS AND KANSAS CITY

By Joseph H. Haslag

Joseph H. Haslag is an associate professor of economics at the University of Missouri, Columbia. He holds a master's degree in economics from the University of Missouri and a Ph.D. from Southern Methodist University.

On the surface, an earnings tax seems like an ideal way for a city to raise revenue. After all, cities—especially their downtown business districts—possess substantial competitive advantages relative to the surrounding suburbs. Many businesses need to be located near clients, customers, and complementary businesses. Hence, many city policymakers have traditionally assumed that they could impose a small earnings tax with minimal economic damage.

In practice, this analysis is too simplistic. Although some existing businesses will not be willing or able to move to avoid the earnings tax, new investment is more mobile. When deciding where to start a new business, entrepreneurs will choose to locate where their rate of return—after taxes—is the highest. Moreover, as more and more businesses choose to locate outside of the city's downtown, the convenience of a downtown location begins to diminish.

Improvements in transportation have worsened the problem: over the last half-century, freeways and widespread automobile ownership have made both residents and businesses more mobile. As a result, the cost of locating businesses in the suburbs has declined. The competitive advantages of a city's downtown have declined with it.

The Earnings Tax in Missouri

Ironically, the increased mobility of residents was a major motivation for Missouri's adoption of an earnings tax. In the postwar years, families began purchasing cars and moving to the suburbs, causing a decline in property tax revenues. In 1947, the Missouri legislature responded by authorizing cities with populations of at least 70,000 to levy an earnings tax. The tax rate was capped at 1 percent. Both St. Louis and Kansas City chose to enact an earnings tax, in the belief that businesses would prove less mobile than residents.

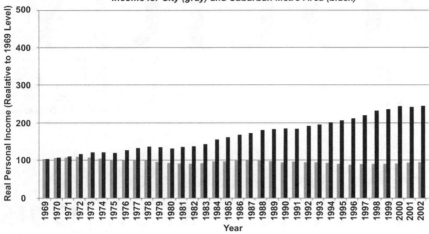

ST. LOUIS
Income for City (gray) and Suburban Metro Area (black)

earnings tax because in addition to two cities with an earnings tax—St. Louis and Kansas City—the state also has a third major city—Springfield—that has chosen not to impose an earnings tax. This presents an opportunity to compare the economic performance of the Springfield area with the performance of its larger neighbors to look for clues about the economic impact of this tax.

Economic Performance of Missouri Cities

A good way to evaluate the economic performance of a region is by looking at growth of total personal income. By comparing the total income of city residents to that of suburban residents, we can gauge how well a city's economy has performed relative to the rest of its Metropolitan Statistical Area (MSA).

Of the three metropolitan areas under consideration, St. Louis has fallen the furthest behind its suburbs. Total real income in the city of St. Louis actually declined between 1969 and 2002, while in the suburbs, it increased about two and a half times. In contrast, Springfield

If bad tax policy drives St. Louis and Kansas City residents into the suburbs, the state of Missouri will lose tax revenue to Ilinois and Kansas.

The effects of an earnings tax should be of particular interest to Missouri policymakers because the St. Louis and Kansas City metropolitan areas each straddle a border with a neighboring state. If bad tax policy drives St. Louis and Kansas City residents into the suburbs, not only will the cities lose tax revenue to neighboring suburbs, but the state of Missouri will lose tax revenue to Illinois and Kansas.

Missouri also makes an interesting case study for the economics of the

KANSAS CITY
Income for City (gray) and Suburban Metro Area (black)

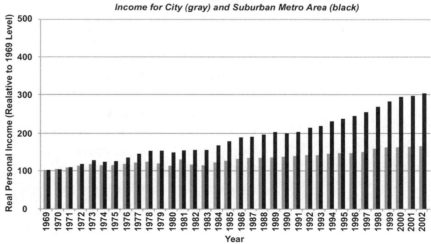

has been the most successful at keeping pace with its suburbs, although it too has seen its share of MSA income fall slightly. Real income in Springfield tripled between 1969 and 2002, while it quintupled in the Springfield suburbs. Kansas City's performance has been middling. The city's total real income in 2002 was one and a half times its 1969 level—while its suburbs increased threefold.

Similar trends can be seen in employment data. In 1969, more than half of all employment in the St. Louis metropolitan area was located in the city of St. Louis. By 2002, only 22 percent of the area's workers had jobs in the city. Kansas City has had greater success at keeping employment in the city. In 1969, about 83 percent of jobs in the Kansas City MSA were located within the city limits. That number fell to 70 percent in 2002. Springfield has done the best job of competing with its suburbs for new investment—the city's share of the region's jobs dropped by only about four percentage points during the same period.

National Evidence

These statistics suggest that the earnings tax might be driving businesses and residents out of St. Louis and Kansas City. But, of course, many other factors could explain the discrepancy. It might be explained by other policy variables—such as the regulatory climate or education system—or by purely accidental characteristics of the three cities.

However, I find the same relationship between the earnings tax and economic performance in statistics across the nation. I perform two regressions using

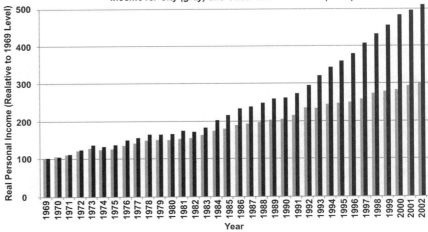

SPRINGFIELD
Income for City (gray) and Suburban Metro Area (black)

data from 101 of the largest metropolitan areas: one from the 1990 census, and the other from the 2000 census. In 23 of those metropolitan areas, the central city has an earnings tax. I find that an earnings tax is systematically associated with lower city per-capita income relative to the surrounding suburbs. For example, consider the city of St. Louis, which had a 2000 per capita income of $19,518. My regressions suggest if St. Louis's earnings tax had been one percentage point higher, its per capita income would have been $995 smaller.

Modeling the Impact of an Earnings Tax

Thus, the evidence—both in Missouri and nationwide—suggests that an earnings tax redistributes jobs and investment from a city to its suburbs. When an earnings tax is imposed only in the city part of a metropolitan area, as it is in St. Louis and Kansas City, it discourages new investment in that part. I present a model of capital investment in an MSA that accounts for this process.

An earnings tax is systematically associated with lower city per-capita income relative to the surrounding suburbs.

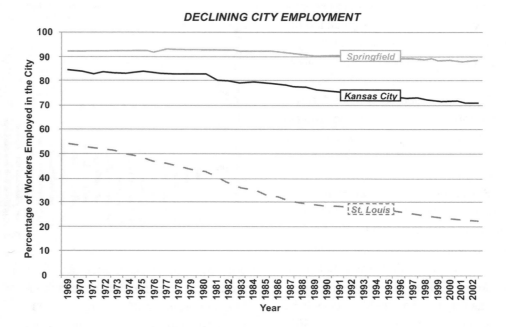

DECLINING CITY EMPLOYMENT

The evidence—both in Missouri and nationwide—suggests that an earnings tax redistributes jobs and investment from a city to its suburbs.

In the model, investors seek to deploy their capital where they can obtain the greatest after-tax rate of return. Because the city has built-in advantages such as convenient access to businesses in the city's downtown, the most profitable place to invest initially will be in the city. However, as the market becomes more crowded, the profitability of new capital invested in the city will begin to drop, and some investors will begin investing in the suburbs.

We can expect that to occur even without an earnings tax—which explains the growth of the Springfield suburbs. However, an earnings tax greatly accelerates the process and permanently lowers the rate of return on capital invested in the city. In a city with an earnings tax, diverting investment to the suburbs becomes profitable sooner than it would have without the earnings tax.

The model predicts that once a city with an earnings tax reaches a certain size, it will stagnate, with all subsequent development occurring in the suburbs. That is a good description of the plight of St. Louis over the last three decades. The model can also account for Kansas City's experience. It seems that Kansas City has not yet reached the growth ceiling imposed by the earnings tax. However, my model predicts that the city's growth will not continue forever. At some point, Kansas City, too, may reach a maximum size, and subsequent investment will occur only in the suburbs. Kansas City's leaders would do well to study how St. Louis has fared in recent decades, and consider whether it's a record they wish to emulate.

For more details, please see Show-Me Policy Study no. 1, which is available at www.showmeinstitute.org.

7777 BONHOMME AVE.
SUITE 2150
ST. LOUIS, MO 63105

WWW.SHOWMEINSTITUTE.ORG

Beet a Retreat
The European Union scales down its sugar subsidies

IT IS twice as costly to produce sugar from beets, in the temperate climes where these crops take root, than to make it from cane, which grows tall, year-round, in the tropics. And yet the European Union is one of the world's biggest exporters of sugar.

This is possible only because Europe's sugar farmers are as adept at extracting favours from Brussels as they are at extracting sucrose from beet. The EU is obliged to buy sugar from its beet growers at euro632 ($768) a tonne, almost three times the world price. Such high prices attract imports from overseas, and encourage overproduction and underconsumption at home. The EU deters imports by raising tariffs, and it clears its sugar mountains by subsidising exports. EU producers have shipped more than 3m tonnes annually in recent years, accounting for about 10% of world exports.

This sugar regime, untouched since 1968, is now ripe for reform. Despite beet growers' angry opposition, the European Commission on June 22nd unveiled its proposals for a radical overhaul. By 2009, the price it sets for white sugar will be cut by 39%. In partial compensation for their loss, farmers will be given a handout that rewards them for their "respect" for the land, not their output of sugar.

The commission also proposes to pay sugar factories to go out of business. If they quit in the first year of the new regime, they will receive euro730 for each tonne of sugar they used to produce. This amount falls in each subsequent year. If factories wait until the fifth year to throw in the towel, they will get nothing.

The proposals must wait until November to secure the approval of ministers, which may not be straightfoward. "The easy option would be to sit on my hands," admitted Mariann Fischer Boel, the EU's agriculture commissioner. But that is not really an option at all. The World Trade Organisation recently ruled that the EU's subsidised exports of sugar breached legal limits. One way or another, Europe must scale down its sugar industry, either through a painful process of attrition or by inviting the least profitable producers to make a prompt and graceful exit.

Michael Mann, spokesman for Ms Fischer Boel, hopes that America and Japan, both generous sugar daddies in their own right, will now follow the EU's example. The stakes are quite high. In 1999, Brent Borrell, of the Centre for International Economics, an Australian research institution, and David Pearce, now of University College, London, calculated that unhindered and unsubsidised trade in sugar would improve the world's lot by the equivalent of $4.7 billion each year. And according to Donald Mitchell, of the World Bank, net imports by Japan, Europe, America and Indonesia would increase by 15m tonnes a year, creating almost 1m jobs in poor countries. In western Europe, sugar prices would fall by 40%.

But the commission's sugar reform will leave a sour taste in the mouth of 46 African, Caribbean and Pacific-island nations that now enjoy privileged access to the EU's sheltered market. Under the current rules, these countries can sell about 1.3m tonnes of sugar, at a price of euro524 a tonne. Under the commission's proposals, this price is due to fall to euro303, depriving them of revenues worth about euro287m. The commission has earmarked euro40m in 2006 to help some of these countries adapt, and may give more once its budget is settled for 2007 and beyond. But this is scant compensation for their loss.

Mr Mitchell reports that the beet industry got started in Europe in the early 1800s only because difficulties in the colonies disrupted the supply of cane sugar. The battle between beet and cane has raged ever since. The Africans, the Caribbean nations and the Pacific islanders are caught in the middle, but the world still has lots to gain from beet's steady retreat.

American apple growers fear Chinese invasion

Published <u>Monday, June 25, 2007</u>

GETTYSBURG, Pa. (AP) - Farmers have been growing apples here since before the Civil War, and as times have changed, they have changed with them, planting smaller trees to speed up harvests and growing popular new varieties to satisfy changing tastes.

But the growers who have made this mountainous region the core of apple growing in Pennsylvania worry that they face a new challenge that might be too big to overcome and could change their way of life.

Like farmers in the bigger apple-producing states, they are becoming increasingly anxious about the prospect of China flooding the U.S. market with their fresh apples - an event many believe is inevitable, even if it could be years away.

They saw what happened in the 1990s when Chinese apple juice concentrate made it into the United States. Prices got so low, some U.S. juice companies were forced out of the U.S. market. Growers could no longer afford to grow apples for making juice.

With the Farm Bill up for renewal this year for the first time since 2002, apple growers are pressing for an unprecedented amount of federal funding to develop technologies to make harvesting less costly and aid to develop overseas markets.

"We're facing a threat that we've never faced before in terms of their ability to come in and essentially replace every apple that we produce in this country numerically and at a much lower cost," said John Rice, a seventh-generation grower.

Rice's family today owns 1,000 acres of orchards and packs and markets apples for 50 area growers primarily in Pennsylvania's historic growing area in Adams County, on the Maryland border.

"We have to" do "whatever it takes," Rice said.

Fifteen years ago, China grew fewer apples than the United States. Today, it grows five times as many - nearly half of all apples grown in the world.

China's advantage is its cheap labor. A picker makes about 28 cents an hour, or $2 per day, according to the U.S. Apple Association. In 2005, workers in Pennsylvania made about $9 to $10 per hour, and those in Washington state about $14 per hour, the association said.

Japan plans to slap tariffs on steel imports from U.S.

Published Monday, August 1, 2005

TOKYO (AP) - Japan will slap 15 percent levies on U.S. steel imports starting Sept. 1 in retaliation for American steel industry protection measures, the trade ministry said today, turning up the heat on a long-festering dispute between the world's two largest economies.

The tariffs, which could run as high as $51 million, will target ball bearings, airplane parts and other steel products, the Ministry of Economy, Trade and Industry said.

Japan has long demanded the repeal of duties imposed by the United States on Japanese steel products under the so-called Byrd amendment, an anti-dumping law ruled illegal by the World Trade Organization.

Trade Minister Shoichi Nakagawa said Tokyo had no choice but to move after realizing there was little chance that the amendment would be repealed before the end of the fiscal year, Sept. 30.

"Therefore, the Japanese government has decided that there is a need to more effectively pressure the U.S. by implementing retaliatory measures and promoting the repeal of the amendment in Congress," he said in a statement.

The tariffs would not be imposed if the Byrd amendment - named after West Virginia Sen. Robert Byrd - were repealed by Sept. 1, trade officials said.

Neither the U.S. Embassy nor the American Chamber of Commerce in Japan had an immediate reaction.

The Japanese decision follows similar moves by the 25-nation European Union and Canada, which slapped penalty tariffs on millions of dollars' worth of U.S. imports in retaliation for the amendment on May 1.

Washington placed tariffs on hot-rolled steel from Japan, Brazil and other countries starting in 1999 on allegations that those countries were selling their products at unfairly low prices.

Passed in October 2000, the Byrd amendment imposed penalty tariffs and also awarded American companies the revenue collected by the U.S. government on those duties.

Previously, the extra border taxes went into the government's coffers instead of being turned over to U.S. companies.

Foreign companies complain not only that their products being hit with penalty tariffs but also that their U.S. competitors are getting a windfall from those tariffs.

The WTO ruled in January 2003 that the U.S. measure unlawfully protected the American steel industry. When it was not repealed by the end of that year, Japan, the European Union and six other countries won the right to impose a total of $150 million in economic sanctions against the United States.

Japanese officials have said they have the right to take countermeasures after repeatedly urging American officials to repeal the duties.

Deal's impact expected to be small yet positive

CAFTA will benefit few industries greatly.
Published Sunday, July 31, 2005

WASHINGTON (AP) - U.S. shoppers should get price breaks on shirts and pants made in Central America. American farmers and manufacturers are hoping to gain new sales in the region.

U.S. sugar growers, however, are fretting about increased competition now that Congress has passed and sent to President George W. Bush a trade deal that eliminates barriers between the United States and Costa Rica, the Dominican Republic, El Salvador, Guatemala, Honduras and Nicaragua.

Most analysts predict that the political fallout from the Central American Free Trade Agreement, which Bush plans to sign Tuesday, will outweigh the economic impact. They note that the six CAFTA countries have economies that are very small in comparison with the U.S. economy.

The debate over the pact was the most contentious free trade fight in Congress in more than a decade.

The U.S. International Trade Commission, which did the most extensive study of the agreement, found that it will have a tiny but positive impact on the U.S. economy - a gain of 0.01 percent in output in an $11 trillion economy.

Overall price breaks for U.S. consumers will be small because 80 percent of goods from the six nations already come into the U.S. duty-free under federal programs to help poor nations.

Yet the effect on some industries will be significant.

The commission estimated that after full phasing in of the agreement, U.S. exports of textiles and clothing to the six countries will increase by $802.8 million. Machinery exports will rise by $400.6 million. Auto shipments will go up by $180.4 million. Sales of wheat and other grains will climb by $157.3 million.

Total U.S. exports to the CAFTA nations will rise by $2.7 billion, or 14.8 percent, according to the study.

The value of goods sent from those countries to the United States will jump by $3.1 billion for textile and clothing shipments, and shipments of processed sugar will increase by $113.2 million. The total increase in imports will come to $2.8 billion at the time of full phase-in.

"The biggest winners from the passage of CAFTA will be the people of Central America. This will solidify the tremendous gains they have made in economic and political reforms," said Dan Griswold, head of trade studies at the Cato Institute, a libertarian think tank in Washington.

In addition to promoting the pact on foreign policy grounds, the Bush administration and Republican leaders participated in a frenzy of deal-making to win votes.

One deal meant passage of House legislation to make it easier to impose penalty tariffs on China in trade disputes.

Also, there were agreements sought by textile state lawmakers to ensure that U.S. plants now shipping yarn and fabric to Latin America, where they are made into finished clothing, will not lose out to competition from China and other low-cost suppliers.

Despite all the horse-trading, the legislation passed by only two votes, 217-215, on Thursday night after House leaders held the normal 15-minute vote open for an hour to allow more arm-twisting.

"Passing CAFTA required last-minute procedural stunts even after weeks of the president's personal attention, ... months of GOP leadership threats and goodies, and an army of corporate lobbyists," said Lori Wallach, head of Public Citizen's Global Trade Watch, a CAFTA opponent.

U.S. and China seek deal on textile quotas
Negotiations set to open in San Francisco.
Published Tuesday, August 16, 2005

WASHINGTON (AP) - Shoppers who enjoyed a sustained drop in clothing prices over the past year are likely to see markups on pants, shirts and dresses if the Bush administration gets China to agree to comprehensive limits on its clothing and textile exports.

Since a three-decade system of clothing and textile quotas expired Jan. 1, there has been a flood of clothing and textile imports entering the United States from China.

Those shipments are up 58 percent so far this year, an increase that has played a big part in pushing the cost of clothing down at an annual rate of 5.9 percent for the three months ending in June.

American textile and clothing manufacturers blame the import flood for the loss of 26,000 jobs so far this year and the closing of 19 textile plants.

They want the administration to stop the losses by re-imposing quotas on Chinese goods.

"By using its currency as an economic weapon and by pouring billions of dollars of illegal subsidies into its textile sector, the Chinese government has effectively declared war on U.S. textile producers," said Cass Johnson, president of the National Council of Textile Organizations, which is pushing the administration to reach a comprehensive deal.

U.S. and Chinese textile negotiators were scheduled today to begin two days of talks in San Francisco to see whether agreement can be reached.

Experts say America's annual clothing bill could rise $6 billion - or $20 for each U.S. consumer - if China agrees to restrain exports.

Gary Hufbauer, a trade expert at the Institute for International Economics, a Washington think tank, said that could turn out to be a low estimate, given that China's massive production capacity also affects clothing makers in other countries.

"A comprehensive trade agreement would take the downward pressure off not only for American producers but for other countries as well," Hufbauer said.

Under the rules by which China was admitted to the World Trade Organization in 2001, the United States and other countries could re-impose quotas on Chinese clothing and textile imports if shipments of the Chinese products began surging once the global quotas were removed and the increase was found to be harming the domestic industry.

Under this "safeguard" provision, the administration can cap imports in specific clothing and textile categories to growth of just 7.5 percent annually through 2008.

Rather than impose quotas on a category by category basis, the European Union in June negotiated a comprehensive arrangement with China that covered 10 categories and allowed growth in shipments of 8.5 percent to 12.5 percent annually through 2007.

The U.S. industry, while seeking a comprehensive deal as well, has branded the French agreement unacceptable, contending it allows too much growth in shipments each year and does not extend through 2008.

"No comprehensive deal is better than a bad deal," said Lloyd Wood, spokesman for the American Manufacturing Trade Action Coalition, another group representing clothing and textile manufacturers.

CAN EXTREME POVERTY BE
ELIMINATED?

BY JEFFREY D. SACHS

Market economics and globalization are lifting the bulk of humanity out of extreme poverty, but special measures are needed to help the poorest of the poor

Almost everyone who ever lived was wretchedly poor. Famine, death from childbirth, infectious disease and countless other hazards were the norm for most of history. Humanity's sad plight started to change with the Industrial Revolution, beginning around 1750. New scientific insights and technological innovations enabled a growing proportion of the global population to break free of extreme poverty.

Two and a half centuries later more than five billion of the world's 6.5 billion people can reliably meet their basic living needs and thus can be said to have escaped from the precarious conditions that once governed everyday life. One out of six inhabitants of this planet, however, still struggles daily to meet some or all of such critical requirements as adequate nutrition, uncontaminated drinking water, safe shelter and sanitation as well as access to basic health care. These people get by on $1 a day or less and are overlooked by public services for health, education and infrastructure. Every day more than

20,000 die of dire poverty, for want of food, safe drinking water, medicine or other essential needs.

For the first time in history, global economic prosperity, brought on by continuing scientific and technological progress and the self-reinforcing accumulation of wealth, has placed the world within reach of eliminating extreme poverty altogether. This prospect will seem fanciful to some, but the dramatic economic progress made by China, India and other low-income parts of Asia over the past 25 years demonstrates that it is realistic. Moreover, the predicted stabilization of the world's population toward the middle of this century will help by easing pressures on Earth's climate, ecosystems and natural resources—pressures that might otherwise undo economic gains.

Although economic growth has shown a remarkable capacity to lift vast numbers of people out of extreme poverty, progress is neither automatic nor inevitable. Market forces and free trade are not enough. Many of the poorest regions are ensnared in a

EXTREME POVERTY could become a thing of the past in a few decades if the affluent countries of the world pony up a small percentage of their wealth to help the planet's 1.1 billion indigent populations out of conditions of dire poverty. At the right, a Ghanaian village is served by a single water standpipe.

poverty trap: they lack the financial means to make the necessary investments in infrastructure, education, health care systems and other vital needs. Yet the end of such poverty is feasible if a concerted global effort is undertaken, as the nations of the world promised when they adopted the Millennium Development Goals at the United Nations Millennium Summit in 2000. A dedicated cadre of development agencies, international financial institutions, nongovernmental organizations and communities throughout the developing world already constitute a global network of expertise and goodwill to help achieve this objective.

This past January my colleagues and I on the U.N. Millennium Project published a plan to halve the rate of extreme poverty by 2015 (compared with 1990) and to achieve other quantitative targets for reducing hunger, disease and environmental degradation. In my recent book, *The End of Poverty*, I argue that a large-scale and targeted public investment effort could in fact eliminate this problem by 2025, much as smallpox was eradicated globally. This hypothesis is controversial, so I am pleased to have the opportunity to clarify its main arguments and to respond to various concerns that have been raised about it.

Beyond Business as Usual

ECONOMISTS HAVE LEARNED a great deal during the past few years about how countries develop and what roadblocks can stand in their way. A new kind of development economics needs to emerge, one that is better grounded in science—a "clinical economics" akin to modern medicine. Today's medical professionals understand that disease results from a vast array of interacting factors and conditions: pathogens, nutrition, environment, aging, individual and population genetics, lifestyle. They also know that one key to proper treatment is the ability to make an individualized diagnosis of the source of illness. Likewise, development economists need better diagnostic skills to recognize that economic pathologies have a wide variety of causes, including many outside the traditional ken of economic practice.

Public opinion in affluent countries often attributes extreme poverty to faults with the poor themselves—or at least with their governments. Race was once thought the deciding factor. Then it was culture: religious divisions and taboos, caste systems, a lack of entrepreneurship, gender inequities. Such theories have waned as societies of an ever widening range of religions and cultures have achieved relative prosperity. Moreover, certain supposedly immutable aspects of culture (such as fertility choices and gender and caste roles) in fact change, often dramatically, as societies become urban and develop economically.

Most recently, commentators have zeroed in on "poor governance," often code words for corruption. They argue that extreme poverty persists because governments fail to open up their markets, provide public services and clamp down on bribe taking. It is said that if these regimes cleaned up their acts, they, too, would flourish. Development assistance efforts have become largely a series of good governance lectures.

The availability of cross-country and time-series data now allows experts to make much more systematic analyses. Although debate continues, the weight of the evidence indicates that governance makes a difference but is not the sole determinant of economic growth. According to surveys conducted by Transparency International, business leaders actually perceive many fast-growing Asian countries to be more corrupt than some slow-growing African ones.

Geography—including natural resources, climate, topography, and proximity to trade routes and major markets—is at least as important as good governance. As early as 1776, Adam Smith argued that high transport costs inhibited devel-

CROSSROADS FOR POVERTY

THE PROBLEM:

- Much of humankind has succeeded in dragging itself out of severe poverty since the onset of the Industrial Revolution in the mid-18th century, but about 1.1 billion out of today's 6.5 billion global inhabitants are utterly destitute in a world of plenty.

- These unfortunates, who get by on less than $1 a day, have little access to adequate nutrition, safe drinking water and shelter, as well as basic sanitation and health care services. What can the developed world do to lift this huge segment of the human population out of extreme poverty?

THE PLAN:

- Doubling affluent nations' international poverty assistance to about $160 billion a year would go a long way toward ameliorating the terrible predicament faced by one in six humans. This figure would constitute about 0.5 percent of the gross national product (GNP) of the planet's rich countries. Because these investments do not include other categories of aid, such as spending on major infrastructure projects, climate change mitigation or postconflict reconstruction, donors should commit to reaching the long-standing target of 0.7 percent of GNP by 2015.

- These donations, often provided to local groups, would need to be closely monitored and audited to ensure that they are correctly targeted toward those truly in need.

Food for young African refugees

Although chronically poor people live in all regions of the world, they are concentrated in certain places. According to many studies, the problem of extreme poverty (those living on less than $1 a day) is least tractable in sub-Saharan Africa, the Andean and Central American highlands, and the landlocked nations of Central Asia. In the map below, produced by the Chronic Poverty Research Center, country size scales to the number of chronically poor people it harbors, and color indicates the income level of most impoverished inhabitants of each country. When sufficient official data were unavailable, the researchers estimated national poverty rates and numbers.

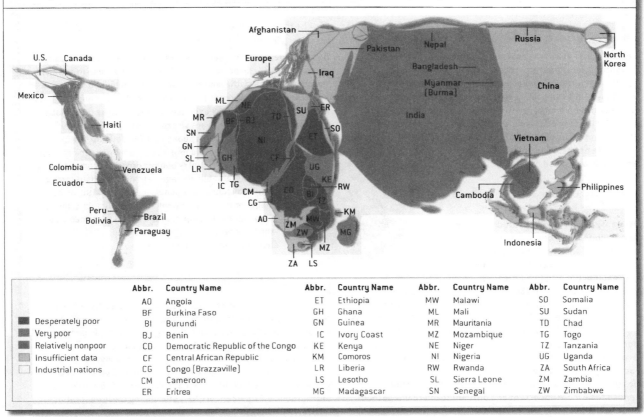

	Abbr.	Country Name	Abbr.	Country Name	Abbr.	Country Name	Abbr.	Country Name
■ Desperately poor	AO	Angola	ET	Ethiopia	MW	Malawi	SO	Somalia
■ Very poor	BF	Burkina Faso	GH	Ghana	ML	Mali	SU	Sudan
■ Relatively nonpoor	BI	Burundi	GN	Guinea	MR	Mauritania	TD	Chad
■ Insufficient data	BJ	Benin	IC	Ivory Coast	MZ	Mozambique	TG	Togo
□ Industrial nations	CD	Democratic Republic of the Congo	KE	Kenya	NE	Niger	TZ	Tanzania
	CF	Central African Republic	KM	Comoros	NI	Nigeria	UG	Uganda
	CG	Congo (Brazzaville)	LR	Liberia	RW	Rwanda	ZA	South Africa
	CM	Cameroon	LS	Lesotho	SL	Sierra Leone	ZM	Zambia
	ER	Eritrea	MG	Madagascar	SN	Senegal	ZW	Zimbabwe

SOURCE: CHRONIC POVERTY RESEARCH CENTER (WWW.CHRONICPOVERTY.ORG)

opment in the inland areas of Africa and Asia. Other geographic features, such as the heavy disease burden of the tropics, also interfere. One recent study by my Columbia University colleague Xavier Sala-i-Martin demonstrated once again that tropical countries saddled with malaria have experienced slower growth than those free from the disease. The good news is that geographic factors shape, but do not decide, a country's economic fate. Technology can offset them: drought can be fought with irrigation systems, isolation with roads and mobile telephones, diseases with preventive and therapeutic measures.

The other major insight is that although the most powerful mechanism for reducing extreme poverty is to encourage overall economic growth, a rising tide does not necessarily lift all boats. Average income can rise, but if the income is distributed unevenly the poor may benefit little, and pockets of extreme poverty may persist (especially in geographically disadvantaged regions). Moreover, growth is not simply a free-market phenomenon. It requires basic government services: infrastructure, health, education, and scientific and technological innovation. Thus, many of the recommendations of the past two decades emanating from Washington—that governments in low-income countries should cut back on their spending to make room for the private sector—miss the point. Government spending, directed at investment in critical areas, is itself a vital spur to growth, especially if its effects are to reach the poorest of the poor.

THE AUTHOR
JEFFREY D. SACHS

SACHS directs the Earth Institute at Columbia University and the United Nations Millennium Project. An economist, Sachs is well known for advising governments in Latin America, eastern Europe, the former Soviet Union, Asia and Africa on economic reforms and for his work with international agencies to promote poverty reduction, disease control and debt reduction in poor countries. A native of Detroit, he received his B.A., M.A. and Ph.D. degrees from Harvard University.

GLOBALIZATION, POVERTY AND FOREIGN AID

Average citizens in affluent nations often have many questions about the effects of economic globalization on rich and poor nations and about how developing countries spend the aid they receive. Here are a few brief answers:

Is globalization making the rich richer and the poor poorer?

Generally, the answer is no. Economic globalization is supporting very rapid advances of many impoverished economies, notably in Asia. International trade and foreign investment inflows have been major factors in China's remarkable economic growth during the past quarter century and in India's fast economic growth since the early 1990s. The poorest of the poor, notably in sub-Saharan Africa, are not held back by globalization; they are largely bypassed by it.

Is poverty the result of exploitation of the poor by the rich?

Affluent nations have repeatedly plundered and exploited poor countries through slavery, colonial rule and unfair trade practices. Yet it is perhaps more accurate to say that exploitation is the result of poverty (which leaves impoverished countries vulnerable to abuse) rather than the cause of it. Poverty is generally the result of low productivity per worker, which reflects poor health, lack of job-market skills, patchiness of infrastructure (roads, power plants, utility lines, shipping ports), chronic malnutrition and the like. Exploitation has played a role in producing some of these conditions, but deeper factors (geographic isolation, endemic disease, ecological destruction, challenging conditions for food production) have tended to be more important and difficult to overcome without external help.

Will higher incomes in poor countries mean lower incomes in rich countries?

By and large, economic development is a positive-sum process, meaning that all can partake in it without causing some to suffer. In the past 200 years, the world as a whole has achieved a massive increase in economic output rather than a shift in economic output to one region at the expense of another. To be sure, global environmental constraints are already starting to impose themselves. As today's poor countries develop, the climate, fisheries and forests are coming under increased strain. Overall global economic growth is compatible with sustainable management of the ecosystems on which all humans depend—indeed, wealth can be good for the environment—but only if public policy and technologies encourage sound practices and the necessary investments are made in environmental sustainability.

Do U.S. private contributions make up for the low levels of U.S. official aid?

Some have claimed that while the U.S. government budget provides relatively little assistance to the poorest countries, the private sector makes up the gap. In fact, the Organization for Economic Cooperation and Development has estimated that private foundations and nongovernmental organizations give roughly $6 billion a year in international assistance, or 0.05 percent of U.S. gross national product (GNP). In that case, total U.S. international aid is around 0.21 percent of GNP—still among the lowest ratios of all donor nations. —J.D.S.

The Poverty Trap

SO WHAT DO THESE INSIGHTS tell us about the region most afflicted by poverty today, Africa? Fifty years ago tropical Africa was roughly as rich as subtropical and tropical Asia. As Asia boomed, Africa stagnated. Special geographic factors have played a crucial role.

Foremost among these is the existence of the Himalaya Mountains, which produce southern Asia's monsoon climate and vast river systems. Well-watered farmlands served as the starting points for Asia's rapid escape from extreme poverty during the past five decades. The Green Revolution of the 1960s and 1970s introduced high-yield grains, irrigation and fertilizers, which ended the cycle of famine, disease and despair.

It also freed a significant proportion of the labor force to seek manufacturing jobs in the cities. Urbanization, in turn, spurred growth, not only by providing a home for industry and innovation but also by prompting greater investment in a healthy and skilled labor force. Urban residents cut their fertility rates and thus were able to spend more for the health, nutri-

tion and education of each child. City kids went to school at a higher rate than their rural cousins. And with the emergence of urban infrastructure and public health systems, city populations became less disease-prone than their counterparts in the countryside, where people typically lack safe drinking water, modern sanitation, professional health care and protection from vector-borne ailments such as malaria.

Africa did not experience a green revolution. Tropical Africa lacks the massive floodplains that facilitate the large-scale and low-cost irrigation found in Asia. Also, its rainfall is highly variable, and impoverished farmers have been unable to purchase fertilizer. The initial Green Revolution research featured crops, especially paddy rice and wheat, not widely grown in Africa (high-yield varieties suitable for it have been developed in recent years, but they have not yet been disseminated sufficiently). The continent's food production per person has actually been falling, and Africans' caloric intake is the lowest in the world; food insecurity is rampant. Its labor force has remained tethered to subsistence agriculture.

EMILY HARRISON

140

Compounding its agricultural woes, Africa bears an overwhelming burden of tropical diseases. Because of climate and the endemic mosquito species, malaria is more intensively transmitted in Africa than anywhere else. And high transport costs isolate Africa economically. In East Africa, for example, the rainfall is greatest in the interior of the continent, so most people live there, far from ports and international trade routes.

Much the same situation applies to other impoverished parts of the world, notably the Andean and Central American highlands and the landlocked countries of Central Asia. Being economically isolated, they are unable to attract much foreign investment (other than for the extraction of oil, gas and precious minerals). Investors tend to be dissuaded by the high transport costs associated with the interior regions. Rural areas therefore remain stuck in a vicious cycle of poverty, hunger, illness and illiteracy. Impoverished areas lack adequate internal savings to make the needed investments because most households live hand to mouth. The few high-income families, who do accumulate savings, park them overseas rather than at home. This capital flight includes not only financial capital but also the human variety, in the form of skilled workers—doctors, nurses, scientists and engineers, who frequently leave in search of improved economic opportunities abroad. The poorest countries are often, perversely, net exporters of capital.

Put Money Where Mouths Are

THE TECHNOLOGY TO OVERCOME these handicaps and jump-start economic development exists. Malaria can be controlled using bed nets, indoor pesticide spraying and improved medicines. Drought-prone countries in Africa with nutrient-depleted soils can benefit enormously from drip irrigation and greater use of fertilizers. Landlocked countries can be connected by paved highway networks, airports and fiber-optic cables. All these projects cost money, of course.

Many larger countries, such as China, have prosperous regions that can help support their own lagging areas. Coastal eastern China, for instance, is now financing massive public investments in western China. Most of today's successfully developing countries, especially smaller ones, received at least some backing from external donors at crucial times. The critical scientific innovations that formed the underpinnings of the Green Revolution were bankrolled by the Rockefeller Foundation, and the spread of these technologies in India and elsewhere in Asia was funded by the U.S. and other donor governments and international development institutions.

We in the U.N. Millennium Project have listed the investments required to help today's impoverished regions cover basic needs in health, education, water, sanitation, food production, roads and other key areas. We have put an approximate price tag on that assistance and estimated how much could be financed by poor households themselves and by domestic institutions. The remaining cost is the "financing gap" that international donors need to make up.

For tropical Africa, the total investment comes to $110 per person a year. To place this into context, the average income

JEN CHRISTIANSEN: SOURCE: WORLD BANK GROUP'S WORLD DEVELOPMENT INDICATORS (WWW.WORLDBANK.ORG/DATA/WDI2005/WDITEXT/SECTION1_1_1.HTM)

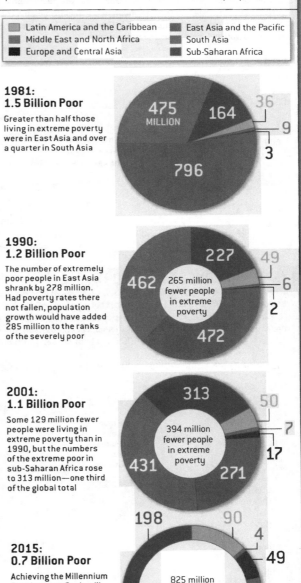

EXTREME POVERTY: WHERE WE STAND

The number of people mired in the lowest depths of poverty has shrunk since the early 1980s, as the global economy has grown stronger. But these gains were concentrated in East Asia, leaving behind more than a billion unfortunates in sub-Saharan Africa, Central Asia and the mountainous parts of Central America and the Andean region. A determined push to help those lagging populations during the coming decade could cut the ranks of poor in half. The numbers below indicate millions of people.

Latin America and the Caribbean
Middle East and North Africa
Europe and Central Asia
East Asia and the Pacific
South Asia
Sub-Saharan Africa

1981:
1.5 Billion Poor
Greater than half those living in extreme poverty were in East Asia and over a quarter in South Asia

475 MILLION 164 36 9 3 796

1990:
1.2 Billion Poor
The number of extremely poor people in East Asia shrank by 278 million. Had poverty rates there not fallen, population growth would have added 285 million to the ranks of the severely poor

227 49 6 2 462 472 265 million fewer people in extreme poverty

2001:
1.1 Billion Poor
Some 129 million fewer people were living in extreme poverty than in 1990, but the numbers of the extreme poor in sub-Saharan Africa rose to 313 million—one third of the global total

313 50 7 17 431 271 394 million fewer people in extreme poverty

2015:
0.7 Billion Poor
Achieving the Millennium Development Goals will mean that by 2015 more than 500 million people will be lifted out of extreme poverty as compared with 1990 and that millions of lives will be saved

198 90 4 49 317 825 million fewer people in extreme poverty

At the United Nations Millennium Summit in 2000, the nations of the world promised to make the investments necessary to help today's impoverished regions improve their residents' welfare in key areas, including health, education, water, sanitation and food production. The U.N. specified eight broad Millennium Development Goals (MDG) to reduce extreme poverty substantially across the globe by 2015. The data on these two pages illustrate the challenges of meeting those goals. Measurement of progress is based on statistical levels that existed in 1990.

GOAL 1 ERADICATE EXTREME POVERTY AND HUNGER

Target: Halve the proportion of people living on less than $1 a day and the proportion of those who suffer chronic hunger.

Status: Between 1990 and 2001, the fraction of the populations in sub-Saharan Africa, Latin America and the Caribbean living in extreme poverty remained stagnant and, ominously, increased in Central Asia. Food intake is rising, but hunger is still widespread in several regions.

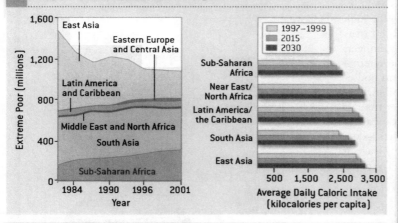

GOAL 2 ACHIEVE UNIVERSAL PRIMARY EDUCATION

Target: Ensure that by 2015 all children complete a full course of primary education.

GOAL 3 PROMOTE GENDER EQUALITY AND EMPOWER WOMEN

Target: Eliminate gender disparity in primary, secondary and tertiary education by 2015.

Status: Education is probably the best way to promote gender equality. The greatest challenges are in sub-Saharan Africa, where overall school completion rates have hovered around 50 percent. Women and girls fare even worse, as shown below by the ratio of literate females to males on the African continent.

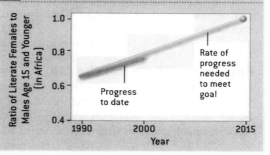

GOAL 4 REDUCE CHILD MORTALITY

Target: Reduce by two thirds the mortality rate of children younger than five years.

Status: Child mortality rates fell in every region except the former Soviet republics in the Commonwealth of Independent States (CIS), but rates remain high in sub-Saharan Africa and in South Asia. For comparison, the child mortality rate in high-income countries in 2000 was about six per 1,000 births.

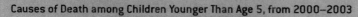

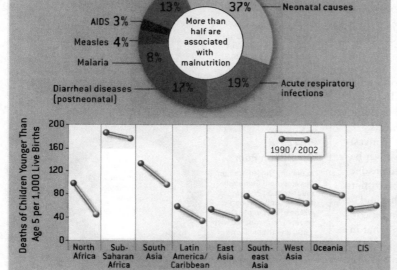

GOAL 5 IMPROVE MATERNAL HEALTH

Target: Reduce by 75 percent the maternal mortality rate by 2015.

Status: Maternal mortality rates remain shockingly high in every developing region of the world. Increasing the proportion of deliveries attended by skilled health workers will be critical to lowering maternal mortality.

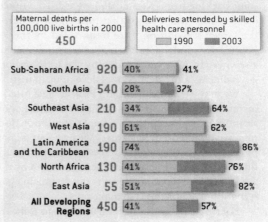

SARA BEARDSLEY (*data compilation*); JEN CHRISTIANSEN (*illustrations*); SOURCES: GOAL 1: WWW.WORLDBANK.ORG/DATA/WDI2005/WDITEXT/SECTION1_1_1.HTM (*graph*); WWW.FAO.ORG/DOCREP/007/Y5650E/Y5650E04.HTM (*bar chart*); GOALS 2 AND 3: *ACHIEVING THE MILLENNIUM DEVELOPMENT GOALS IN AFRICA*, JUNE 2002 (*graph*); GOAL 4: *THE MDG REPORT 2005* (*pie chart*); HTTP://UNSTATS.UN.ORG/UNSD/MI/MI_COVERFINAL.HTM (*line graph*); GOAL 5: *THE MDG REPORT 2005* (*bar chart*)

GOAL 6 COMBAT HIV/AIDS, MALARIA AND OTHER DISEASES

Targets: Halt and begin to reverse the spread of HIV/AIDS. Slow the spread of malaria and other diseases.

Status: HIV, now affecting about 40 million people, is widespread in parts of sub-Saharan Africa and poses a serious threat to other developing regions. Meanwhile malaria kills around three million people a year, mostly in Africa, the vast majority of them children. In recent years, the distribution of mosquito nets has expanded, but hundreds of millions in malarious regions still need nets.

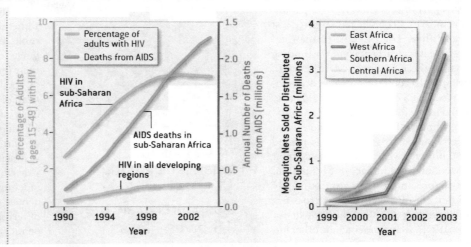

GOAL 7 ENSURE ENVIRONMENTAL SUSTAINABILITY

Target: Halve by 2015 the proportion of people without sustainable access to safe drinking water and basic sanitation.

Status: With the exception of sub-Saharan Africa, access to drinking water in urban areas is generally relatively high, although rural access remains limited. Low availability of sanitation services in sub-Saharan African and South Asia contributes to widespread diarrheal disease.

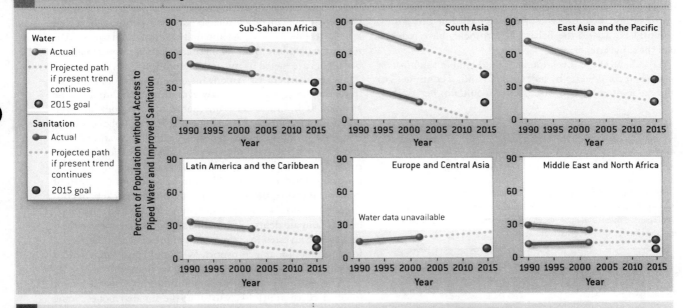

GOAL 8 DEVELOP A GLOBAL PARTNERSHIP FOR DEVELOPMENT

Target: Address the special needs of the least developed countries (including more generous development assistance).

Status: Rich countries have repeatedly pledged to give 0.7 percent of their national income as foreign aid, yet 17 of 22 donors have failed to reach that target. Some progress has occurred, however: European Union countries recently committed to attaining the 0.7 percent mark by 2015. Meanwhile other donors claim that poor countries are too corrupt to achieve economic growth. The table at the right helps to dispel that myth; in fact, many fast-growing Asian economies have higher levels of perceived corruption than some slow-growing African ones.

CORRUPTION AND ECONOMIC GROWTH

		Rank of perceived corruption levels (lower means less corrupt)	Average yearly percent growth in GDP per capita, 1980–2000
Sub-Saharan Africa	Ghana	70	0.3
	Senegal	76	0.5
	Mali	78	−0.5
	Malawi	83	0.2
East Asia	India	83	3.5
	Pakistan	92	2.4
	Indonesia	122	3.5
	Bangladesh	133	2.0

GOAL 6: *THE MDG REPORT 2005 (graphs)*; GOAL 7: *GLOBAL MONITORING REPORT 2005: MDG: FROM CONSENSUS TO MOMENTUM (data)*; GOAL 8: *GLOBAL CORRUPTION REPORT, BY TRANSPARENCY INTERNATIONAL, 2004 (table)*

in this part of the world is $350 per annum, most or all of which is required just to stay alive. The full cost of the total investment is clearly beyond the funding reach of these countries. Of the $110, perhaps $40 could be financed domestically, so that $70 per capita would be required in the form of international aid.

Adding it all up, the total requirement for assistance across the globe is around $160 billion a year, double the current rich-country aid budget of $80 billion. This figure amounts to approximately 0.5 percent of the combined gross national product (GNP) of the affluent donor nations. It does not include other humanitarian projects such as postwar Iraqi reconstruction or Indian Ocean tsunami relief. To meet these needs as well, a reasonable figure would be 0.7 percent of GNP, which is what all donor countries have long promised but few have fulfilled. Other organizations, including the International Monetary Fund, the World Bank and the British government, have reached much the same conclusion.

We believe these investments would enable the poorest countries to cut poverty by half by 2015 and, if continued, to eliminate it altogether by 2025. They would not be "welfare

Hungry children in Sudan

When polled, Americans greatly overestimate how much foreign aid the U.S. gives—by as much as 30 times.

payments" from rich to poor but instead something far more important and durable. People living above mere subsistence levels would be able to save for their futures; they could join the virtuous cycle of rising incomes, savings and technological inflows. We would be giving a billion people a hand up instead of a handout.

If rich nations fail to make these investments, they will be called on to provide emergency assistance more or less indefinitely. They will face famine, epidemics, regional conflicts and the spread of terrorist havens. And they will condemn not only the impoverished countries but themselves as well to chronic political instability, humanitarian emergencies and security risks.

The debate is now shifting from the basic diagnosis of extreme poverty and the calculations of financing needs to the practical matter of how assistance can best be delivered. Many people believe that aid efforts failed in the past and that care is needed to avoid the repetition of failure. Some of these concerns are well grounded, but others are fueled by misunderstandings.

When pollsters ask Americans how much foreign aid they think the U.S. gives, they greatly overestimate the amount—by as much as 30 times. Believing that so much money has been donated and so little has been done with it, the public concludes that these programs have "failed." The reality is rather different. U.S. official assistance to sub-Saharan Africa has been running at $2 billion to $4 billion a year, or roughly $3 to $6 for every African. Most of this aid has come in the form of "technical cooperation" (which goes into the pockets of consultants), food contributions for famine victims and the cancellation of unpaid debts. Little of this support has come in a form that can be invested in systems that improve health, nutrition, food production and transport. We should give foreign aid a fair chance before deciding whether it works or not.

A second common misunderstanding concerns the extent to which corruption is likely to eat up the donated money. Some foreign aid in the past has indeed ended up in the equivalent of Swiss bank accounts. That happened when the funds were provided for geopolitical reasons rather than development; a good example was U.S. support for the corrupt regime of Mobutu Sese Seko of Zaire (now the Democratic Republic of the Congo) during part of the cold war. When assistance has been targeted at development rather than political goals, the outcomes have been favorable, ranging from the Green Revolution to the eradication of smallpox and the recent near-eradication of polio.

The aid package we advocate would be directed toward those countries with a reasonable degree of good governance and operational transparency. In Africa, these countries include Ethiopia, Ghana, Mali, Mozambique, Senegal and Tan-

FOREIGN AID: HOW SHOULD THE MONEY BE SPENT?

Here is a breakdown of the needed investment for three typical low-income African countries to help them achieve the Millennium Development Goals. For all nations given aid, the average total annual assistance per person would come to around $110 a year. These investments would be financed by both foreign aid and the countries themselves.

Investment Area	Average per Year between 2005–2015 ($ per capita)		
	Ghana	Tanzania	Uganda
Hunger	7	8	6
Education	19	14	15
Gender equality	3	3	3
Health	25	35	34
Water supply and sanitation	8	7	5
Improving slum conditions	2	3	2
Energy	15	16	12
Roads	10	22	20
Other	10	10	10
Total	100	117	106

Calculated from data from Investing in Development (U.N. Millennium Project, Earthscan Publications, 2005). Numbers do not sum to totals because of rounding.

Mexico City

"RICH MAN ON TOP, poor man below" describes the state of human society since the dawn of civilization, but the realization that all people on this planet are profoundly interdependent means that for the sake of our future, no one—not even the poorest among us—can be left behind.

zania. The money would not be merely thrown at them. It would be provided according to a detailed and monitored plan, and new rounds of financing would be delivered only as the work actually got done. Much of the funds would be given directly to villages and towns to minimize the chances of their getting diverted by central governments. All these programs should be closely audited.

Western society tends to think of foreign aid as money lost. But if supplied properly, it is an investment that will one day yield huge returns, much as U.S. assistance to western Europe and East Asia after World War II did. By prospering, today's impoverished countries will wean themselves from endless charity. They will contribute to the international advance of science, technology and trade. They will escape political instability, which leaves many of them vulnerable to violence, narcotics trafficking, civil war and even terrorist takeover. Our own security will be bolstered as well. As U.N. Secretary-General Kofi Annan wrote earlier this year: "There will be no development without security, and no security without development." 𝕊𝔸

MORE TO
EXPLORE

Institutions Matter, but Not for Everything. Jeffrey D. Sachs in *Finance and Development (IMF)*, Vol. 40, No. 2, pages 38–41; June 2003. www.sachs.earth.columbia.edu

Determinants of Long-Term Growth: A Bayesian Averaging of Classical Estimates (BACE) Approach. X. Sala-i-Martin, Germot Doppelhofer and Ronald I. Miller in *American Economic Review*, Vol. 94, No. 4, pages 813–835; September 2004.

Ending Africa's Poverty Trap. J. D. Sachs, J. W. McArthur, G. Schmidt-Traub, M. Kruk, C. Bahadur, M. Faye and G. McCord in *Brookings Papers on Economic Activity*, Vol. 1: *2004*, pages 117–216. www.sachs.earth.columbia.edu

The Development Challenge. J. D. Sachs in *Foreign Affairs*, Vol. 84, No. 2, pages 78–90; March/April 2005. www.sachs.earth.columbia.edu

The End of Poverty: Economic Possibilities for Our Time. J. D. Sachs. Penguin Press, 2005. www.earth.columbia.edu/endofpoverty

Investing in Development: A Practical Plan to Achieve the Millennium Development Goals. United Nations Millennium Project, 2005. www.unmillenniumproject.org

Profits over people

Sep 27th 2001
From The Economist print edition

Critics argue that globalisation hurts workers. Are they right?

THE liberty that makes economic integration possible is desirable in itself. In addition, advocates of globalisation argue, integration is good for people in material terms—that is why free people choose it. Sceptics disagree on both points: globalisation militates against liberty and democracy, they say, and while it makes some people who are already rich even richer, it does this by keeping the poor in poverty. After all, globalisation is merely capitalism writ large. A later chapter of this survey will deal with the implications of globalisation for democracy. But first, is it true that globalisation harms the poor?

In a narrow sense, the answer is yes: it does harm some of the poor. Free trade and foreign direct investment may take jobs from workers (including low-paid workers) in the advanced industrial economies and give them to cheaper workers in poor countries. Thanks to the North American Free-Trade Agreement (NAFTA), for instance, there are no tariffs or investment restrictions to stop an American manufacturer closing an old factory in the United States and opening a new one in Mexico.

Sceptics score this strategy as a double crime. The rich-country workers, who were probably on low wages by local standards to begin with, are out of work. That increase in the local supply of labour drives down other wages. Meanwhile, the poor-country workers are drawn into jobs that exploit them. How do you know that the poor-country workers are being exploited? Because they are being paid less, often much less, than their rich-country counterparts got before trade opened up—and in all likelihood they are working longer hours in shabbier premises as well. The only gain from this kind of trade, the indictment continues, accrues to the owners of the companies who have shifted their operations from low-wage factories in industrialised countries to poverty-wage factories in the south.

Some of this is true. Trade displaces workers in the industrialised countries; other things equal, this will have some depressing effect on the wages of other workers; and pay and conditions in developing-country factories are likely to be worse than in their rich-country counterparts. But whereas the displaced rich-country workers are plainly worse off than they were before, the newly employed poor-country workers are plainly better off. They must be, because they have chosen to take those jobs.

As for profits, yes, that is the spur for moving production to a lower-wage area. But no company can expect to hang on to this windfall for long, because it will be competed away as other companies do the same thing and cut their prices. That lowering of prices is crucial in understanding the broader benefits of the change. It is what makes consumers at large—including poor consumers—better off, raising real incomes in the aggregate.

Altogether, given freer trade, both rich-country and poor-country living standards will rise

What about the rich-country workers who are not displaced, but whose wages may nonetheless come under downward pressure? It is hard to generalise. On the one hand, their wages may fall, or fail to rise as quickly as they would have done otherwise; on the other, they benefit from lower prices along with everybody else. On balance, you would expect that some will lose, some will gain, and some will be about as well off as they were before. In developing countries, the labour-market side of this process will tend to work in the other direction. The increase in demand for poor-country labour ought to push up wages even for workers who are not employed in the new trade-related jobs.

So capitalism-globalisation is not mainly concerned with shifting income from workers to investors, as the sceptics maintain. Rather, it makes some workers worse off while making others (including the poorest ones of all, to begin with) better off. And in the aggregate it makes consumers (that is, people with or without a job) better off as well. Altogether, given freer trade, both rich-country and poor-country living standards rise. That gives governments more to spend on welfare, education and other public services.

Changing gear

Note that all this counts only the so-called static gains from trade: the effects of a once-and-for-all shift in the pattern of production and consumption. Modern economics also emphasises the importance of dynamic gains, arising especially from the economies of scale that freer trade makes possible. The aggregate long-term gain for rich and poor countries alike is likely to be far bigger than the simple arithmetic would suggest.

Moreover, few displaced rich-country workers are likely to be permanently out of work. Most will move to other jobs. Also, new jobs will be created by the economic opportunities that trade opens up. Overall, trade neither reduces the number of jobs in the economy nor increases them. In principle, there is no reason to expect employment or unemployment to be any higher or lower in an open economy than in a closed economy—or, for that matter, in a rich economy as compared to a poor economy. Still, none of this is to deny that the displaced rich-country workers lose out: many, perhaps most, of those who find alternative work will be paid less than they were before.

In thinking through the economic theory of liberal trade, it is helpful to draw a parallel with technological progress. Trade allows a country to shift its pattern of production in such a way that, after exporting those goods it does not want and importing those it does, it can consume more without there having been any increase in its available resources. Advancing technology allows a country to do something very similar: to make more with less. You can think of trade as a machine (with no running costs or depreciation): goods you can make cheaply go in at one end, and goods that would cost you a lot more to make come out at the other. The logic of protectionism would demand that such a miraculous machine be dismantled and the blueprint destroyed, in order to save jobs.

No question, technological progress, just like trade, creates losers as well as winners. The Industrial Revolution involved hugely painful economic and social dislocations—though nearly everybody would now agree that the gains in human welfare were worth the cost. Even in far milder periods of economic transformation, such as today's, new machines and new methods make old skills obsolete. The Luddites understood that, which made them more coherent on the subject than some of today's sceptics, who oppose integration but not technological progress. Logically, they should oppose both or neither.

Politically, of course, it is essential to keep the two separate. Sceptics can expect to win popular support for the view that freer trade is harmful, but could never hope to gain broad backing for the idea that, so far as possible, technological progress should be brought to a halt. Still, it might be better if the sceptics concentrated not on attacking trade as such, but on demanding help for the workers who suffer as a result of economic progress, whether the cause is trade or technology.

Winners and losers

So much for the basic theory. What does the evidence say? For the moment, concentrate on the prospects for workers in rich countries such as the United States (the next section will look in more detail at workers in poor countries). By and large, the evidence agrees with the theory—though things, as always, get more complicated the closer you look.

A first qualification is that most outward foreign direct investment (FDI) from rich countries goes not to poor countries at all, but to other rich countries. In the late 1990s, roughly 80% of the stock of America's outward FDI was in Canada, Japan and Western Europe, and nearly all of the rest was in middle-income developing countries such as Brazil, Mexico, Indonesia and Thailand. The poorest developing countries accounted for 1% of America's outward FDI (see table 1). Capital is hardly flooding to the world's poorest countries—more's the pity, from their point of view.

Where the money goes 1

America's stock of direct investment overseas, 2000

	$bn	% of total
High-income countries	982.8	81.0
Middle-income countries	218.1	18.0
Low-income countries	12.2	1.0
All countries	1,213.1	100.0

Sources: Edward M. Graham, Institute for International Economics; *The Economist*

The notion that outward FDI reduces the demand for labour in the sending country and increases it in the receiving one needs to be revised as well. It was based on the assumption that when rich-country firms invest in poor countries, rich-country exports (and jobs) are replaced by poor-country domestic production. In fact, evidence from the United States and other countries suggests that outward FDI does not displace exports, it creates them: FDI and exports are, in the jargon, net complements. This is because the affiliates of multinationals trade with each other. Figures for 1995 show that America's exports to its foreign-owned affiliates actually exceeded its imports from them (see table 2).

Before FDI, the companies exported finished goods. After FDI, they ship, let us suppose, a mixture of finished goods and intermediate goods. The intermediate goods will be used to make finished goods in the FDI-receiving country. The corresponding increase in exports of intermediate goods outweighs the fall, if any, in exports of finished goods. Overall, then, exports from the FDI-sending country rise. At the same time, the sending country's imports rise as well, partly because the affiliate sells goods back to the sending country. Exports rise, which increases the demand for labour; and imports rise, which decreases the demand for labour.

What does all this mean for the labour markets of the rich, FDI-sending countries? Jobs are created in exporting industries which will tend to be relatively high-paying, but overall employment will not rise, for reasons explained earlier. For every job created, another one somewhere else will be destroyed. The jobs that go will tend to be in industries that compete with imports. On average, studies suggest, those jobs pay lower wages.

Keeping it in the family [2]

American exports to, and imports from, American-owned affiliates abroad, 1995, $bn

	Intra-company	Inter-company	Total
All countries			
Exports	145.5	24.5	170.0
Imports	123.9	19.4	143.3
Balance	21.6	5.1	26.7
High-income countries			
Exports	129.0	20.8	149.9
Imports	94.0	15.1	109.1
Balance	35.0	5.7	40.7
Middle-income countries			
Exports	28.9	5.4	34.3
Imports	31.5	1.9	33.4
Balance	-2.6	3.5	0.8
Low-income countries			
Exports	1.6	0.2	1.8
Imports	1.8	0.4	2.2
Balance	-0.2	-0.2	-0.4

Source: Edward M. Graham, Institute for International Economics

On balance, then, you could say that the economy has gained: it now has more higher-paying jobs and fewer lower-paying jobs. A policy which attempted to resist a shift like that would be difficult to defend on its merits. Unfortunately, though, the people getting the higher-paying jobs are not necessarily the ones who have lost the lower-paying jobs. Because of the boost to exports, the overall effect of outward FDI on jobs and wages in the sending country is more benign than the simple theory suggests—but some people still lose.

Another implication of the shift in the demand for labour in the rich, FDI-sending countries is a possible widening of income inequality. In a country such as the United States, the combined action of trade and capital flows is likely to raise the demand for relatively skilled labour and lower the demand for relatively unskilled labour. Some hitherto low-wage workers may succeed in trading up to higher-paid jobs, but many others will be left behind in industries where wages are falling. In this scenario, high and average wages may be rising, but wages at the bottom may be falling—and that means greater inequality.

You would expect to see a similar pattern in an economy that was undergoing rapid technological change. So in the United States, which fits that description better than most in the 1990s, you could say that economic integration may have added to the already powerful pressures that were acting to increase inequality. Since those same pressures were raising living standards in the aggregate—not just for the very rich— it would be a misleading summary, but not a false one.

Explaining inequality

Of these two unequalising forces, economic integration and technological progress, which is likely to be more powerful? If it were the latter, that would raise doubts over the sceptics' focus on globalisation as the primary cause of social friction. The evidence suggests that technology is indeed much the more powerful driver of inequality. One study, by William Cline, estimated that technological change was perhaps five times more powerful in widening inequality in America between 1973 and 1993 than trade (including trade due to FDI), and that trade accounted for only around six percentage points of all the unequalising forces at work during that period. That is just one study, but it is not unrepresentative. The consensus is that integration has exerted a far milder influence on wage inequality than technology.

Mr Cline's study in fact deserves a closer look. It found to begin with that the total increase in the ratio of skilled to unskilled wages in the two decades to the early 1990s was 18%. This was the net result of opposing influences. An increase in the supply of skilled labour relative to the supply of unskilled labour acted to equalise wages, by making unskilled labour relatively scarce. By itself, this would have driven the wage ratio down by 40% (see table 3). But at the same time a variety of unequalising forces pushed the ratio up by 97%, resulting in the net increase of 18%. These unequalising forces included not just trade and technology, but also immigration, reductions in the real value of the minimum wage, and de-unionisation.

Two things strike you about the numbers. First, trade has been relatively unimportant in widening income inequality. Second, this effect is overwhelmed not just by technology but also by the main force operating in the opposite, equalising, direction: education and training.

This means that globalisation sceptics are missing the point if they are worried mainly about the effect of integration on rich-country losers: trade is a much smaller factor than technology. Some people in rich countries do lose out from the combination of trade and technology. The remedy lies with education and training, and with help in changing jobs. Spending in those areas, together perhaps with more generous and effective help for people forced to change jobs by economic growth, addresses the problem directly—and in a way that adds to society's economic resources rather than subtracting from them, as efforts to hold back either technological progress or trade would do.

Getting less equal 3

Illustrative sources of increase in the ratio of skilled to unskilled wages in the United States 1973-93, %

A. Equalising forces

Increase in stock of skilled relative to unskilled labour	-40

B. Unequalising forces

Trade:	7
Lower transport and communication costs	3
Liberalisation	3
Outsourcing	1
Immigration	2
Falling minimum wage	5
Deunionisation	3
Skill-biased technological change	29
Other unexplained	29
TOTAL	**97**

C. Net effect	**18**

Note: Percentages for unequalising forces must be chained, not added, to equal total unequalising effect. Similarly, "A" and "B" must be chained to calculate "C".

Source: William R. Cline, Institute for International Economics

The Brookings Institution
POLICY BRIEF

April 2004   Policy Brief #132

"Offshoring" Service Jobs: Bane or Boon — and What to Do?

LAEL BRAINARD AND ROBERT E. LITAN

Americans worry the economy is permanently shedding jobs and compressing wages, not only in manufacturing but also now in services once assumed immune to foreign competition. The digitization of information and expanded bandwidth abroad are enabling companies to outsource to low-wage countries services ranging from routine call center work to higher-value software programming, medical diagnosis, and research and analytical activities.

At a call center in Bangalore, India, employees provide service support to international customers.

The offshoring debate comes during a recovery with unusually low job creation, causing anxiety about employment and trade. Concern runs across political and demographic lines, prompting calls for measures to slow down or even halt offshoring.

The nation still has a lot to learn about offshoring because existing data are incomplete or contradictory. Economic theory and past performance suggest that although offshoring provides overall economic gains, it also is redistributive, with affected workers facing possible job loss and wage pressures. The challenges are to ensure that American workers have the critical skills to compete successfully in the global economy, that America remains the most attractive location for high value services and manufacturing, and that the playing field does not artificially induce U.S. firms to go abroad. Most immediately, lawmakers must address the serious challenges faced by permanently displaced workers.

The Brookings Institution

1775 Massachusetts Ave., N.W.
Washington, DC 20036

SERVICES OFFSHORING: HOW MUCH, HOW FAST?

Despite the headlines, we know surprisingly little about how many jobs have moved offshore in the recent past, let alone how many are likely to do so in the future. Goldman Sachs estimates that offshoring has accounted for roughly half a million layoffs in the past three years. Looking forward, perhaps

All Policy Briefs are available on the Brookings website at www.brookings.edu.

Lael Brainard is director
of the Initiative on Poverty
and the Global Economy
and New Century Chair
in International Economics
at Brookings.

Robert Litan is a senior
fellow in Economic Studies
at Brookings and vice
president for research
and policy at the
Kauffman Foundation.

the best-known projection is by Forrester, an information technology consulting firm, which expects the number of U.S. jobs outsourced to grow from about 400,000 in 2004 to 3.3 million by 2015. If this estimate turns out to be accurate, then offshoring could result in roughly 250,000 layoffs a year.

How should we think about that number? It is small relative to total U.S. employment of 137 million, and accounts for less than 2 percent of the roughly 15 million Americans who involuntarily lose their jobs each year. But to workers who lose their jobs, and to the far larger number of workers who worry that they will lose theirs, the foreign outsourcing total, whatever it is, resonates powerfully. Indeed, a recent study by Ashok Deo Bardhan and Cynthia A. Kroll at the University of California, Berkeley, suggests that up to 14 million Americans now work in occupations—including financial analysts, medical technicians, paralegals, and computer and math professionals—that could reasonably be considered "at risk."

Gathering more accurate official data about the extent of offshoring may be difficult. The data on services collected by the Bureau of Economic Analysis, for example, do not show any noticeable upticks in net imports in the services where outsourcing is believed to be prevalent—a finding that raises questions about the accuracy of those numbers.

Meanwhile, the Labor Department surveys employers regularly, asking if they have had significant layoffs attributable to

moving offshore. But firms are reluctant to offer such information, and without extensive (and expensive) verification of their survey responses, Washington is unlikely to get a good handle on the real numbers any time soon.

THE ECONOMIC THEORY OF OFFSHORING

Economic theory points to two quite robust conclusions about the likely economic impact of offshoring. Overall, offshoring will offer economic gains. But some American workers, companies, and possibly communities will just as surely lose out in the process.

Offshoring is closely related to technological advance: both are driven by competitive pressures to reduce costs and both result in displacement of existing jobs. Productivity gains and the displacement of existing jobs associated with technological advance have been features of the U.S. economy since its inception. Indeed, manufacturing productivity has been increasing roughly 3.5 percent per year over the last two decades, which helps explain why the share of U.S. workers engaged in producing "things" has declined significantly, although the pace has been very uneven.

International trade works much the same way. Economists such as Catherine Mann of the Institute for International Economics and, more recently, the President's Council of Economic Advisers point to the overall benefits of offshoring to the U.S. economy. They typically argue that it helps lower costs and prices. A recent study by the consulting firm

McKinsey and Company estimates that the net cost savings of moving some jobs offshore is about 50 percent. This is far lower than the wage differential between U.S. and foreign workers, which sometimes runs from 80 percent to 90 percent because of costs incurred for coordination and telecommunications. Nonetheless, it is still sizable. In turn, lower inflation and higher productivity allow the Federal Reserve to run a more accommodative monetary policy, meaning that overall and over time the economy will grow faster, creating the conditions for higher overall employment. Catherine Mann has estimated that GDP growth would have been lower by 0.3 percent a year between 1995 and 2002 without foreign outsourcing of jobs in information technology.

Foreign outsourcing may also accelerate the formation of innovative products and services—an effect that has thus far been unmeasured but may be important. Some new and young firms, especially those that rely on information technology, are using highly trained foreign technicians (principally in India and China) to build prototypes of new products and services. In this way, U.S.-based firms that ultimately employ highly trained U.S. employees to bring new products and services to market can develop those products and services at far lower cost, and often more quickly, than if the activities that took place at the "proof of concept" stage were conducted solely in the United States.

But if fewer people are needed in existing jobs and occupations, then won't total employment fall over time? Historically, the number of jobs has closely followed the growth of the labor force, despite major increases in foreign trade and the advent of a host of new job-displacing technologies, such as voicemail, word processors, and optical scanners. Indeed, despite a surge in openness, the U.S. economy since 1985 has added 30 million workers to its payrolls, even taking into account the recent recession and the unusually low job creation during the recovery. At the same time, median family income has jumped 20 percent. Structural changes, including trade and technology, influence where the jobs are, not the total number of jobs.

The policy challenge arises from the second sure bet from economic theory and practice. Offshoring, like trade and technology, is a process of creative destruction whereby workers in affected industries face the very real possibility of losing not only their jobs but also their health care. Even worse, some workers fall down the economic ladder when they have no choice but to take new jobs at lower pay and thus face the prospect of lower lifetime earnings.

This concern is particularly acute because it comes at a moment when anxieties about jobs and wages are running high. Against the backdrop of a breathtaking acceleration in manufacturing job losses over the past few years, the jobs picture remains murky two years into recovery. Stephen Roach of Morgan Stanley estimates that the current "jobless" recovery is short 2.4 million jobs compared with the previous "jobless" recovery of the early 1990s, and Laura Tyson, dean of the London Business

" Economic theory points to two quite robust conclusions... Overall, offshoring will offer economic gains. But some American workers, companies, and possibly communities will just as surely lose out in the process."

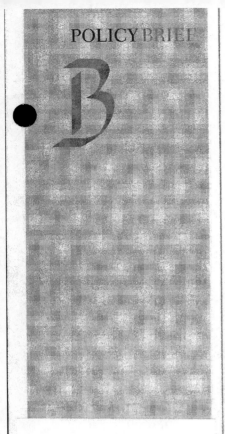

School, estimates that even those Americans who have jobs are short about $350 billion in "missing income."

In this kind of economic climate, it is easy to understand why many Americans lack interest in parsing out how much dislocation is due to offshoring and how much to other causes and instead simply want to put on the brakes.

Just how redistributive is offshoring likely to be? Here, both the theory and the evidence only give partial answers. As an example, the McKinsey study estimates that for every dollar of U.S. services activity that is offshored, there is a global gain of $1.47, suggesting a net gain of 47 cents. In their analysis, India captures 33 cents of the total, leaving the United States with the remaining $1.14. How is this $1.14 distributed? "Reemployed" workers get 47 cents (a substantial reduction), additional exports account for a relatively modest 5 cents, and shareholders and

Figure 1:

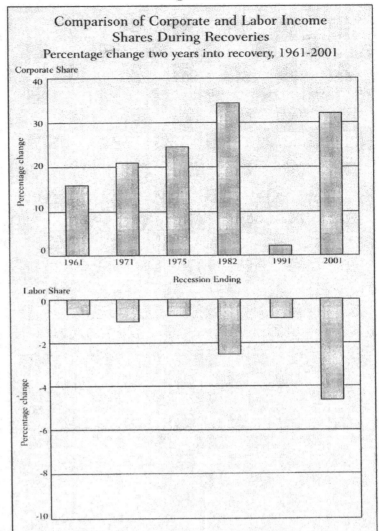

Source: *The Economic Report of the President, 2004*

consumers of the firms doing the offshoring gain the other 62 cents. U.S. shareholders and consumers win while U.S. workers lose.

Indeed, this plays into a broader set of distributive trends that have been quite negative for workers since the end of the 2001 recession, although current data are not adequate to determine how big a role offshoring has played. The administration's tax policies have exacerbated

Policy Brief #132

April 2004

rather than offset these developments. Figure 1 (page 4) shows that on a pre-tax basis, the profit share has grown much more strongly in the current recovery than in the recovery of 1992-93, while worker compensation has suffered a more pronounced decline than in any previous recovery in the last four decades, a point also highlighted by Jared Bernstein of the Economic Policy Institute.

This new allocation may be only temporary. Over the longer run, competition among firms should drive down profits, and consumers should benefit from lower prices. Historically, as shown in figure 2, there does not appear to be a long-term trend in the share of income going to profits relative to labor compensation.

Even so, longer term averages often conceal what is happening to individual workers. Economic research has established that the wages of low-skilled workers—those in the bottom of the income distribution—were pushed down in the 1980s and early 1990s by a combination of foreign trade, immigration, and a drop in demand caused by changes in technology that favor greater skills. This downward pressure increased income inequality during this period until the mid-1990s, when the rising tide of the

Figure 2:

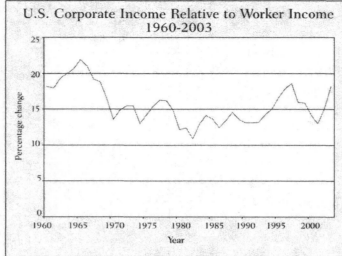

Source: *The Economic Report of the President, 2004*

overall economy lifted all boats. Now that college-educated, white-collar American workers will increasingly be in competition with highly qualified workers in the developing world whose wages are a fraction of their own, won't they be subject to the same pressures?

In a forthcoming book, *Business Week's* chief economist, Michael Mandel, worries that the answer to this question is "yes," and he may well be right. If Mandel's assumption is correct, the "skills premium" that educated workers earned in the past may be pushed down in the future, thus reversing a decades-long trend. At the same time, however, wages within sectors may diverge. In services, for example, some workers whose jobs are vulnerable to offshoring could suffer erosion of their wages while others in supervisory positions may see compensation gains. With all these possible changes, it is no wonder that fears about foreign outsourcing resonate across a broad spectrum of society.

"*Manufacturing productivity has been increasing roughly 3.5 percent per year over the last two decades, which helps explain why the share of U.S. workers engaged in producing 'things' has declined significantly.*"

B

POLICY AGENDA

One thing is clear. Unless policymakers get out ahead of the offshoring debate, they will find themselves reacting to a host of band-aid proposals that do more harm than good. They should be proactive and take five important steps:

Improve the data that the government collects. Despite the challenges associated with gathering accurate, official data on offshoring, policymakers must make it a priority to greatly improve the statistics on this phenomenon so that policymakers, education and training experts, companies, and workers can make informed decisions sooner rather than later. Data collection on services must be expanded to include smaller transactions and be conducted on a more regular basis. Both the Bureau of Economic Analysis and the Bureau of Labor Statistics should look at developing additional survey questions to better measure the extent of services activity moving offshore and the concomitant changes to domestic employment, wages, and productivity. Because of the importance of this challenge, the Brookings Institution is organizing a data workshop to explore gaps between the key policy questions and the existing data available to address them.

Ensure that America remains the most attractive location in the world for high-value services and manufacturing. Policymakers should take a hard look at distortions in the tax code that may artificially encourage offshoring, such as the current corporate tax system that permits deferral of taxation on foreign earnings but not on domestic earnings, and that results in the highest corporate tax burden among industrialized countries. Recent proposals that would end the preferential tax treatment of foreign earnings and lower the corporate tax on domestic earnings merit special attention. A second critical priority is to strengthen support for research and development—the key to creating jobs of the future. Instead, recent budgets have cut federal support for R&D in engineering and the physical sciences relative to the size of the economy. Another policy long advocated by economists is to make permanent the federal tax credit for R&D. Finally, it is important to reduce reliance on an employer-based system of health insurance that adds to costs of U.S. firms and to the overall insecurity of displaced workers.

Give American workers the knowledge and skills they need to compete in the global economy. Cultivating a competitive, highly skilled workforce means strengthening the kindergarten through twelfth-grade curriculum, investing in science and engineering higher education, and restoring funding to community colleges and retraining programs that have suffered large cuts in recent years. America will not be able to hold onto the highest paying jobs in the world if the number of college graduates with degrees in physical sciences, math, and engineering continue on a downward trend.

Designing policies to strengthen the skills of the American workforce is particularly critical because the American economy is likely to confront a rapidly increasing skill shortage on the heels of the offshoring debate. In separate reports, Anthony Carnevale and Donna M. Derochers of Educational

Testing Service and David Ellwood of Harvard University have written about a looming "skilled-worker gap." Carnevale and Derochers forecast a gap of 5.3 million skilled workers by 2010 and 14 million by 2020. This is attributable both to the aging American workforce and to the expectation that increases in average educational attainment achieved over the past two decades will level off over the next two decades. Meanwhile, the demand for skills will continue growing at a rapid pace.

Do more on trade, not less. Policymakers must make sure trade agreements are being enforced and must also regain the market-opening momentum that has disappeared in recent years. Ultimately, it will not be feasible to sustain political support for the relative openness of U.S. services markets while countries such as India maintain high barriers on entry into their own services markets.

Pay attention to legitimate regulatory issues. While policymakers should refrain from blunt, potentially counterproductive approaches, they must address oversight of consumer privacy, cyber security, and consumer protection when services—especially those dealing with sensitive medical and financial information—are produced in other countries with different laws, regulations, and professional credentials. Moreover, consumers have a right to know in services, no less than in manufacturing, where country of origin labeling is mandated by law.

Address the dislocation faced by workers in the services sector through wage insurance, adjustment assistance, **and training.** This is the most urgent priority. Although Congress made far-reaching reforms to the Trade Adjustment Assistance program in 2002—including adding a health care benefit—it ultimately rejected efforts by Democratic Senators Max Baucus of Montana, Jeff Bingaman of New Mexico, Minority Leader Tom Daschle of South Dakota, and others to extend its reach to services workers. Software programmers are now suing the Department of Labor to gain access to the same extended unemployment insurance and retraining benefits long guaranteed to trade-impacted manufacturing workers. Congress could make the suit moot by making clear that service workers are covered by TAA.

Wage insurance should be a central part of the safety net for displaced services workers. In 2002, Congress amended the Trade Promotional Authority Act (TPA) to include a program providing wage insurance to workers older than fifty who can prove that trade is a "major cause" of their displacement. The goals of the wage insurance program were not only to ease the economic dislocations associated with trade-induced displacement, but also to encourage affected workers to search for and accept new jobs quickly. Payments start when workers take new jobs and stop two years from the date they were laid off. Workers who qualify receive, temporarily, half the earnings they lose when taking a new job, up to an annual ceiling of $10,000.

One easy way to address worker displacement by offshoring, then, would be to make such workers eligible for wage insurance, albeit with some qualifications: lowering or eliminating the age requirement and possibly raising the

"*Although Congress made far-reaching reforms to the Trade Adjustment Assistance program in 2002...it ultimately rejected efforts...to extend its reach to services workers. Wage insurance should be a central part of the safety net.*"

The authors are grateful to Gary Burtless, Bill Dickens, Isabel Sawhill, and Charles Schultze of the Brookings Institution and Catherine Mann of the Institute for International Economics for helpful comments.

compensation limit to reflect the likely higher income of many dislocated services workers.

Limiting the kinds of benefits available under the Trade Adjustment Assistance law to workers displaced by trade and offshoring more generally raises fundamental questions of fairness—in addition to the difficulties of identifying the cause of displacement. Why should those protections not also be available to workers who are permanently displaced for other reasons, notably improvements in technology and shifts in consumer demand?

Because there is no satisfactory answer to this question—other than one of cost to the federal government—one author of this brief (Litan) proposed three years ago, with Professor Lori Kletzer of the University of California at Santa Cruz, to offer wage insurance to all permanently displaced workers, regardless of age. The proposed insurance would be identical to that in the TPA program except that it would also provide a federal subsidy for up to six months of health insurance coverage. Had both programs been in place in 1997, for example, when the national unemployment rate was 4.9 percent, the annual total cost would have been $3.6 billion. With today's 5.6 percent unemployment rate, and the likelihood that average wage losses suffered by displaced workers have increased since 1997, a reasonable estimate is that the two programs would now cost roughly $4.5 to $5 billion. Over ten years, a program costing about $50 billion could easily be refunded out of just a small portion of the revenues from repealing the 2001 tax cut for those few in the top bracket. B

Tell us what you think of this Policy Brief.
E-mail your comments to yourview@brookings.edu.

The Brookings Institution
1775 Massachusetts Ave., NW
Washington, DC 20036

8

Policy Brief #132

April 2004

CEI Competitive Enterprise Institute

The Market and Nature
Smith Op-Ed in The Freeman

Op-Eds & Articles
by Fred L. Smith, Jr.
September 1, 1993

(Originally appeared in The Freeman, September 1993)

Many environmentalists are dissatisfied with the environmental record of free economies. Capitalism, it is claimed, is a wasteful system, guilty of exploiting the finite resources of the Earth in a vain attempt to maintain a non-sustainable standard of living. Such charges, now raised under the banner of "sustainable development," are not new. Since Malthus made his dire predictions about the prospects for world hunger, the West has been continually warned that it is using resources too rapidly and will soon run out of something, if not everything. Nineteenth century experts such as W.S. Jevons believed that world coal supplies would soon be exhausted and would have been amazed that over 200 years of reserves now exist. US timber "experts" were convinced that North American forests would soon be a memory. They would similarly be shocked by the reforestation of eastern North America—reforestation that has resulted from market forces and not mandated government austerity.

In recent decades, the computer-generated predictions of the Club of Rome enjoyed a brief popularity, arguing that everything would soon disappear. Fortunately, most now recognize that such computer simulations, and their static view of resource supply and demand, have no relation to reality. Nevertheless, these models are back, most notably in the book *Beyond the Limits*, and enjoying their newly-found attention. This theme of imminent resource exhaustion has become a chronic element in the annual Worldwatch Institute publication, *State of the World*. (This book is, to my knowledge, the only gloom-and-doom book in history which advertises next year's edition.) Today, sustainable-development theorists from the World Bank's Herman Daly and the United Nations' Maurice Strong to Vice President Albert Gore and Canadian author David Suzuki, seem certain that, at last, Malthus will be proven right. It was this environmental view on display at the United Nations' "Earth Summit" in Rio de Janeiro in June, 1992. This conference, vast in scope and mandate, was but the first step in the campaign to make the environment the central organizing principle of global institutions.

If such views are taken seriously, then the future will indeed be a very gloomy place, for if such disasters are in the immediate future, than drastic government action is necessary. Consider the not atypical view of David Suzuki:

> [T]here has to be a radical restructuring of the priorities of society. That means we must no longer be dominated by global economics, that the notion that we must continue to grow indefinitely is simply off, that we must work towards, not zero growth, but negative growth.

For the first time in world history, the leaders of the developed nations are being asked to turn their backs on the future. The resulting policies could be disastrous for all mankind.

The Environmental Challenge

The world does indeed face a challenge in protecting ecological values. Despite tremendous success in many areas, many environmental concerns remain. The plight of the African elephant, the air over Los Angeles, the hillsides of Nepal, the three million infant deaths from water-borne diseases throughout the world, and the ravaging of Brazilian rain forests all dramatize areas where problems persist and innovative solutions are necessary.

Sustainable development theorists claim these problems result from "market failure": the inability of capitalism to address environmental concerns adequately. Free market proponents suggest such problems are not the result of market forces, but rather of their absence. The market already plays a critical role in protecting those resources which are privately owned and for which political interference is minimal. In these instances there are truly sustainable practices. Therefore, those concerned with protecting the environment and ensuring human prosperity should seek to expand capitalism, through the extension of property rights, to the broadest possible range of environmental resources. Our objective should be to reduce, not expand, political interference in both the human and natural environments.

Private stewardship of environmental resources is a powerful means of ensuring sustainability. Only people can protect the environment. Politics *per se* does nothing. If political arrangements fail to encourage individuals to play a positive role, the arrangements can actually do more harm than good. There are tens of millions of species of plants and animals that merit survival. Can we imagine that the 150 or so governments on this planet—many of which do poorly with their human charges—will succeed in so massive a stewardship task? Yet, there are in the world today over five billion people. Freed to engage in private stewardship, the challenge before them becomes surmountable.

Sustainable Development and Its Implications

The phrase *sustainable development* suggests a system of natural resource management that is capable of providing an equivalent, or expanding, output over time. As a concept, it is extremely vague, often little more than a platitude. Who, after all, favors non-sustainable development? The basic definition promoted by Gro Harlem Brundtland, former Prime Minister of Norway and a prominent player at the 1992 Earth Summit, is fairly vague as well: "[S]ustainable development is a notion of discipline. It means humanity must ensure that meeting present needs does not compromise the ability of future generations to meet their own needs."

In this sense, sustainability requires that as resources are consumed one of three things must occur: New resources must be discovered or developed; demands must be shifted to more plentiful resources; or, new knowledge must permit us to meet such needs from the smaller resource base. That is, as resources are depleted, they must be renewed. Many assume that the market is incapable of achieving this result. A tremendous historical record suggests exactly the opposite.

Indeed, to many environmental "experts," today's environmental problems reflect the failure of the market to consider ecological values. This market-failure explanation is accepted by a panoply of political pundits of all ideological stripes, from Margaret Thatcher to Earth First! The case seems clear. Markets, after all, are short-sighted and concerned only with quick profits. Markets undervalue biodiversity and other ecological concerns not readily captured in the marketplace. Markets ignore effects generated outside of the market, so-called externalities, such as pollution. Since markets fail in these critical environmental areas, it is argued, political intervention is necessary. That intervention should be careful, thoughtful, even scientific, but the logic is clear: Those areas of the economy having environmental impacts must be politically controlled. Since, however, every economic decision has some environmental effect, the result is an effort to regulate the whole of human activity.

Thus, without any conscious decision being made, the world is moving decisively toward central planning for ecological rather than economic purposes. The Montreal Protocol on chlorofluorocarbons, the international convention on climate change, the convention on biodiversity, and the full range of concerns addressed at the UN Earth Summit—all are indicative of this rush to politicize the world's economies. That is unfortunate, for ecological central planning is unlikely to provide for a greener world.

Rethinking the Market Failure Paradigm

The primary problem with the market-failure explanation is it demands too much. In a world of pervasive externalities—that is, a world where all economic decisions have environmental effects—this analysis demands all economic decisions be politically managed. The world is only now beginning to recognize the massive mistake entailed in economic central planning; yet, the "market failure" paradigm argues that we embark on an even more ambitious effort of ecological central planning. The disastrous road to serfdom can just as easily be paved with green bricks as with red ones.

That markets "fail" does not mean that governments will "succeed." Governments, after all, are susceptible to special interest pleadings. A complex political process often provides fertile ground for economic and ideological groups to advance their agendas at the public expense. The US tolerance of high-sulfur coal and the massive subsidies for heavily polluting "alternative fuels" are evidence of this problem. Moreover, governments lack any means of acquiring the detailed information dispersed throughout the economy essential to efficiency and technological change.

More significantly, if market forces were the dominant cause of environmental problems then the highly industrialized, capitalist countries should suffer from greater environmental problems than their centrally-managed counterparts. This was once the conventional wisdom. The Soviet Union, it was argued, would have no pollution because the absence of private property, the profit motive, and individual self-interest would eliminate the motives for harming the environment. The opening of the Iron Curtain exploded this myth, as the most terrifying ecological horrors ever conceived were shown to be the Communist reality. The lack of property rights and profit motivations discouraged efficiency, placing a greater stress on natural resources. The result was an environmental disaster.

Do Markets Fail——Or Do We Fail to Allow Markets?

John Kenneth Galbraith, an avowed proponent of statist economic policies, inadvertently suggested a new approach to environmental protection. In an oft-quoted speech he noted that the United States was a nation in which the yards and homes were beautiful and in which the streets and parks were filthy. Galbraith then went on to suggest that we effectively nationalize the yards and homes. For those of us who believe in property rights and economic liberty, the obvious lesson is quite the opposite.

Free market environmentalists seek ways of placing these properties in the care of individuals or groups concerned about their well-being. This approach does not, of course, mean that trees must have legal standing, but rather is a call for ensuring that behind every tree, stream, lake, air shed, and whale stands at least one owner who is able and willing to protect and nurture that resource.

Consider the plight of the African elephant. On most of the continent, the elephant is managed like the American buffalo once was. It remains a political resource. Elephants are widely viewed as the common heritage of all the peoples of these nations and are thus protected politically. The "common property" management strategy being used in Kenya and elsewhere in East and Central Africa has been compared and contrasted with the experiences of those nations such as Zimbabwe which have moved decisively in recent years to transfer elephant-ownership rights to regional tribal councils. The differences are dramatic. In Kenya, and indeed all of eastern Africa, elephant populations have fallen by over 50 percent in the last decade. In contrast, Zimbabwe's elephant population has been increasing rapidly. A program of conservation through use that relies upon uniting the interest of man and the environment succeeds where political management has failed.

The Market and Sustainability

The prophets of sustainability have consistently predicted an end to the world's abundant resources, while the defenders of the free market point to the power of innovation—innovation which is encouraged in the marketplace. Consider the agricultural experience. Since 1950, improved plant and animal breeds, expanded availability and types of agri-chemicals, innovative agricultural techniques, expanded irrigation, and better pharmaceutical products have all combined to spur a massive expansion of world food supplies. That was not expected by those now championing "sustainable development." Lester Brown, in his 1974 Malthusian publication *By Bread Alone*, suggested that crop-yield increases would soon cease. Since that date, Asian rice yields have risen nearly 40 percent, an approximate increase of 2.4 percent per year. This rate is similar to that of wheat and other grains. In the developed world it is food surpluses, not food shortages, that present the greater problem, while political institutions continue to obstruct the distribution of food in much of the Third World.

Man's greater understanding and ability to work with nature have made it possible to achieve a vast improvement in world food supplies, to improve greatly the nutritional levels of a majority of people throughout the world in spite of rapid population growth. Moreover, this has been achieved while reducing the stress to the environment. To feed the current world population at current nutritional levels using 1950 yields would require plowing under an additional 10 to 11 million square miles, almost tripling the world's agricultural land demands (now at 5.8 million square miles). This would surely come at the expense of land being used for wildlife habitat and other applications.

Moreover, this improvement in agriculture has been matched by improvements in food distribution and storage, again encouraged by natural market processes and the "profit incentive" that so many environmentalists deplore. Packaging has made it possible to reduce food spoilage, reduce transit damage, extend shelf life, and expand distribution regions. Plastic and other post-use wraps along with the ubiquitous Tupperware have further reduced food waste. As would be expected, the United States uses more packaging than Mexico, but the additional packaging results in tremendous reductions in waste. On average, a Mexican family discards 40 percent more waste each day. Packaging often eliminates more waste than it creates.

Despite the fact that capitalism has produced more environment-friendly innovations than any other economic system, the advocates of sustainable development insist that this process must be guided by benevolent government officials. That such efforts, such as the United States' synthetic fuels project of the late 1970s, have resulted in miserable failures is rarely considered. It is remarkable how many of the participants at the UN Earth Summit seemed completely oblivious to this historical reality.

In the free market, entrepreneurs compete in developing low-cost, efficient means to solve contemporary problems. The promise of a potential profit, and the freedom to seek after it, always provides the incentive to build a better mousetrap, if you will. Under planned economies, this incentive for innovation can never be as strong, and the capacity to reallocate resources toward more efficient means of production is always constrained.

This confusion is also reflected in the latest environmental fad: waste reduction. With typical ideological fervor, a call for increased efficiency in resource use becomes a call to use less of everything, regardless of the cost. Less, we are told, is more in terms of environmental benefit. But neither recycling nor material or energy use reductions *per se* are a good thing, even when judged solely on environmental grounds. Recycling paper often results in increased water pollution, increased energy use, and, in the United States, actually discourages the planting of new trees. Mandating increased fuel efficiency for automobiles reduces their size and weight, which in turn reduces their crashworthiness and increases highway fatalities. Environmental policies must be judged on their results, not just their motivations.

Overcoming Scarcity

Environmentalists tend to focus on ends rather than processes. This is surprising given their adherence to ecological teaching. Their obsession with the technologies and material-usage patterns of today reflects a failure to understand how the world works. The resources people need are not chemicals, wood fiber, copper, or the other raw materials of concern to the sustainable-development school. We demand housing, transportation, and communication services. How those demands are met is a derivative result based on competitive forces—forces which respond by suggesting new ways to meet old needs as well as improving the ability to meet needs in older ways.

Consider, for example, the fears expressed in the early post-war era that copper would soon be in short supply. Copper was the life-blood of the world's communication system, essential to linking together humanity throughout the world. Extrapolations suggested problems and copper prices escalated accordingly. The result? New sources of copper in Africa, South America, and even the United States and Canada, were found. That concern, however, also prompted others to review new technologies, an effort that produced today's rapidly expanding fiber optics links.

Such changes would be viewed as miraculous if not now commonplace in the industrialized, and predominantly capitalistic, nations of the world. Data assembled by Lynn Scarlett of the Reason Foundation noted that a system requiring, say, 1,000 tons of copper can be replaced by as little as 25 kilograms of silicon, the basic component of sand. Moreover, the fiber-optics system has the ability to carry over 1,000 times the information of the older copper wire. Such rapid increases in communication technology are also providing for the displacement of oil as electronic communication reduces the need to travel and commute. The rising fad of telecommuting was not dreamed up by some utopian environmental planner, but was rather a natural outgrowth of market processes.

It is essential to understand that physical resources are, in and of themselves, largely irrelevant. It is the interaction of man and science that creates resources: Sand and knowledge become fiber optics. Humanity and its institutions determine whether we eat or die. The increase of political control over physical resources and new technologies only increases the likelihood of famine.

Intergenerational Equity

Capitalism is ultimately attacked on grounds of unsustainability for its purported failure to safeguard the needs of future generations. Without political intervention, it is argued, capitalists would leave a barren globe for their children. Thus, it is concluded, intergenerational equity demands that politics intervene. But are these criticisms valid?

Capitalists care about the future because they care about today's bottom line. Market economies have created major institutions—bond and stock markets, for example—which respond to changes in operating policies that impact future values. A firm that misuses capital or lowers quality standards, a pet store that mistreats its stock, a mine that reduces maintenance, a farmer that permits erosion—all will find the value of their capital assets falling. Highly specialized researchers expend vast efforts ferreting out changes in management practices that might affect future values; investment houses pay future-analysts very well indeed to examine such questions.

Markets, of course, are not able to foresee all eventualities, nor do they consider consequences hundreds of years into the future. Yet, consider the time horizon of politicians. In the United States, at least, they are concerned with only one thing: getting re-elected, a process that provides them at best a two-to-six-year time horizon. Politically-managed infrastructure is routinely undermaintained; funds for new roads are more attractive than the smaller sums used to repair potholes; national forests are more poorly maintained than private forests; erosion is more serious on politically-controlled lands than on those maintained by private corporations. If the free market is shortsighted in its view of the future, then the political process is even more so. It is therefore the free market which best ensures that there will be enough for the future.

Warring Paradigms

The two alternative perspectives on environmental policy—free markets and central planning—differ dramatically. One relies upon individual ingenuity and economic liberty to harness the progressive nature of market forces. The other rests upon political manipulation and government coercion. In point of fact, these approaches are antithetical. There is little hope of developing a "third way." Yet, there has been little debate on which approach offers the greatest promise in enhancing and protecting environmental concerns. The political approach has been adopted on a wide scale throughout the world, with more failure than success, while efforts to utilize the free-market approach have been few and far between.

Nevertheless, there are numerous cases where private property rights have been used to complement and supplement political environmental strategies. One excellent example is a case in England in the 1950s where a fishing club, the Pride of Derby, was able to sue upstream polluters for trespassing against private property. Even the pollution issuing from an upstream municipality was addressed. This ability to go against politically-preferred polluters rarely exists where environmental resources are politically managed.

At the heart of the division between statist and free market environmentalists is a difference in moral vision. Free market environmentalists envision a world in which man and the environment live in harmony, each benefiting from interaction with the other. The other view, which dominates the environmental establishment, believes in a form of ecological apartheid whereby man and nature must be separated, thus protecting the environment from human influence. From this view rises the impetus to establish wilderness lands where no humans may tread, and a quasi-religious zeal to end all human impact on nature.

Thus, the establishment environmentalists view pollution—human waste—as an evil that must be eliminated. That waste is an inevitable by-product of human existence is of secondary concern. To the environmentalist that endorses this ideology, nothing short of civilization's demise will suffice to protect the earth.

The view that free market environmentalists endorse is somewhat different. Not all waste is pollution, but only that waste which is transferred involuntarily. Thus, it is pollution to dispose of garbage on a neighbor's lawn, but not to store it on one's own property. The voluntary transfer of waste, perhaps from an industrialist to the operator of a landfill or recycling facility, is merely another market transaction.

Conclusion

The United Nations Earth Summit considered an extremely important issue: What steps should be taken to ensure that economic and ecological values are harmonized? Unfortunately, the Earth Summit failed to develop such a program, opting instead to further the flawed arguments for ecological central planning.

The world faces a fateful choice as to how to proceed: by expanding the scope of individual action via a system of expanded private property rights and the legal defenses associated with such rights, or by expanding the power of the state to protect such values directly. In making that choice, we should learn from history. Much of the world is only now emerging from decades of efforts to advance economic welfare via centralized political means, to improve the welfare of mankind by restricting economic freedom, by expanding the power of the state, to test out the theory that market forces are inadequate to protect the welfare of society. That experiment has been a clear failure on economic, civil liberties, and even ecological grounds. Economic central planning was a utopian dream; it became a real world nightmare.

Today, the international environmental establishment seems eager to repeat this experiment in the ecological sphere, increasing the power of the state, restricting individual freedom, certain that market forces cannot adequately protect the ecology. Yet, as I've quickly sketched out here, this argument is faulty. Wherever resources have been privately protected, they have done better than their politically managed counterparts—whether we are speaking of elephants in Zimbabwe, salmon streams in England, or beaver in Canada. Where such rights have been absent or suppressed, the results have been less fortunate. Extending property rights to the full array of resources now left undefended, now left as orphans in a world of protected properties, is a daunting challenge. Creative legal arrangements and new technologies will be necessary to protect the oceans and airsheds of the world, but those tasks can be resolved if we apply ourselves. The obstacles to ecological central planning are insurmountable. The need for centralized information and a comprehensive system of controls in order to coerce the population of the world to act in highly restricted ways, as well as that for omniscient decision-makers to choose among technologies, can never be met.

Ecological central planning cannot protect the environment, but it can destroy our civil and economic liberties. There is too much at stake to allow the world to embark upon this course. The environment can be protected, and the world's peoples can continue to reach new heights of prosperity, but it is essential to realize that political management is not the proper approach. Rather, the leaders of the world should follow the path of the emerging nations of Eastern Europe and embrace political and economic freedom. In the final analysis, the free market is the only system of truly sustainable development.

How to Lose the Brain Race

By STEVEN CLEMONS AND MICHAEL LIND (NYT) 797 words
Published: April 10, 2006

Washington - IS the United States importing too many immigrant physicists and not enough immigrant farm workers? You might think so, to judge from two provisions that Senator Dianne Feinstein, Democrat of California, added to the comprehensive immigration reform package that just fell apart in the Senate. Senator Feinstein insisted that the bill call for some fees for foreign students applying to study at American colleges and universities to be doubled, and also demanded that agribusiness get the right to 1.5 million low-wage foreign guest workers over five years. Combined, the two proposals sent a message to the rest of the world: send us your brawn, not your brains.

Whether Senator Feinstein's amendments will resurface in any reconstituted legislation on immigration reform remains unclear. But her priorities reflect in many ways those of Congress as a whole. Congress seems to believe that while the United States must be protected from an invasion of educated, bright and ambitious foreign college students, scientists, engineers and entrepreneurs, we can never have too many low-wage fruit-pickers and dishwashers.

In making immigration laws, Congress caters to cheap-labor industries like agribusiness and sweatshop manufacturing while shortchanging the high-tech, high-wage industries on which the future of the American economy depends. Witness the Senate bill's provision to admit 400,000 temporary workers a year, or roughly four million a decade, in addition to the 12 million mostly low-wage illegal immigrants already here, many of whose status would be legalized. Few if any of those guest workers would go to universities, corporate campuses or innovation clusters like Silicon Valley. They would head straight to restaurants, hotels and plantation-like farms.

While the United States perversely tries to corner the market in uneducated hotel maids and tomato harvesters, other industrial democracies are reshaping their immigration policies to invite the skilled immigrants that we turn away. Britain is following Australia and Canada in adopting a points system that gives higher scores to skilled immigrants with advanced education and proficiency in English. British, Canadian, German and even French universities are overflowing in undergraduate and graduate enrollment as they absorb the foreign talent that America is repelling.

Whereas Senator Feinstein fears that foreigners are snatching places at American universities from deserving American students, the fact is that our universities are weakened when fewer talented international students enter their programs.

In recent years, skilled immigration to the United States has been accommodated chiefly by the H-1B visa program. But like all guest-worker programs, the H-1B program pits American workers against foreign workers lacking full legal and political rights. Because H-1B workers depend on employer sponsorship to remain in this country, unscrupulous employers can blackmail them into working longer hours for lower pay than American workers. Skilled workers admitted under a points system, by contrast, would be able to quit their employers in the United States and find new ones at will without risk of deportation.

Will admitting more immigrants drive down the wages of American workers? That may be true in unskilled jobs, since there is a fixed number of bedpans to be emptied and restaurant meals to be cooked in the United States.

But it isn't necessarily true for skilled workers, at least not in the long run. That's because more talent means more innovation and opportunities for all, immigrant and native alike. The growth economist Paul Romer has spoken of the prospector theory of human capital. The more prospectors there are, the more likely it is that some will find gold. As the history of Silicon Valley and other tech centers proves, brain work migrates to where the brain workers are. It's a kind of Field of Dreams in reverse: You will build it, if they come.

Even if a skill-based immigration system did reduce incomes for the elite, that would not be the end of the world. For a generation, college-educated Americans have enjoyed a seller's market in professional services and a buyer's market in the labor of landscapers and nannies. If skilled immigration were increased while unskilled immigration were reduced, the wages of janitors would go up while the salaries and fees of professionals would fall, creating a broader middle class and a more equal society.

The United States can always use another Albert Einstein or Alexander Graham Bell. But with the vast pool of poorly paid, ill-educated laborers already within our borders, we do not need a third of a million new ones a year.

What the space race was to the cold war, the "brain race" is to today's peaceful global economic competition. The comprehensive immigration reform America needs is one that slashes unskilled immigration and creates a skill-rewarding points system modeled on those of Australia, Britain and Canada. In encouraging skilled labor, Congress for a change might perform some of its own.

REFLECTIONS ON THE CORPORATION
AS A SOCIAL INVENTION

Michael C. Jensen
Harvard Business School
MJensen@hbs.edu

William H. Meckling
University of Rochester

Abstract

The corporation as an organizational form is an enormously productive social invention. Partly because of its success it is under increasing attack from various quarters, often under the guise of "protecting" investors from self-interested managers. Some of these attacks are successful simply because the corporation is a poorly understood entity. This paper discusses what the corporation is, what it is not, and how certain misconceptions about the corporate form are fostered by its critics as part of their attack.

Keywords: social responsibility, survival, definition of corporation, corporate democracy, federal chartering, Corporate Democracy Act, corporate control, government involvement.

Controlling the Giant Corporation: A Symposium, Center for Research in Government Policy and Business, Graduate School of Management, University of Rochester, 1982.

Reprinted in the *Midland Corporate Finance Journal*, Vol. 1, No. 3 (Autumn, 1983); reprinted in International Institute for Economic Research, Reprint Paper 18 (November, 1983).

REFLECTIONS ON THE CORPORATION

AS A SOCIAL INVENTION

Michael C. Jensen
Harvard Business School
MJensen@hbs.edu

William H. Meckling
University of Rochester

Controlling the Giant Corporation: A Symposium, Center for Research in Government Policy and Business, Graduate School of Management, University of Rochester, 1982.

Reprinted in the *Midland Corporate Finance Journal,* Vol. 1, No. 3 (Autumn, 1983); reprinted in International Institute for Economic Research, Reprint Paper 18 (November, 1983).

"At least until the 1940's, modern business enterprise grew in spite of public and government opposition. Many Americans—probably a majority—looked on large-scale enterprise with suspicion . . . the coming of modern business enterprise in its several forms brought strong political and legislative action. The control and regulation of the railroads, of the three types of mass retailers— department stores, mail order houses, and the chains—and of the large industrial enterprise became major political issues. In the first decade of the twentieth century, the control of the large corporation was, in fact, the paramount political question of the day."[1]

Big business has never suffered from a dearth of critics. The language employed by these critics, the tactics and the rationale they advance for their hostility, even the faces of the players in the game, perpetually change, but the basic theme seems immutable. Recently, big business has been cast in the role of villain by various activist groups—anti-war protesters, consumer advocates, environmentalists, and the like.[2] Since

---

[1]   Chandler (1977, p. 497).

[2]   One economist noted that ". . . those who wish to use the power of the state to pervert the corporate arrangement are not confined to the intellectually unwashed among politicians, social activists, and

most "big businesses" are organized as corporations,[3] the corporation as an institutional form has become one focus of the hostility.

Separation of Ownership and Control

Nowadays, the attack on the corporation is comprised of two distinctly different themes. One of these themes—concern over the so-called "separation of ownership from control" which characterizes large corporations—has been around at least since 1776, when Adam Smith denounced joint stock companies on those grounds. In Smith's day, of course, joint stock companies were the exception rather than the rule—individual proprietorships dominated the conduct of business.

Use of the corporate form of organization grew throughout the 19th century, but early 19th century corporations tended to be "closely held" rather than "publicly held." During the latter part of the 19th century in the United States sizeable businesses which had been owned and managed by a single entrepreneur, or by a closely-knit entrepreneurial cadre (sometimes all members of one family), began to be transformed into the large publicly held corporations[4] which dominate the business scene today—corporations in which no single stockholder or small group of stockholders had anything like a controlling interest. Because responsibility for operation of these firms has devolved into the hands of "professional managers," "ownership" is said to be separated from "control." As a result of this separation, management is alleged to be insensitive to

---

Hollywood stars: astonishingly, they include some representatives of major corporations. Allen (1982, p. 40).

[3] It is worth noting that there are many "big businesses" operated by governments, e.g., the U.S. Post Office, state universities, metropolitan school systems, the TVA and other power authorities, municipal airports, metropolitan mass transit systems, metropolitan sanitary and waste disposal services, metropolitan water systems, and the New York Port Authority. Government big businesses are not without their critics, but the criticism is of an entirely different sort. Government managers such as school superintendents and postal administrators, for example, are seldom depicted in the media as ruthless and power hungry.

[4] Chandler, op. cit. documents the history of this transformation. He refers to the new organizational form as "managerial capitalism".

the welfare of investors. Corporate management, so the story goes, possesses vast discretionary power which it uses to operate firms to suit itself.

Corporate Social Responsibility

A second line of attack against the corporation—one that in an important sense is contradictory to the first—charges corporations with anti-social behavior on a broad front. Corporations pollute the environment; bribe foreign officials; ignore the impact of plant relocations on local communities; discriminate against the handicapped, minorities, women and the elderly in hiring and promotion; support and help elect dictatorial governments in developing countries, etc. It is this kind of charge that has led to the popular prescription that corporations must be "socially responsible."[5]

It is important to distinguish these two lines of attack. Indictment of the corporation on grounds that management is not responsible to investors is one thing; indictment on grounds that management behaves anti-socially is an entirely different affair. Concern over whether or to what extent management in the modern corporation is controlled by investors, implicitly takes as given the idea that management ought to behave in the interest of investors. In technical language it implies acceptance of investor welfare as "the objective function" of the firm.[6] Thus, it is consistent with conventional views regarding corporate "purposes" in particular, the view that investors are willing to hold wealth in the form of claims on such organizations, because (or to the extent that) management acts on their behalf.

The allegation that investors are the victims of management expropriation or neglect also differs from the anti-social behavior charge in another important way.

---

[5] The more politic interest groups avoid specifically indicting corporations while nonetheless maintaining that corporations have an obligation to do more good, i.e., be more socially responsible.

[6] While this is not the place to address the issue in detail, behaving in the interest of investors is, under a very broad range of circumstances, equivalent to maximizing the value of the firm, i.e., maximizing the net present value of future cash flows.

Whether or to what extent managers act in the interest of investors is an empirical question—a question of fact; one, which in principle is scientifically answerable. Since the motive for investors holding claims on corporations is overwhelmingly the earnings therefrom (including appreciation in value), investors' welfare is something we can define and measure. Research can provide evidence about whether or to what extent modern corporate management behaves in the interest of investors.

The second line of attack on the corporation, the charge that corporations display anti-social behavior, does not stem from any concern, real or professed, over the welfare of investors. Indeed, the charges levied often implicitly or explicitly presume that the corporation behaves badly <u>in pursuit of</u> profits i.e., when it behaves in the interest of investors. More importantly, the antidotes for corporate anti-social behavior prescribed by these critics characteristically imply wealth transfers from investors to other groups in society.[7] Those who contend that management has too much discretion can (and do) prescribe policies which will make investors worse off rather than better off. This raises the question of whether the "separation of ownership from control" charge isn't simply a guise used to discredit the corporation rather than evidence of concern over investors' well being. When individuals and organizations attack the corporation for failure to adhere to the interest of stockholders, and simultaneously prescribe policies which transfer wealth from investors to others, one is led to suspect that the appearance of concern for investor welfare is a pretense.

What constitutes either "anti-social" behavior, or its converse, "socially responsible" behavior, of course, depends on how "anti-social" and "socially responsible"

---

[7] It is not uncommon for policies, which purport to deal with anti-social behavior by some corporations to end up bestowing benefits on investors in other corporations. Investors in firms producing water or air purification equipment are likely to be delighted with strict air and water pollution statutes. Wealth transfers from one group of investors to another, however, are usually incidental to larger transfers from investors (and others, particularly consumers) to non-investor interest groups. Firms likely to benefit from coerced social responsibility, i.e. statutory decrees which requires firms to engage in wealth transfers, will, of course, be members of the interest group lobbying for enactment of such laws.

are defined, and those terms cannot be defined except by appeal to some value or set of values—some specification of what is "good" and what is "bad." Social responsibility is a normative catch-all, something which each of us is likely to define very differently.

Serious examination of the notion of social responsibility suggests that the popularity it enjoys stems more from what it conceals than from what it adds. Since "social" is a "good' (as distinct from a "bad"), the term arouses the right sentiments on the side of whatever cause is being pressed. Meanwhile "social" is a word that is vague enough to encompass any cause. Most importantly, the term social responsibility has, from the standpoint of proponents, the advantage that it disguises what they really have in mind, namely, that managers should deliberately take actions which adversely affect investors in order to bestow benefits on other individuals. While various advocate groups would disagree about what constitutes socially responsible behavior, they will all agree that investor welfare must be rejected as the corporate objectives.[8] Otherwise, why introduce the notion of "social responsibility."

The Corporation and the Organizational Test of Survival

Critics of the corporation are confronted by a striking historical phenomenon not readily reconciled with their views. The corporation has come to dominate production and commerce, not only in the United States, but in all of the world's highly developed nations. If the corporation is such a defective institution, how do we explain its chronicle of success? Freedom to choose among organization forms provides an "organizational" test of survival just as markets provide a survival test for individual firms.[9] There are no

[8] Associate Professor James W. Evans of San Diego State University puts the point very directly: . . . "corporate social responsibility means simply that business firms have an obligation to act for the social good even if this might lower their economic profits", University of San Diego Newsletter, Autumn 1982, Vol. 6, No. 1.

[9] The unconditional proposition that "the fittest survive," of course, is not testable. The notion of "survival processes" is, however, not scientifically useless. The concept of survival provides a vehicle for structuring scientific inquiry. It focuses scientific attention on the factors which determine "fitness."

private rights in organizational ideas. Organizational innovations cannot be copyrighted or patented. Entrepreneurs and promoters are free both to replicate and innovate organizational forms. In such an environment more costly organizational forms will tend to be replaced by less costly forms because cost reducing modifications to organizations will yield (short run) rents. The organizational forms that survive and prosper will be those that satisfy consumer demands at lowest cost.

Wherever competition among organizational forms is open and unfettered, the large corporation has demonstrated its strength and durability. It has not, however, won the survival race in all areas. Non-profit forms dominate in certain service areas such as museums and private education at the undergraduate and graduate levels in the United States. In the legal, accounting, and consulting businesses, professional partnerships dominate. In retailing, proprietorships coexist with private corporations, and in the financial industry, private corporations and mutuals coexist. In the capital-intensive industries, such as manufacturing, private corporations with widespread stock ownership have swept the field.[10] The role which the corporation has come to play in society during the last 150 years suggests not that it is a social menace, but that it represents an enormously productive social invention.

What The Corporation Is

Understanding the success of the corporation involves understanding what the corporation is and what it is not. Stripped to its essentials, the corporation is simply a legal fiction which serves as a nexus of contracts. Individuals and organizations— employees, investors, suppliers, customers, etc.—contract with each other in the name of

---

Moreover, survival propositions which specify the criterion (criteria) that serve as a basis for selection are testable, so long as the criterion itself is observable. Statutes which increase (or decrease) the costs of using particular organizational forms, for example, provide what amounts to an experiment from which we can glean evidence regarding the importance of costs to organizational survival.

[10] Fama and Jensen (1983a; 1983b).

a fictional entity—the corporation. Two points about the development of the corporation are worth noting at this juncture. First, it is misleading and inaccurate to view the corporate organizational form as a static institution. The corporation is the product of hundreds of years of individual human ingenuity—hundreds of years during which individuals have fashioned a complex network of contractual relations to more effectively serve the objectives of the parties to the legal fiction. Corporate financial officers, financial consultants, potential investors, et al, for example, have spawned a remarkably diverse set of corporate financial claims (contracts). Moreover, the development of the claims themselves has been accompanied by an equally remarkable development of markets in which the claims are traded.

The second point worth emphasizing at this juncture is that the corporation is neither the creature of the state nor the object of special privileges extended by the state. The corporation did not draw its first breath of life from either a minister of state or civil servant. More importantly, the corporation requires for its existence only freedom of contract. Corporate vitality in no way is dependent on special dispensation from the authorities. Limited liability, for example, is not an idea specialized to corporations. Non-profit organizations, partnerships, and individual proprietorships, for example, all exhibit various forms of limited liability. And, even if private corporations were the only organizations which invoked limited liability, that would not constitute a special privilege. Freedom of contract surely encompasses the right of parties to prescribe limits to liability in contracts. When the state requires those who wish to organize and operate in the corporate form to be chartered or licensed, they are not thereby extending a special privilege to the promoters or stockholders. They are curtailing the freedom of individuals to contract. The truth is, the corporation has survived and prospered despite unfavorable treatment by the state—despite unfavorable taxation and despite costly legal restrictions not applicable to many of its competitors.

What the Corporation Is Not

"A corporation is an artificial being, invisible, intangible, and existing only in contemplation of law." Dartmouth College v. Woodward, 4 Wheat. (U.S.) 518, 636, 4 L.Ed. 629 (1819), Chief Justice Marshall.

The disposition to treat corporations as if they were individuals has venerable roots in both law and economics. In the legal arena this practice serves a function which is of great practical importance—it provides a focus for legal actions. Suits can be brought in the name of the "corporation" and the "corporation" can serve as the object of legal action.

Economists have found it convenient to treat the corporation as if it were a (wealth) maximizing individual in explaining how market systems function. For many purposes, assuming that corporations choose and maximize like an individual simplifies our analysis without seriously impairing the usefulness of the theory. More generally, of course, ascribing human characteristics to the corporation is often a useful linguistic expedient.

That anthropomorphic practice, however, has not been an unmixed blessing. Until very recently, at least, it has distracted social scientists away from the study of the corporation as an organizational form. More importantly, it has distorted both popular and academic understanding of the corporation by obfuscating analysis and public discussion of the impact of government policies when those policies operate <u>through</u> the corporation. The source of this obfuscation is the illusion that the impact of such policies falls <u>on</u> the corporation.

The corporation is not an individual. It does not feel; it does not choose; it cannot bear the burden of taxes; it cannot bear the costs of regulation; it cannot benefit from tariffs or subsidies. All such actions, of course, can and generally do benefit or harm <u>individuals</u> who have some relationship with the corporation such as investors, employees or customers, but it is literal nonsense to say that the <u>corporation</u> is benefitted or is harmed. The viability and the prevalence of the corporation as an organizational form, of course, depends on the cost of doing business as a corporation. Government policies which impose costs on firms who do business as a corporation will discourage the use of that organizational form. But those costs cannot be borne by the corporation, costs can only be borne by "real" as distinct from artificial beings.

More to the point, the corporation cannot be socially (or otherwise) responsible! However we end up defining it, the notion of "being responsible" is a normative concept strictly relevant only to human beings. A corporation can no more be responsible than can a lump of coal.

Vulnerability of the Corporation

Calling attention to the vagarious nature of "social responsibility" is not mere semantic quibbling. The case against the corporation is not being brought, nor will it be decided, on the basis of scientific analysis and research. The corporation is on trial in the political and public opinion arenas, not in academic circles. It will not pay the individual citizen to invest much in understanding the issues surrounding the corporation controversy. If he is at all realistic he will understand that he is virtually powerless to do anything to effect the outcome. Politicians and bureaucrats on the other hand have a powerful incentive to join forces with corporate critics. Corporations control substantial accumulations of wealth. Politicians and bureaucrats can expand their own role in life if they can transfer rights to decide the use of that wealth from the corporation to government. The right to decide how corporate assets will be used is a form of power, and politicians and bureaucrats have a strong incentive to accumulate power in government. It is not surprising, given these circumstances that public discussion of the corporation is fraught with semantic ambushes.

Corporate Democracy and Federal Chartering

One of the captions which has become the vogue in more recent proposals for rehabilitating the corporation is "corporate democracy." Those who argue for "corporate democracy" have again chosen a label that evokes favorable "vibes." Who could oppose "corporate democracy?" When we look at the embodiment of corporate democracy in the Corporate Democracy Act, however, we find that it means:

(1) limiting freedom of contract to work for, buy from, sell to, lend to or own stock in a corporation that does not meet certain rules regarding membership on its board of directors.

(2) limiting freedom of contract to work for, buy from, sell to, lend to or own stock in a corporation that does not disclose certain kinds of information.

(3) limiting freedom of contract to work for, buy from, sell to, lend to or own stock in a corporation that does not include certain contractual guarantees against discipline and firing of employees.[11]

It is difficult to see what the word "democracy" has to do with any of the provisions of this Act. Presuming honesty, Nader, et al, who are the authors of this Act, either misunderstand the essential nature of the proposed Act or are deliberately deceiving the unsuspecting public. In their book[12] they quote the following provision in Delaware's 1899 Incorporation Act—a provision which is perfectly consistent with the notion of freedom of contract:

> "The certification of incorporation may also contain any provision which the incorporators may choose to insert for the management of the business and for the conduct of the affairs of the corporation, and any provision creating, defining, limiting, and regulating the powers of the corporation, the directors and stockholders; provided, such provisions are not contrary to the laws of this State."

---

[11]   In addition, Title V of the "Corporate Democracy Act" provides for various penalties and sanctions to be imposed on corporations and their executives for violating federal or state law. Nader, Green, and Seligman (1976).

[12]   Ibid, p. 52.

They then go on to say:

> "These sanguine little words literally turned corporate law inside out. The first hundred years of the corporation's history in the United States had established one rule above all else: The business corporation could only exercise powers explicitly provided or necessarily implied in its charter with the state. Delaware's 'self-determination' provision allowed the corporation to be a lawmaker itself. The corporation could conduct business in any way it chose as long as the state did not explicitly prohibit it."

Using the term "lawmaker" to describe the corporation under the 1899 Delaware Incorporation Act is either deliberate deception or gross ignorance. The provisions of the Act did not turn over lawmaking powers of the state to the corporation.[13] The language is clear. The Act simply allows individuals to voluntarily agree to whatever contractual provisions they choose in organizing a corporation so long as they do not contravene state laws.

"Our Largest Corporations are Governments"[14]

The pièce de résistance of the anti-corporation rhetoric is the charge that corporations have become governments in their own right. This assertion is simply the extreme version of the cliché that corporations have "too much" power. It is, of course, absurd to claim that corporations have become governments. The distinguishing feature of government is its role as the locus of the police powers or to put it more directly, its legal monopoly over the use of physical violence. Be they democratic or otherwise, governments are governments in precisely this sense. Corporations do not fit this bill.

Corporate managers are delegated rights to decide many questions—how corporate assets will be used, what contracts will be executed in the name of the corporation, who will be hired, who will be fired, where plants will be located, etc., but

---

[13] Robert Hessen (1982) points out that the first two sentences of the paragraph are factually incorrect since versions of the policy existed in earlier New Jersey and Connecticut statutes going back in the latter case as far as 1837. Hessen goes on to document numerous errors and inadequacies in the documentation for the one chapter of the book he examined.

[14] Green (1980, p. 21).

they cannot decide what the law will be, nor can they enforce the law. Managers can and do attempt to influence what the law is and how it is enforced.[15] Moreover, they have the right to resort to the courts and the police where the corporation's rights are infringed. In that respect, however, they are not different from any other citizen. The government has an obligation to protect the rights of private citizens even if it happens that those citizens are acting through a legal fiction, i.e., the corporation. That is why the police powers exist, and are lodged in government.

Fiat Labeled Democracy

There is one rather persuasive reason for adopting a skeptical attitude toward those who promote corporate democracy. The specific measures which they wish to impose by law such as what the composition of Boards of Directors will be, how discretion over employment is to be limited, or what information is to be supplied to the public are all measures which the parties to the corporate nexus could voluntarily put into effect if they chose to do so. It is important to emphasize that all of the contracts between the "corporation" and other individuals are voluntary. Barring intervention by the state, corporate organizers could choose whatever Board make-up they like. It if was truly in the interest of investors to deny management membership on Boards of Directors, we would expect to observe that stipulation written into articles of incorporation. Corporate organizers or reorganizers who adopted such a policy thereby would be able to market shares in the organization at higher prices to reflecting the higher value investors attach to their increased welfare. Since we do not observe corporations which deliberately deny the top managers membership on the Board of Directors, we must presume that it is not in the interest of investors to do so.

---

[15] One recent success of the anti-corporation forces is the constraints which have been imposed on corporate contributions to political campaigns.

Similarly, there is nothing to prevent corporations from guaranteeing tenure in contracts with employees. Indeed, it is clear that if employees value tenure at more than it costs, the corporation can make investors better off by offering it. Again, we must presume that to the extent that employees value security more than "current" salary, corporations provide that amount of security. The same argument, of course, applies with respect to the provision of information.

The Alleged Failure of State Chartering

Corporate democracy proponents contend that State chartering has failed. They allege that the revenues generated by having corporations chartered in the various states leads to competition among states to enact chartering statutes enabling managers to exploit stockholders. The corporations themselves then engage in a "movement towards the least common denominator" or a "race for the bottom."[16] They migrate for their charters to states with the most lax statutes. The prescription advocated to protect shareholders from exploitation by management is the imposition of federal minimum standards on corporate charters.

Delaware is generally regarded as the most pro-management charterer, which explains why a disproportionate share of corporations are chartered there. The charge that corporations choose Delaware as the state of charter in order to exploit stockholders is not based on any scientific study of the effects of corporate chartering on shareholders' welfare. In fact, a careful study of the effects on shareholder wealth of 140 changes in the state of incorporation during the period 1928-1967 has been performed (126 of these changes were to Delaware). Peter Dodd and Richard Leftwich, the authors of the study, find that in the 25 months prior to and including the month of the switch, stockholders of firms which switched the state of incorporation earned a positive abnormal return (after

---

[16]   Carey (1974, pp. 663-707).

adjusting for marketwide effects and risk) of slightly over 30 percent. For a period up to five years after the switch, the abnormal stockholder returns are insignificantly different from zero. This evidence is inconsistent with the hypothesis that the switch enables management to exploit the stockholders. It is consistent with the converse proposition, however, that management is switching the state of incorporation for the benefit of stockholders. As the news of the intended switch becomes available in investment markets, even before the switch is actually effected, investors revise upward their evaluation of the firms prospects. That revolution leads to an increase in the price of the shares which in turn generates the abnormal returns to shareholders. Professors Dodd and Leftwich conclude:

> "The evidence presented here lends no support to the arguments that stockholders are harmed by management's choice of a state of incorporation. Stockholders do not earn negative abnormal returns when managements initiate a change in the state of incorporation to a state which is supposedly more promanagement (such as Delaware). Indeed, the change follows a period of abnormal positive returns. Subsequent to the change, stockholders earn normal returns, contrary to the basic arguments of the proponents of federal chartering regulation."[17]

Control of Managerial Behavior Analysis and Evidence

The charge that management exploits investors is, as we have pointed out earlier, a testable proposition. In recent years, scholars have devoted substantial effort to assessing the validity of that charge. The result is a growing body of analysis and evidence bearing on the question of how managerial behavior is controlled. The study of corporate chartering cited above is an example. Much of this research has focused on the ''market for corporate control,'' as it has come to be known.

The charge that managers can disregard the wishes of investors is deduced from a very simple model of the factors controlling managerial behavior. It begins with the

---

[17]   Dodd and Leftwich (1980, p. 261).

proposition that ownership of stock in large corporations tends to be widely dispersed.[18] Individual stockholders, it is said, thereby have little influence on (or even interest in) the election of Directors. That, in turn, allows management to control membership on Boards of Directors; including arranging to be elected themselves. Boards of Directors are therefore captives of management rather than watchdogs representing investors. This is why managers can run corporations to suit themselves.

This chain of logic is incomplete in one very important respect. It ignores the market for corporate control. Whenever management exploits stockholders, whether through lack of diligence, incompetence or deliberate depradation, that behavior creates a profit opportunity. Anyone who can replace management and eliminate the exploitation can increase the value of the firm. There is no shortage of individuals and organizations, including other firms, constantly searching for such opportunities. Moreover, it is not necessary to enlist the support of a majority of current stockholders to take over corporate managerial reins. Control can be conveyed to newcomers in a variety of ways, the most common of which is conveyance to other firms through a tender offer or merger. The market for control of corporations differs from the market for control in the political sector in one important respect. Voters do not have the right to sell their political vote in an open market.[19] Since voting rights almost universally follow title to common shares, corporate votes <u>are</u> for sale. Corporate control is always for sale, and in a market to which there is ready access. Contenders for control can also avail themselves of the proxy fight to effect takeovers.

How effectively managerial behavior is controlled depends on how costly it is to exploit the profit opportunities managerial exploitation creates. Specifically, it depends

---

[18] The extent of dispersion of stock ownership itself has been challenged. See Demsetz (1983).

[19] This does not, of course, mean there is no vote buying in the political arena, but it does mean that such buying takes other forms. Interest groups contribute to political candidates' campaigns, and successful candidates repay by taking legislative and/or administrative actions which bestow benefits on their financiers.

on (1) the cost of gathering information reflecting managerial performance, and (2) the cost of exercising the various options for acquiring control. If it is relatively costless to assess managerial performance, and if it is relatively costless for control to be transferred, managers will have very limited opportunity to exploit investors.

Study of the operation of the market for corporate control is still in its infancy.[20] Nonetheless, certain facts about the performance of that market are apparent. There is convincing evidence that stockholders of acquired firms on average earn large positive returns on their shares in the course of a successful takeover. The size of the abnormal return to the acquired firm's shareholders is not independent of the form of the takeover—whether it is a merger, tender offer, or proxy fight—but in all three cases the abnormal return is significantly positive. Evidently, management is not so well entrenched and so indifferent to stockholder welfare that it simply rebuffs every takeover opportunity. Moreover, even where management does ward off potential suitors, there is at best mixed evidence that stockholders suffer. Management sponsorship of anti-takeover charter amendments, for example, is not immediate evidence of managerial actions inimical to shareholders. Apparently, anti-takeover provisions often enhance the price target shareholders ultimately are paid in a subsequent takeover. "Targeted buy-backs" and "stand still" agreements are the only instances where it appears that management of target firms act in their own behalf rather than in the interest of shareholders at large. A targeted buy-back occurs when management, using corporate funds, buys out the interest of a specific large shareholder at a premium. When such buy-back transactions take place, the selling shareholder often agrees to limit his holding of

---

[20] The bibliography of recent articles relevant to this issue includes: Manne (1965, pp. 110-120); Jarrell and Bradley (1980, pp. 371-376); Bradley (1980, pp. 345-376); Dodd (1980, pp. 105-137); Volume 11 of the Journal of Financial Economics is devoted entirely to "The Market for Corporate Control: The Scientific Evidence" (Michael C. Jensen, ed.); the following articles are included in that Volume: Jensen and Ruback (1983); Asquith (1983); Schipper and Thompson (1983); Asquith, Bruner, and Mullins (1983); Ruback (1983); Malatesta (1983); Bradley, Desai, and Kim (1983); Wier (1983); Stillman (1983); Eckbo (1983); Dann and DeAngelo (1983); Bradley and Wakeman (1983); DeAngelo and Rice (1983); Linn and McConnell (1983); Dodd and Warner (1983); Lease, McConnell, and Mikkelson (1983).

shares for some period into the future. The latter is referred to as a "stand still" agreement. Shareholders on average suffer abnormal negative returns as a result of targeted buy-backs and stand still agreements. This is perhaps the single most direct piece of evidence in the market for corporate control literature supporting the proposition that management on occasion, at least, behaves in ways inimical to shareholders.

Whether the shareholders of acquiring firms are made better or worse off as a result of acquisitions activity remains an open question. Some research shows acquisition activity leading to positive abnormal returns to shareholders of acquiring firms; other research leads to the converse conclusion—that acquiring shareholder returns are negative. While the jury is still out on the precise fate of acquiring firm shareholders, it would be surprising if future research concluded that acquisition activity led either to very large benefits or very large losses.

The surge of interest in corporate control research that has occurred in recent years suggests that a much more detailed and authentic assessment of managerial performance will be available. Such an assessment is not possible yet.

Will the Corporation Survive?

"The private corporation has been an enormously productive social invention, but it is on the way to being destroyed. Large corporations will become more like Conrail, Amtrak and the Post Office. One scenario seems clear. It begins with the creation of a crisis by the politicians and the media. In some cases the crisis will be blamed on the 'bad' things corporations do or might do, e.g., the multi-nationals. In any case the remedy will be more and more controls on the corporations (something like what is happening in the transportation and oil industries). When the controls endanger the financial structure of the corporations they will be subsidized by the public sector at the cost of more controls. When the controls bring the industry to the brink of collapse the government will take over. The details of the scenario will no doubt vary. Moreover, some firms will simply be driven out of business because of regulatory costs and the inability to raise capital."

These words were written by the authors in 1976 in an article entitled "Can the Corporation Survive?"[21] Little has transpired since that time that suggests we ought to change our prediction. Since the mid-1960's the stock market has performed remarkably poorly. The real value of the Dow Jones stocks fell by 62 percent over the 18 year period from December 1964 to the end of 1982. The real (after inflation) rate of return on all common stocks on the NYSE in the 40 year period from 1926 to 1965 was about 8.6 percent per year.[22] If stocks included in the Dow Jones Index had risen in price in the period 1965-1982 to provide that same 8.6 percent inflation adjusted rate of return, the index would have had to be about 5,600 on January 1, 1983 instead of 1,047.

Despite its record of success (or perhaps because of it), the large corporation is a highly vulnerable organizational form. The viability of the corporation critically depends on society's respect for the rights of the parties to the corporate contract, particularly the rights of stockholders who hold residual claims on net cash flows. Over the years, the right of managers to use corporate assets in the interest of stockholders has gradually been eroded away. Special interest groups of various sorts have joined forces with politicians to severely limit managerial decision rights. The special interest groups thereby transfer wealth from parties to the corporate contract to themselves, and politicians enhance their role in society by transferring decision rights to the government. Investors, on the other hand, will not for long, turn over their wealth to organizations from which it will, with high probability, be expropriated. We believe the attack on the corporation lies behind the poor performance of the stock market during the last 18 years. It is hard to imagine any change in the political process in Western Democracies that could be implemented that would reverse this trend.

---

[21] Jensen and Meckling (1978).

[22] Calculated from data given in Ibbotson and Sinquefield (1979).

References

Allen, William R. 1982. "Midnight Economist: Broadcast Essays IV": International Institute for Economic Research. Original paper #39.

Asquith, Paul. 1983. "Merger Bids, Uncertainty, and Stockholder Returns." *Journal of Financial Economics,* V. 11, No. 1-4: pp 51-83.

Asquith, Paul, Robert F. Bruner, and David W. Mullins, Jr. 1983. "The Gains to Bidding Firms from Merger." *Journal of Financial Economics,* V. 11, No. 1-4: pp 121-39.

Bradley, Michael. 1980. "Interfirm Tender Offers and the Market for Corporate Control." *Journal of Business,* V. 53, No. 4: pp 345-76.

Bradley, Michael, Anand Desai, and E. Han Kim. 1983. "The Rationale Behind Interfirm Tender Offers: Information or Synergy?" *Journal of Financial Economics,* V. 11, No. 1-4: pp 183-206.

Bradley, Michael and Lee M. Wakeman. 1983. "The Wealth Effects of Targeted Share Repurchases." *Journal of Financial Economics,* V. 11, No. 1-4: pp 301-28.

Carey, William L. 1974. "Federalism and Corporate Law: Reflections Upon Delaware." *Yale Law Journal,* V. 83: March, pp 663-707.

Chandler, Alfred D., Jr. 1977. *The Visible Hand: The Managerial Revolution in American Business*. Cambridge, Mass: Belknap Press.

Dann, Larry Y. and Harry DeAngelo. 1983. "Standstill Agreements, Privately Negotiated Stock Repurchases, and the Market for Corporate Control." *Journal of Financial Economics,* V. 11, No. 1-4: pp 275-300.

DeAngelo, Harry and Edward M. Rice. 1983. "Antitakeover Charter Amendments and Stockholder Wealth." *Journal of Financial Economics,* V. 11, No. 1-4: pp 329-60.

Demsetz, Harold. 1983. "The Structure of Ownership and the Theory of the Firm." *Journal of Law and Economics,* V. 26: pp 375-390.

Dodd, Peter. 1980. "Merger Proposals, Management Discretion, and Stockholder Wealth." *Journal of Financial Economics,* V. 8, No. 2: pp 105-38.

Dodd, Peter and Richard Leftwich. 1980. "The Market for Corporate Charters: 'Unhealthy Competition' versus Federal Regulation." *Journal of Business,* V. 53, No. 3: pp 259-83.

Dodd, Peter and Jerold B. Warner. 1983. "On Corporate Governance: A Study of Proxy Contests." *Journal of Financial Economics,* V. 11, No. 1-4: pp 401-438.

Eckbo, B. Espen. 1983. "Horizontal Mergers, Collusion, and Stockholder Wealth." *Journal of Financial Economics,* V. 11, No. 1-4: pp 241-273.

Fama, Eugene F. and Michael C. Jensen. 1983a. "Agency Problems and Residual Claims." *Journal of Law and Economics,* V. 26, No. 2: pp 327-349. Available at the Social Science Research Network eLibrary at: http://papers.ssrn.com/Abstract=94032. Reprinted in Michael C. Jensen, *Foundations of Organizational Strategy*, Cambridge: Harvard University Press, 1998.

Fama, Eugene F. and Michael C. Jensen. 1983b. "Separation of Ownership and Control." *Journal of Law and Economics,* V. 26, No. 2: pp 301-325. Available at the Social Science Research Network eLibrary at: http://papers.ssrn.com/Abstract=94034. Reprinted in Michael C. Jensen, *Foundations of Organizational Strategy*, Cambridge: Harvard University Press, 1998.

Green, Mark. 1980. "The Case for Corporate Democracy." *Regulation,* V. May/June.

Hessen, Robert. 1982. "Credible Crusader? An Assessment of Ralph Nader's Scholarship," in ed. Michael C. Jensen, *Controlling the Giant Corporation.*

Ibbotson, R. G. and R. A. Sinquefield. 1979. "Stocks, Bonds, Bills, and Inflation: Updates." *Financial Analysts Journal.*

Jarrell, Gregg and Michael Bradley. 1980. "The Economic Effects of Federal and State Regulations of Cash Tender Offers." *Journal of Law and Economics,* V. 23: pp 371-407.

Jensen, Michael C. and William H. Meckling. 1978. "Can the Corporation Survive?" *Financial Analysts Journal,* V. 34, No. 1. Available at the Social Science Research Network eLibrary at: http://papers.ssrn.com/Abstract=244155.

Jensen, Michael C. and Richard S. Ruback. 1983. "The Market for Corporate Control: The Scientific Evidence." *Journal of Financial Economics,* V. 11, No. 1-4: pp 5-50. Available at the Social Science Research Network eLibrary at: http://papers.ssrn.com/Abstract=244158. Reprinted in *The Modern Theory of Corporate Finance*, Michael C. Jensen and Clifford W. Smith, Jr., Editors, New York: McGraw-Hill, Inc., 1984.

Lease, Ronald C., John J. McConnell, and Wayne H. Mikkelson. 1983. "The Market Value of Control in Publicly-traded Corporations." *Journal of Financial Economics,* V. 11, No. 1-4: pp 439-471.

Linn, Scott C. and John J. McConnell. 1983. "An Empirical Investigation of the Impact of 'Antitakeover' Amendments on Common Stock Prices." *Journal of Financial Economics,* V. 11, No. 1-4: pp 361-99.

Malatesta, Paul H. 1983. "The Wealth Effect of Merger Activity and the Objective Functions of Merging Firms." *Journal of Financial Economics,* V. 11, No. 1-4: pp 155-181.

Manne, Henry G. 1965. "Mergers and the Market for Corporate Control." *Journal of Political Economy*: pp 110-120.

Nader, Ralph, Mark Green, and W. W. Seligman. 1976. *Taming the Giant Corporation.* New York: Norton & Co.

Ruback, Richard S. 1983. "Assessing Competition in the Market for Corporate Acquisitions." *Journal of Financial Economics,* V. 11, No. 1-4: pp 141-53.

Schipper, Katherine and Rex Thompson. 1983. "Evidence on the Capitalized Value of Merger Activity for Acquiring Firms." *Journal of Financial Economics,* V. 11, No. 1-4: pp 85-119.

Stillman, Robert. 1983. "Examining Antitrust Policy Towards Horizontal Mergers." *Journal of Financial Economics,* V. 11, No. 1-4: pp 225-240.

Wier, Peggy. 1983. "The Costs of Antimerger Lawsuits: Evidence from the Stock Market." *Journal of Financial Economics,* V. 11, No. 1-4: pp 207-224.

THE FREEMAN

Home
Political Quiz
Celebrities
Liberator OnLine
Ask Dr. Ruwart
Unbelievable
FAQ
The Freeman
Catalog
EMail
← Index →

Search

Where do you fit?

What do these
celebrities
have in
common?

Find out.

The $100 Tree Fern

by Donald G. Smith

I once owned a $1,000 dog. I got him for $2 and a $998 cat. --old vaudeville joke

Our house in Los Angeles featured a rather impressive planter area adjacent to the front porch. The builder--it was a new house--had put in a few plants to enhance its eye appeal, and one was a large Australian tree fern.

People who entered the house invariably informed me that the plant was worth $100: "That's what they go for in the nurseries." I repeatedly offered to sell them the plant, but they weren't interested. It supposedly was worth $100, but no one would pay it.

Eventually the fern grew to such mammoth proportions that it was starting to take over the porch, and it was clear that it had to go. I offered it for $50, then $25, then free to anyone who would cart it off. There were no takers, and I wound up paying to have it cut up and hauled away. Still, I was often told in subsequent conversations that the plant had a value of-what else? -$100.

What it boils down to is a gross misunderstanding of basic economics. My plant would have been worth $100, $500, or $1,000 if anyone had been willing to pay that amount. The truth was that it was worth nothing-in fact, less than nothing because I had to pay to get rid of it. To put it simply, an item or service is worth only what another person is willing to pay.

This is the very core of the capitalistic system -the marketplace. Those who understand it generally prosper, and those who don't haven't a chance.

We have all read, for example, that no baseball player is worth $5 million a year. In the days of Ted Williams and Joe DiMaggio, we heard that no player

The Freeman is the monthly publication of The Foundation for Economic Education, Inc., Invington-on-Hudson, NY 10533. Phone (914)591-7230. FAX (914)591-8910. E-mail: freeman@fee.org. FEE, established in 1946 by Leonard E. Read, is a non-political, educational champion of private property, the free market, and limited government. FEE is classified as a 26 USC 501(c)(3) tax-exempt organization.

This article appeared in the August 1992 issue of *The Freeman*. Copyright © 1992 by The Foundation for Economic Education. Permission to reprint this article is granted provided appropriate credit is given and two copies of the reprinted material

was worth $100,000. Whatever the amount, it is a naive statement because it is the marketplace that dictates what a ballplayer, or anyone else, is worth. One can't compare a professional athlete with, say, a classical musician, or a real estate agent with a locksmith. A person's services are worth what he can command in the market.

I have talked with people who believe that we should place a dollar value on occupationsthrough government, of course. They envision a great chart in which a typist might make X dollars, a plumber Y dollars, and a college professor Z dollars. But market values aren't static. The typist is worth more than the plumber or the college professor if a writer has to get a manuscript in the overnight mail, and the plumber's value goes up when the basement is flooded.

Where, in this great chart of human values, would we place a high-school-dropout rock musician who cannot name his state capital but who can sell out the Los Angeles Coliseum in a matter of hours? The great chart-maker might put him at a minimum wage level, but the marketplace says he is worth millions. There is no set value for an entertainer. If he sells tickets, he is a valuable property. If no one will pay to see him or buy his cassettes, he is worth very little.

This brings us back to the premise that the economic value of anything is determined solely by what it will bring in the marketplace.

Price controls, rent ceilings, minimum wage laws, and other artificial constraints are really worthless because they are injected into the economy to hold back a tide that isn't going to be held back. If a person is worth less to an employer than the minimum wage, he isn't going to be hired. If a price ceiling is far below the real value of a product or service, the item either goes off the market or follows an illegal path to its realistic level. The market value will prevail one way or another.

All of which leads back to my marvelous Australian tree fern. Whatever pleasure I derived was from the delusion that I had a $100 item greeting guests as they entered my house. It wound up as a great disappointment, but now I have something even better. This is my $5,000 pine-cone collection. I have decided never to sell it.

_____

Mr. Smith, a frequent contributor to The Freeman, lives in Santa Maria, California.

CHAPTER 16

WHY POPCORN COSTS MORE AT THE MOVIES AND WHY THE OBVIOUS ANSWER IS WRONG

"They *pay* you to think about things like that?" My airline seatmate didn't come right out with the question, but despite his best efforts, his expression revealed all. "Are you really," he wanted to continue, "the only person in America who doesn't know the answer to that question? Or are all economists equally dense?"

I'd been thinking idly about one of the recurring problems of modern economics, one that has occupied great minds and boosted great careers. My seatmate had expressed some mild curiosity about the equations and diagrams I was scribbling. I had a feeling I'd be best off muttering something about the magnetodynamics of the solar system, but I opted for the truth instead. I was working on the mystery of why popcorn is so expensive at the movie theater.

Actually, I'm not 100% certain that popcorn *is* so expensive at the movie theater. My guess is that when a quart of popcorn sells for $3 or so, the theater owner is earning back substantially more than his expenses. Perhaps I'm wrong about this; there may be a lot of hidden costs to running those concession stands that are not so obvious to the casual moviegoer. Still, there is no evident reason why costs should be so much higher in the theater than they are at the candy store, where you can buy the same size popcorn at one-third the price. So it seems a worthwhile exercise to assume that the theater's markup really is enormous and to look for an explanation.

My seatmate, of course, already had an explanation. Popcorn is expensive because, once you have entered the movie theater, the theater owner has a monopoly. If there were only one candy store in town, and if that were the only place to buy popcorn, it would cost $3 a quart at the candy store. When you are trapped in the theater, the concession stand might as well be the only candy store in town.

As my seatmate wanted so badly to tell me, you don't have to know any economics to see the logic of that simple story. As I wanted so badly to tell him—he wasn't the only one restraining himself for politeness' sake—you actually *do* need to *not* know any economics to see the logic. Because the story makes no sense.

Once you enter the theater, the owner has a monopoly on a lot of things. He is the only supplier of rest rooms, for example. Why doesn't he charge you a monopoly price to use the rest room? Why isn't there a monopoly price for the right to proceed from the box office to the outer lobby, another to proceed from the outer lobby to the inner lobby, another to pass through the double doors so that you can see the screen, and another to take a seat?

The answer, of course, is that a rest room fee would make the theater less attractive to moviegoers. To maintain his clientele, the owner would be forced to sell tickets at a lower price. What he collected at the rest room door would be lost at the box office.

As with rest rooms, so with popcorn. When I go to watch a movie and buy a quart of popcorn, I am quite indifferent between paying $1 for the popcorn and $7 for the ticket or paying $3 for the popcorn and $5 for the ticket. By the end of the evening, the owner collects $8 from me under either strategy.

This calculation makes it look like a matter of indifference how the popcorn is priced. But it leaves out one thing, and that one thing argues for making the popcorn cheap and the tickets expensive: *If popcorn is cheap, I might buy two quarts instead of one.* That's good for the owner, because if I am willing to pay $8 for a movie plus a quart of popcorn, I might be willing to pay $10 for a movie plus *two* quarts of popcorn. He can extract the additional $2 by raising the ticket price.

Shall I run through that again? The cheaper the popcorn, the more I eat. The more I eat, the more I enjoy going to the theater. The more I enjoy going to the theater, the more I am willing to pay for an evening there (counting the ticket price plus popcorn). The more I am willing to pay for an evening at the theater, the more coins end up in the owner's pocket.

With a little more argument along lines like these, it is not difficult to establish that the owner's best strategy is to sell me popcorn at a price equal to the cost of production, earning *no profit whatsoever* at the concession stand. This leads me to buy a lot of popcorn, which makes me happy and willing to pay a very high price at the box office.

Which returns me to my question. Why is popcorn so expensive at the movie theater?

Of course, a possible answer is that the owner doesn't know enough economics to realize that his pricing strategy is suboptimal. But it is probably a safe bet that theater owners know more about running theaters profitably than economists do. So the right question is, What does the owner know that my analysis ignores?

I believe he knows this: *some moviegoers like popcorn more than others.* Cheap popcorn attracts popcorn lovers and makes them willing to pay a high price at the door. But to take advantage of that willingness, the owner must raise ticket prices so high that he drives away those who come only to see the movie. If there are enough nonsnackers, the strategy of cheap popcorn can backfire.

My seatmate's clear intuition to the contrary, the purpose of expensive popcorn is *not* to extract a lot of money from customers. *That* purpose would be better served by cheap popcorn and expensive movie tickets. Instead, the purpose of expensive popcorn is to extract *different* sums from *different* customers. Popcorn lovers, who have more fun at the movies, pay more for their additional pleasure.

In fact, expensive popcorn makes sense *only* if popcorn lovers are really willing to pay more than other people for their evenings at the theater. If things were otherwise, and nonsnackers were all cinemaphiles happy to pay $15 a ticket, then the owner would be best advised to mark the popcorn down and the tickets up. Then every moviegoer would have some incentive to buy those expensive tickets—in some cases to see the movie, and in others to gain access to the concession stand. In fact, it would be even better to sell popcorn *below* cost. To exploit the cinemaphiles, the admission fee should be $15; at this price popcorn lovers need a special inducement to get them into the theater.

The owner's objective is not to set a uniformly high price but to match the price to the customer. When you go to buy a car, the salesman is likely to ask a question like "How much do you want to pay?" (Personally, I always answer "zero.") What he really means to ask is "What is the *most* you are *willing* to pay?" or in economists' jargon, "What is your reservation price?" If he could get an honest answer to that question, he would charge each customer accordingly. In practice, he connives to estimate your reservation price by engaging you in conversation about what other cars you have been looking at, what you do for a living, and the size of your family. Then he does the best he can.

In a seller's paradise, each customer would be charged exactly his reservation price and not a penny less. In the worldly realm we inhabit, sellers concoct mechanisms for charging a little more on average to those who are willing to pay a little more and a little less on average to those who would otherwise walk away.

I recently bought a new car myself and was offered the opportunity to add a decorative rear spoiler bar at a price that I believe was much greater than the cost of production. If everybody took the spoiler bars, there would be no point in this. It is a matter of indifference whether you pay $20,000 for the car and $3,000 for the spoiler or $22,000 for the car and $1,000 for the spoiler. But if the manufacturer believes that people who like spoilers are willing to pay $23,000 for a car that most people think is worth no more than $20,000, then the pricing strategy begins to make sense.

Fads and tastes evolve over time, and there may come a year in which low-income people are generally fond of spoiler bars and high-income people are generally not. If that year arrives, I expect to see spoiler bars selling for a *negative* price: $20,000 for a bare car, $18,000 if you take it with the spoiler. Like popcorn at the theater, the spoiler helps the seller match the customer to the appropriate price.

A movie theater is in the business of selling neither movies nor popcorn but evenings at the theater that, at the customer's option, include both. Like any seller, the owner seeks to charge the highest price to those most willing to pay it. Cheap tickets and expensive popcorn effectively charge a higher price to those who eat a lot of popcorn. This works—but only because those who are willing to pay high prices and those who eat a lot of popcorn are, on average, the same people. If popcorn lovers were generally from low income groups who needed special inducements to come to the theater, popcorn would be free and you'd get a discount at the box office for agreeing to eat at least a quart of it.

When you buy a Polaroid camera or a ticket to Disneyland, your expenses have only just begun. To get any use out of your purchase, you must also buy Polaroid film or Disneyland ride tickets.* If all customers were identical, the seller would provide film or ride tickets at cost to maximize the value of the camera or the park admission. The only reason why Polaroid film is expensive is because some people are willing to pay more for the ability to take pictures than others are. Expensive film extracts more from the heavy users, and Polaroid sensibly believes that the heaviest users are willing to pay the most.

Why do supermarkets print discount coupons in the newspaper? No doubt my seatmate on the airplane could have explained it to me in a sentence: To lure customers with the prospect of a bargain. But why should a coupon for 50 cents off a bottle of detergent be a more effective lure than an ad announcing that the price of detergent had been slashed by 50 cents? The "obvious" explanation is wrong.

Discount coupons are intended *not* to lure customers in general but to lure a certain *class* of customers—namely, those who would shop elsewhere in the absence of a bargain. The device works only if the discounts end up in the right hands: It must be the case that coupon clippers, on average, are more sensitive to price. Most economists believe that the connection is established by the fact that some people have more free time than others. Those with a lot of free time are both more likely to be clipping coupons *and* more likely to be shopping around for

*This statement was true when I wrote it but is false today because Disneyland has changed its pricing policy. The right question for an economist to be asking now is, Why did they change it?

bargains. The correlation is imperfect, but it probably means that the average coupon clipper is more likely than the average non clipper to leave the store if the price isn't right.

It is worth stressing that if everybody clipped coupons, they would serve no purpose. They make sense only as a device to charge more to those who are willing to pay more.

Sometimes an easily identifiable group, such as students or senior citizens, is particularly sensitive to price. In such cases, sellers give discounts to those groups directly. It has been remarked that senior citizen discounts are an odd convention in a country where the elderly, despite stereotypes, are on average quite well-to-do. The remark overlooks the fact that price sensitivity is not a function of income alone. Most senior citizens are retired and have time to shop for bargains. Their sons and daughters, though far less financially secure, are often strapped for time and willing to pay a higher price to avoid a time-consuming search.

Did you buy this book in hardcover or in paperback? It might interest you to know that the production costs for the two kinds of binding are very close to equal. By pricing the hardback several dollars higher, the publisher effectively charges different prices to different classes of customers. As in all these examples, the scheme works only if those who choose the paperback are those who were initially more frugal in what they were willing to spend for the book. Perhaps the connection is that real booklovers insist on hardcovers because they expect to keep their books a long time.

I have known economists who made hobbies of collecting examples of price discrimination. (*Price discrimination* is economic jargon for selling the same product at more than one price.) Airlines charge different prices depending on whether you stay over a Saturday, hotels charge different prices depending on whether you make reservations in advance, car rental agencies charge different prices depending on whether you belong to a frequent flyer program, doctors charge different prices depending on your income and your insurance status, and universities charge different prices depending on your grades and your family's income. Any giveaway that is claimed by only some buyers (such as trading stamps or free delivery) can be a form of price discrimination, as is a policy of "ten cents apiece, three for a quarter." Leaded gasoline sells for less than unleaded gasoline despite comparable production costs, free coffee refills mean that some people pay more per cup than others, and two prices at the salad bar depend on whether you order a complete meal or just the salad. Price discrimination, in short, appears ubiquitous.

Yet there is a good theoretical reason to believe that price discrimination should be relatively rare, and therein lies a puzzle. To see the problem, let's return to the movies.

I have argued that $3 popcorn makes sense only as a form of price discrimination. Popcorn lovers have more fun at the movies and are therefore asked to pay more. But if this is the whole story, then why don't popcorn lovers simply patronize a different theater?

Presumably my airline seatmate would have had no trouble with this one; he could have told me that shopping elsewhere is not an option because the situation is the same all over town. But it is extremely difficult to see how such an outcome could persist. According to my seatmate's model, each theater makes huge profits selling popcorn. The theater that sold a quart for $2.50 instead of $3 could attract all of the big popcorn eaters and under most circumstances would more than make up in volume what was lost by cutting the price. Other theaters, having lost the bulk of their popcorn business, would be forced to cut prices. Why don't we see popcorn price wars?

Even if for some reason existing theaters were insufficiently competitive to bring down the price, the lure of high popcorn profits should suffice to spur new theater construction. Newcomers would offer discounts and the price wars would be underway.

So one more ingredient must be added to the price discrimination story. Price discrimination can work only when the seller has a monopoly of the appropriate kind. (The theater owner needs a monopoly in the *theater* market, not just the popcorn market, to make price discrimination work.) If Wegman's grocery store can profitably sell detergent at 50 cents off to coupon clippers, then it can profitably sell detergent at 50 cents off to anyone. If Wegman's archrival, Tops, advertises "no coupons but all prices 10 cents lower than Wegman's," it can strip away all of Wegman's nonclipping customers and earn 40 cents more on each sale than Wegman's (now catering to clippers only) earns. To retrieve the high-profit business of the nonclippers, Wegman's cuts prices 20 cents. Tops responds with further cuts. If there is real competition, this process must continue until all customers are paying the same price.

The standard textbook example of a perfectly competitive industry is wheat farming. No wheat farmer has any control over market conditions, and no wheat farmer represents a significant share of the market. That is precisely the reason why wheat farmers do not give senior citizen discounts. If all wheat farmers charged $1 a bushel to senior citizens and $2 a bushel to everyone else, I would start a wheat farm and charge $1.90 a bushel to everybody. Let others have the senior citizen business; I'll take all the rest.

Senior citizens don't get wheat discounts because there are too many opportunists like me around. Price discrimination can succeed only where it cannot be competed away.

If price discrimination is viable only for a monopolist, and if price discrimination is as common as our many examples seem to indicate, we are forced to conclude that monopolies are everywhere. But many economists—including most of those whom I know well—are quite skeptical of that conclusion.

From this skepticism, there arises a parlor game. The game is to take examples of apparent price discrimination and debunk them. The goal is to argue convincingly that the single product being sold at two different prices is not a single product at all but two quite different products. One product at two prices requires monopoly power, but two products at two prices is the normal order of things.

Some cases are easy. The salad bar costs more if you don't order dinner. But people who don't order dinner generally take more from the salad bar. There are two prices for the salad bar, but they probably work out, on average, to about the same price per chick-pea or carrot slice. No price discrimination here.

Others are slightly harder. Doctors charge wealthy patients more than they charge poor patients. Is this price discrimination? Perhaps. But perhaps wealthy patients are in general more demanding of the doctor's time, more likely to phone in the middle of the night, and more likely to sue for malpractice when things go wrong. If so, then wealthy patients really purchase a different level of service than poor patients do, and it is not surprising that better service carries a higher price tag.

What about those supermarket coupons? The usual price discrimination story is that clippers get a price break because they have a lot of free time and therefore shop for bargains. When I wrote a college textbook on economic theory, I included this standard example. One reviewer suggested an intriguing alternative: Coupon clippers, because they have more free time, tend to shop in the middle of the day, when the store is not crowded and the checkout clerks are idle. Nonclippers shop on their way home from work when lines are long and tempers are short. Thus nonclippers are actually more expensive to serve than clippers. They pay extra not because of price discrimination, but because they have purchased the right to shop at times that the grocery store finds inconvenient.

I applaud the spirit that concocted this story, though I don't believe it is correct. If grocery stores really wanted to charge extra for shopping between 5 and 7 P.M., it seems to me that the most straightforward way to do it would be to impose a surcharge on all groceries sold between those hours. On the other hand, I am equally uncomfortable with the price discrimination story because it implies a level of monopoly power for which I see no other evidence. More ideas are needed.

Leaded and unleaded gasoline are more or less the same good from the producer's viewpoint in the sense that their production costs are comparable. Yet they sell for substantially different prices. How can this be price discrimination, which requires monopoly power, when there are sometimes three gas stations at a single intersection?

The economists John Lott and Russell Roberts recently gave an ingenious answer when they observed that leaded gasoline is used primarily by older vehicles with larger gas tanks. To sell 30 gallons of leaded gas, the station manager needs to record one sale, write up one credit card slip, and watch other customers shop across the street because his pumps are busy for the length of time that it takes to fill one gas tank. To sell 30 gallons of unleaded, he needs to record two or three sales, with the consequent doubling or tripling of all these related costs. Different prices that result from different retailing costs do not constitute price discrimination and can survive perfectly well in competition.

On a recent trip to New Mexico, I visited the Taos Pueblo, an Indian community that welcomes tourists. The entrance fee is five dollars per car plus five dollars per camera. The more cameras you carry, the more you pay. Is this price discrimination? Maybe, because those who carry many cameras might be most eager not to miss a major tourist attraction. On the other hand, tourists with cameras are likely to be more intrusive in any number of ways that are all too easy to imagine. Less gracious guests can be thought of as consuming more hospitality and paying more for their additional consumption.

Taxis sometimes charge one rate for a couple traveling together and a higher rate for two strangers going to the same destination. To support a diagnosis of price discrimination, one must argue that the couple is more likely to consider alternative transportation than the strangers are. Perhaps people traveling in pairs are more adventurous, or more likely to be from in town and aware of their options. To reject a diagnosis of price discrimination, one must argue that it is genuinely more expensive to serve two strangers than to serve a couple. Here I have no argument that makes me comfortable, but I am looking.

And finally and once again, why is popcorn so expensive at the movie theater? If this be price discrimination, whence the monopoly power? Theaters might have a small amount of monopoly power, at least when they are the exclusive local outlets for popular first-run movies. But this can hardly account for the exorbitant popcorn prices that seem to be the norm.*

Economists Luis Locay and Alvaro Rodriguez recently gave an ingenious answer to this age-old question, and to me it has the ring of truth. People go to movies in groups. Popcorn lovers often travel with companions who eat no popcorn. The usual argument says that you cannot price discriminate against popcorn eaters without losing them to another theater. The Locay/Rodriguez response is that popcorn eaters cannot go to

*My insightful student Jeff Spielberg suggests that the high price you pay for popcorn is not price discrimination at all but a fee for cleaning up after you. He might be right.

another theater without splitting up their social groups. If another theater offers cheap popcorn and high ticket prices, the nonsnackers in the group will vote to stay put. Locay and Rodriguez have constructed a complete argument demonstrating that under plausible hypotheses about the way groups make decisions, theater owners have a degree of monopoly power over popcorn lovers who travel with popcorn nonlovers, and can plausibly exploit this power by pricing popcorn high.

I like that story, but it does leave a thread hanging. It doesn't tell me why the popcorn lover fails to offer his friends a deal: Let's stick to theaters with low-priced popcorn, and I'll occasionally pay for your tickets.

Other cases baffle me even more. Canadian restaurants near the border sometimes accept U.S. currency at above-market exchange rates. This appears to be price discrimination in favor of Americans. Is it? If so, why are Americans more price-sensitive than Canadians? And if not, then what is the alternative explanation? Do Americans demand less service than Canadians?

Disneyland offers discount tickets to its stockholders. Are Disneyland stockholders more price-sensitive than the general public?

In the United States, hotels typically set a price per room that is independent of the number of occupants. In Great Britain, hotels typically set a price per guest that is independent of how many rooms they occupy. Which if either of these is price discrimination? In either case, what is the source of the monopoly power and what makes one group of travelers more price-sensitive than another? If neither is price discrimination, what does account for the differential pricing? And why does the outcome differ so radically across countries?

It might have been fun to discuss these questions with my neighbor on the airplane. But I decided to let him sleep.

Windows à la carte
Mar 25th 2004

Might the European Commission's controversial new antidote to Microsoft's monopoly actually work?

HALF a billion euro? Forget about it. The headline-grabbing €497m ($612m) fine imposed by the European Commission on Microsoft this week is the least of the software giant's worries, for it makes that much profit every two weeks and is sitting on a cash pile nearly 100 times bigger. Far more worrying for Microsoft is the commission's demand that it produce, within 90 days, a version of its Windows operating system stripped of its media-playback capabilities. That sounds trivial, but it would set an important precedent that could be used to make Microsoft remove other bits from Windows in future. Hence Microsoft's recent strenuous efforts to negotiate a settlement to avoid this week's ruling, and its determination to have the ruling overturned on appeal. Allowing PC-makers to pick and choose which bits of Windows they want from an "à la carte" list of features is something Microsoft wants to avoid at all costs.

That is because Microsoft relies on the "bundling" of new features into Windows to protect its existing monopoly and to extend it into new areas. Windows is installed on over 90% of new PCs. So any feature Microsoft adds—a web browser, say, or a media player—quickly becomes ubiquitous. Rival products, such as Netscape's web browser or the RealNetworks media player, which must be installed separately, lose out. Microsoft crushed Netscape this way, and now the commission has ruled that Microsoft's "bundling" of its media player into Windows "is an example of a more general business model which deters innovation and reduces consumer choice in any technologies which Microsoft could conceivably take interest in and tie with Windows in the future."

The next version of Windows, codenamed Longhorn, due in 2006, will include search, database and security add-ons, and will no doubt inspire new legal challenges. By making Microsoft "unbundle" its media player when asked to do so by PC-makers, who can then substitute an alternative, the commission's aim is both to level the playing field today and pave the way for further unbundlings in future.

So great is Microsoft's desire to preserve its ability to bundle that, during settlement talks with the commission, it even offered to include rival media players in Windows, rather than remove its own. But Mario Monti, Europe's competition commissioner, was less interested in winning yesterday's battles than in preventing tomorrow's misdeeds. Attempts to devise a voluntary set of rules to govern future unbundling failed, so Microsoft will now be legally compelled—subject to appeals—to unbundle its media player. This would constitute a big step towards an "à la carte" Windows. But would that actually work?

It might. If Microsoft's various add-ons were optional rather than compulsory parts of Windows, each one would have to compete on merit with rival alternatives. PC-makers could then differentiate themselves from each other by assembling different software bundles for specific markets. Indeed, to some extent, though it would never admit it, Microsoft has started down this path already: it sells several versions of Windows, including a basic version for home users, a more advanced "pro" version for business users, and specially modified versions for tablet computers, media centres and its Xbox games console. It also offers cut-down versions of Windows in some Asian markets.

Pick and choose

Strikingly, Microsoft also sells a version of Windows for use in "embedded" devices such as cash dispensers or supermarket tills. Firms that license this version of Windows can specify which features they want, or do not want. This undermines Microsoft's claim that Windows is a single product that stops working if any part is removed, says Dave Stewart, deputy general counsel for RealNetworks. It is notable, he says, that Microsoft lets licensees modify Windows in embedded markets where it is not dominant, but insists on bundling everything in markets where it is.

Yet there are several problems with the "à la carte" model. One difficulty, to continue with the restaurant analogy, lies in compiling the menu. It would be necessary to decide how to carve Windows up, and how much PC-makers ought to pay once they have decided which bits they want. So far, the commission has said merely that Microsoft should not be allowed to offer incentives to PC-makers to include its media player—in other words, the unbundled version must not cost more than the full version of Windows. Surely it should cost less.

Yet PC-makers might simply prefer to stick with the full version of Windows. Today they can do deals with Microsoft's rivals to add extra software to their PCs. Hewlett-Packard, for example, is to sell PCs with Apple's media-player software, and Dell ships RealNetworks' player on some of its computers. But in both cases, Microsoft's media player is still present. Why antagonise Microsoft by removing it, even if it were for a small cut in the price of Windows? Philip Lowe, the commission's director general of competition, notes that rival software firms already pay PC-makers to carry their software. In future, he says, they might insist that Microsoft's rival product be removed.

The scope of the commission's ruling is limited to the European market. But Thomas Vinje, a lawyer at Clifford Chance, which represented a consortium of Microsoft's opponents in the case, says that Europe is probably a big enough market to act as a laboratory in which to test the "à la carte" model. If it worked, PC-makers would probably be able to insist on the same terms worldwide. Hence the unease at Microsoft: if the commission's ruling is upheld on appeal and the unbundling of media player goes ahead, its current business model could start to unravel.

All this, of course, assumes that the remedy is not overturned. Microsoft says that it will appeal, and will also ask for the commission's remedies to be suspended while the appeal is underway. On past form, says John Kallaugher, an expert on comparative competition law at University College, London, and a partner at Latham & Watkins, a law firm, the decision on whether or not to suspend the remedies could come as early as June. The appeal itself would take several years, however. By then the media-player case may well have become moot, and Longhorn will probably have been released. But a ruling in the commission's favour could still shape future versions of Windows.

By rejecting Microsoft's offer to include rival media players in Windows, says Brad Smith, Microsoft's general counsel, the commission turned down an opportunity to "create a foundation to solve future issues". Such an agreement, he says, would have demonstrated that future bundling disputes could be solved by negotiation, on a case-by-case basis. Of course, that would also leave Microsoft the option of spinning out negotiations indefinitely, to its own advantage. Recognising this, the commission has in effect taken a bold gamble, rejecting a solution to a specific problem now in the hope of establishing a general precedent for the future. If it can get its remedy to stick, there is an outside chance that it might be able to dent the mighty Microsoft monopoly.

ISBN-13: 978-1-4240-7008-4
ISBN-10: 1-4240-7008-2

9 781424 070084